ORGANISED ABUSE

To the children: that we may get it right next time

'Whosoever shall cause one of these little ones to stumble, it were better for him that a millstone were hanged about his neck, and that he were cast into the sea.' – *Jesus of Nazareth*

'Whatever you do, stamp out abuses.' – *Voltaire*

'The greater the power, the more dangerous the abuse.' – *Burke*

'a former Tory whip . . . asserted that . . . [their] generosity extends to helping out MPs "in trouble involving small boys".' – *Care Weekly*, 25 May 1995

Organised Abuse

The Current Debate

Edited by
Peter C. Bibby, MA, DipASS, FIMgt
Foreword by
The Baroness Faithfull, OBE

Published by
Arena
Ashgate Publishing Limited
Gower House
Croft Road
Aldershot
Hants GU11 3HR
England

Ashgate Publishing Company
Old Post Road
Brookfield
Vermont 05036
USA

British Library Cataloguing in Publication Data

Organised abuse: the current debate
  1. Child sexual abuse   2. Sexually abused children   3. Paedophilia
  4. Child molesters   5. Organised crime
  I. Bibby, Peter
  362.7'6

ISBN 1 85742 284 8

Library of Congress Catalog Card Number: 96–83248

Typeset by Raven Typesetters, Chester
Printed in Great Britain by Hartnolls Ltd, Bodmin

Contents

List of figures and tables

Figures

Tables

Authors' details

Arnon Bentovim is a consultant child psychiatrist, family therapist and psychoanalyst and works at the Hospital for Sick Children, Great Ormond Street, and the Tavistock Clinic. He is an expert witness in many child abuse cases and writes and speaks widely at national and international conferences.

Marianne Bentovim is a social worker and psychotherapist and works at the Department of Psychological Medicine, Great Ormond Street Hospital. She has many years' experience of dealing with sexually abused children, and in particular, victims of organised abuse. She has written and trained widely on the impact of abuse and treatment on children and families.

Peter Bibby qualified as a social worker and teacher. He was Founder Chair of the Committee on Child Abuse Networks (COCAN), a former Deputy Director of Social Services and was previously Deputy Director of Child-care for the London Division of Barnardos and Chief Probation Officer for West Glamorgan. He has worked with Rule 43 prisoners in Liverpool Prison, has written and trained on dealing with organised abuse since 1989 and has been a partner in PB SERVICES Care Consultancy since 1993.

Chris Brannan is a qualified social worker, with a Masters in Social Science, who has had experience in a number of social work settings, including residential and fieldwork. His main specialist area is child protection, in which his experience has been as both a social worker and manager over a twelve-year period. He led the social work team into the Castle Hill School inquiry and was a co-author of the *Castle Hill Report* (Shropshire County Council, 1993), commissioned and recommended by the Department of Health and Department of Education. He has also written and presented a number of

articles and papers on organised and institutional abuse and has developed and presented a number of training seminars on the subject.

Hedy Cleaver trained as a social worker and a psychologist. She started her professional life as an educational psychologist, before moving to an academic career. Her research has explored a range of issues, including foster-home breakdown and vulnerable children in mainstream education. More recently, her work has been in the field of child abuse and neglect.

Catherine Doran is currently employed as a service manager responsible for child protection with the London Borough of Haringey. She has worked in the field of child protection for over fifteen years. She has a special interest in child sexual abuse, and more recently, organised abuse, and has taught widely in both areas.

Baroness Lucy Faithfull has worked for children since becoming a social worker in 1933. She retired as Director of Social Services for Oxford in 1972. She is active in over a dozen child-centred charities. Her work for children and social work in the House of Lords is legendary. She is actively pursuing the implementation of three years' professional training for social workers, including probation officers. She launched the Faithfull Foundation in December 1994. Its aim is to reduce the risk of children being abused. It does this through providing services for children, their families, their workers and their abusers.

Pam Freeman is currently employed at the Socio-Legal Centre for Family Studies, based at the University of Bristol, where she is completing a project on parental perspectives on statutory intervention in child protection. She has a background in teaching and social work, but has been engaged as a university researcher since 1989, working at Dartington Social Research Unit until 1993. Her first major joint publication explores parental perspectives in suspected cases of child abuse.

Bernard Gallagher is Research Fellow in the Department of Social Policy and Social Work at the University of Manchester. He has been involved in child protection research for approximately ten years and in the summer of 1995 began a two-year Economic and Social Research Council-funded study of stranger abuse.

Roger Gaspar is Acting Chief Superintendent, Metropolitan Police, in charge of their Central Complaints Investigation Department. He was responsible for the police operational management of Operation Hedgerow, a successful paedophile case in Kilburn, Brent. He was also Project Leader on

the award-winning ACPO/Home Office Investigative Interviewing Project and has trained on joint investigations since 1989.

Perdeep Gill is a former child protection social worker and was the founder of Incest Survivors in Strength. She has worked with survivors' groups, mothers' groups, and Asian children and families. She is a freelance trainer on group work in child protection, and a consultant on the impact of abuse within the Asian communities.

David Gough is Associate Professor at Japan Women's University. His research on child welfare includes a two-year prospective study of child abuse case intervention (1987), a survey of cases of child sexual abuse seen at Glasgow Children's Hospital, the first Scottish child abuse statistics (1988, 1991), and a survey of services for children in Scotland with motor impairment (1992). He was co-editor of *Intervening in Child Sexual Abuse* (Scottish Academic Press, 1991) and author of *Child Abuse Interventions: A Review of the Research Literature* (HMSO, 1993). He is Book Review Editor of *Child Abuse Review* and a member of the Editorial Board of the *Journal of Child Abuse and Neglect*.

Mike Hames joined the Metropolitan Police in 1962. He served for 32 years and held a variety of management positions at senior rank from 1970. During much of this time he specialised in the detection of sex offences. During the last five years of his service he was the Detective Superintendent in charge of the Obscene Publications Branch at New Scotland Yard. The main role of the branch is the proactive detection of paedophile offenders. He was also the UK representative at Interpol on the Standing Working Group on Offences Against Children and a member of the Sexual Offences Steering Committee at Scotland Yard. He has carried out research into organised and ritual abuse of children and is an acknowledged authority on the subject of child sexual abuse from a police perspective. He has lectured widely at home and abroad, has published many articles and has frequently been on television and radio.

Anne Hollows is Principal Lecturer in Social Work at the University of East London, where she is responsible for children and families teaching and for the Diploma in Social Work. She was previously head of the Child Abuse Training Unit, a national training advisory service based at the National Children's Bureau. She is co-editor of *Children as Abusers, Significant Harm* and *Child Protection in the Early Years* and has written and contributed to a number of training packs. She is currently researching the role of independent social workers in child protection and the development of concepts of professional practice in novice social workers.

Jan Horwath combines work as a senior training officer in Sheffield Family and Community Services Department with a part-time lecturing post at Sheffield University, where she is responsible for the training of practice teachers and trainers. She previously worked as the Northern Training Adviser at the Child Abuse Training Unit.

Beverley Hughes is head of the Department of Social Policy and Social Work at the University of Manchester. She has researched on both child sexual abuse and adoption and has written and lectured extensively about these.

Catherine Itzin is Research Professor in Sociology and Social Policy in the School of Social and International Studies at the University of Sunderland. She is the editor and co-author of *Pornography: Women, Violence and Civil Liberties* (Oxford University Press, 1992) and the author of 'Pornographic and Violent Videos' in *Video Violence and Young Offenders*, Home Affairs Committee, 4th Report (HMSO, 1994) and 'Pornography, Harm and Human Rights: The European Context' in *Sexual Politics and the European Union*, edited by A. Elman (Berghann Books, 1995).

Jean La Fontaine is a social anthropologist who taught at the London School of Economics, where she is now Professor Emeritus. She has done research in East and Central Africa and, recently, in Britain. Her publications about sexual abuse include 'Child Sexual Abuse: Defining Organised Sexual Abuse' (in *Child Abuse Review*) and *The Nature and Extent of Organised and Ritual Abuse* (HMSO, 1994). She is currently working on a book about ritual and satanic abuse.

Maureen O'Hara worked at the Children's Legal Centre, where she co-ordinated the legal advice service and carried out policy work relating to child protection. The centre is a national charity which promotes the human rights of children. With other children's charities, she lobbied for full implementation of the Pigot recommendations on child witnesses during the passage of the Criminal Justice Act 1991. She was a member of the Home Office Advisory Group which was consulted about the *Memorandum of Good Practice* on video recording of children's evidence (HMSO, 1992), and contributed to the *Child Witness Pack* published by the NSPCC. Before training in law, she was a teacher for eight years, working in mainstream education as well as teaching children with 'emotional and behavioural difficulties'. She has worked on issues of child protection from a feminist perspective for sixteen years.

Howard Parker is Professor of Social Work at the University of Manchester. In addition to his work on child sexual abuse, he has researched and written on delinquency, the criminal justice system and drug misuse.

Anne Peake is employed as a principal psychologist by Oxfordshire Social Services. She works with professionals and families using family centres, social work teams and children's homes. She runs, with colleagues, a child sexual abuse consultation service, thus reflecting one of her professional interests. She has run many groups for both girls and boys of all ages. She is also involved in group work for mothers of abused children.

Angela Thomas is an occupational therapist with a background in adult mental health. She was seconded to Barnardos in April 1993, where she carried out the study upon which much of her chapter is based. Prior to qualifying as an occupational therapist, she worked as a nursery and infant teacher and as a playgroup leader.

Ray Wyre is nationally acknowledged as an independent consultant and expert in the sexual crime field. He began this work in the Probation Service in the 1970s. In the 1980s he established a group work programme in a top-security prison. Having worked providing sexual counselling, he then founded the Gracewell Clinic and Institute in 1988. He is currently a sessional specialist for the Faithfull Foundation. He has published and broadcast widely. His books include *Women, Men, and Rape* (Hodder and Stoughton, 1986), *Working with Sex Abuse* (Perry Publishers, 1986), and most recently, *The Murder of Childhood* (Penguin, 1995), a study of the multiple child murderer, Robert Black.

Foreword

Baroness Faithfull

There is cause to wonder why child sexual abuse has only risen to the surface of public awareness within the past decade; perhaps the reason is the publicity given to such cases as were cited in the Cleveland Report, in reports of subsequent public inquiries into child abuse in children's homes and schools, the Clyde Report of occurrences in the Orkneys, and increased understanding of child abuse within families.

Whether as victims of a paedophile ring or a family circle, children are so manipulated by perpetrators or a single perpetrator that they remain silent. Shame and unhappiness are borne alone; indeed, some children have said that they thought that such practices within the family were part of normal family life. We now recognise the effects of child sexual abuse on children, as adolescents and into the later years of life; such experiences can never be forgotten; moreover, abused children are likely to become abusers in later life.

In this book there are 19 chapters, each of which has been written by an author with knowledge and experience of a particular aspect of organised child sexual abuse. Peter Bibby is to be congratulated on bringing together such a group of authors able to inform those professionally engaged in the investigation and treatment of organised child sexual abuse. This book will also be of value, and give information, to the general public, to parents, and indeed all those responsible for the care and education of children. In this, I believe the book to be unique.

In Chapter 1, Peter Bibby sets a scene for the ensuing chapters; he outlines his own findings, and these threads are to be found in other chapters in different guises and different settings. He discusses organised abuse, which he first came across in 1987, and which goes under many names: satanic abuse, network abuse, child sex rings or institutional abuse. The perpetrator may or may not be a member of the children's family. Perpetrators choose their victims in a deliberate and sophisticated manner; the children on whom perpe-

trators target their interest are those children most likely to be vulnerable and insecure and therefore easily manipulated. There is a link between the sexually-abused child and the adoption of high-risk behaviour in later life: prostitution, drugs and sexual abuse. Parents of sexually-abused children experience a sense that they themselves have been assaulted. The vulnerable children who are sexually assaulted experience a sense of shame and personal guilt.

This book covers the nature, extent, and history of our understanding of organised abuse (Chapters 1, 2, 4, 7, 15 and 16); the legal issues (Chapter 3); the impact on people – victims, families and staff (Chapters 5, 10 and 17); links with pornography (Chapters 13 and 14); specialist areas (issues concerning the Asian communities, HIV/AIDS and institutions – Chapters 6, 8 and 12), and ways of responding (Chapters 9, 11, 18 and 19).

The authors have made a valuable contribution to the understanding of the issues of organised child sexual abuse, how they arise, and how they may best be dealt with.

This is a unique and valuable book for all those working in the arena of childcare and those who wish to seek an understanding of abusers.

Introduction

Peter Bibby

This book has taken more time than a baby whale in its gestation. It was conceived following Roger Gaspar's and my involvement in the successful breaking up of a paedophile ring in 1987. This resulted in 15 men being sent to prison for a total of more than 150 years. We both felt that what we had achieved had occurred mainly through fortune and flying by the seat of our pants. This did not seem like a good way to approach what we realised was a complex phenomenon that we had not previously studied. Later research led us to believe that no one else had either. This was confirmed when we attended an invitation conference sponsored by ChildLine and the National Children's Homes, together with approximately another 500 people. We, with Liz Webb (Brent's then Child Protection Co-ordinator), made our first presentation.

Further requests for talks led to requests for training. Following the publication of the Clyde Report into the incidents in the Orkneys, and as part of the training provided by the Department of Health on the Children Act 1989, Roger, Marianne Tranter (later Bentovim) and I represented COCAN (the Committee on Child Abuse Networks) in taking a road show on 'Organised Abuse' around the regions to members of each Area Child Protection Committee in England. This led to requests for a formalisation of our understanding of this newly-identified phenomenon.

Our respective employers gave us time to undertake this training (the fees being passed on to them). We became conscious of the dearth of written material about the topic. In 1993, I was able to take an early pension and so had the time, security and freedom to develop my thinking about this subject. Whilst I did not consider that I could write about all aspects of the topic, I felt that I knew people who collectively could. They are drawn from a variety of professions, truly having to 'work together' to achieve our objective of helping children and their families.

At that time, a few books about satanic abuse had been published. I was concerned that the debate about the validity of this would ensure that we did not deal with the bigger problem of tackling organised abuse. This book is therefore intended to cover all aspects of 'common or garden' organised abuse. I hope it will be of use to all child protection workers, and policy-makers, and will give front-line workers, managers and trainers ideas to improve their response. From this, I believe that we will be able to examine other forms of abuse from a more considered perspective.

Baroness Faithfull kindly outlines in her Foreword the areas covered by the chapters. When I started on this enterprise, I had a list that included only 12 of them. Each time I spoke with anyone, more and more ideas came up. There are many gaps left by the structure of this book, partly due to the fast-moving nature of the topic and partly due to difficulties in getting chapters written. The most obvious omissions are chapters on *the impact on African/Caribbean communities* (the designated author was not able to complete the task, for personal reasons, within the time-scale required), on *issues for children with disabilities* (people with expertise in this area were not able to give a commitment to write a chapter as part of their workload), *by a survivor* (as the book has developed, it has become increasingly apparent that this would be useful; the nearest we have are in Chapters 10 and 13, but these are not a substitute for the firsthand voice of a survivor), on *international trafficking* (this is an area that is closely linked with the international use of child pornography; there are issues of compatibility of different jurisdictions and different cultural approaches to sex and children; sexual tourism is but one aspect of this) and on *international comparisons* (although there are some current talks about the possibility of exchanging ideas found in this book across the Atlantic and through the European Forum for Child Welfare, there is no doubt that the methods of abusers internationally are far more advanced than those of the child protection agencies).

In order to avoid the distracting, repetitive use of such expressions as 'he or she' or 's/he' in this book, we have adopted the following conventions: although there is some discussion of the involvement of females as perpetrators of abuse, abusers are generally referred to as 'he'; unless the gender distinction is important to the argument, children or a single child subjected to abuse are referred to as 'they'.

I am truly grateful to each of the authors in this book who found time in addition to their day-jobs to write their contribution. Each has done this with great thought and under great pressure. I am also particularly grateful to Valerie Howarth, Chief Executive of ChildLine, without whose support I might well have fallen at the first hurdle.

Whilst the credit should go to each of the authors for the work they have done, shortcomings, including those mentioned above, in the concept and implementation of this compilation remain my responsibility.

1 Definitions and recent history

Peter Bibby

Introduction

Although sex was discovered, according to Philip Larkin, in 1965, if we go back into history we discover that Tiberius abused many children on his retirement in Capri (Graves, 1957). Only two or three articles on organised abuse appear before the late 1980s. As for me, I discovered it in 1987. If one looks at publications, letters and conferences, there is virtually nothing published before that time on the subject.

British literature started appearing in 1990. North America often identifies sociological issues before the United Kingdom. However, there appears to be no US literature, other than Finkelhor, before 1988, and Canadian literature of that time is descriptive rather than analytical. Some earlier literature looks at the use of pornography, and some looks at child prostitution, but there is no over-arching paradigm linking them with each other or with paedophilia. The early literature is dominated by articles about the more dramatic forms of organised abuse that have been given the titles 'ritual' or 'satanic abuse'.

How was it then, for me? When we came across our first sex ring in Brent in 1987, it was necessary to research quickly, and then act. There was a faint recollection of a ring in Leeds, a few years earlier, but no reference to it could be found in social work literature. In fact, articles were published in *Child Abuse and Neglect* and *Paediatrics*, but only at a later date.

Why should something that is now seen as such a serious violation of children have been unidentified for so long? I feel that society can only recognise something when it is ready to do so. Like peeling an onion, society can only go to the next layer of difficulty when it has come to terms with the layer above.

When I was trained, the general approach to domestic violence was to

1

explain it as wives (sic) who subconsciously wanted to be dominated by their husbands. The police dealt with such assaults as 'domestics', where the women always returned home. It was only when Erin Pizzey brought the women's refuge concept to Britain that women found an alternative: somewhere to go, where they were able to take action to counteract the oppression they were suffering. At that time, there were major debates about the nature and depth of the problem of 'battered wives'. This was the first occasion in modern times when the image of the 'protective' family was broken.

Society was only then ready to consider the possibility of battered children, resulting, in Britain in 1974 following the death of Maria Colwell, in the first co-ordinated response, with the setting up of Area Review Committees. Having swallowed hard at the discovery that child abuse covered all classes and all ages, by the 1980s we became ready to accept the fact of sexual abuse by parents and close family. However, in November 1985, the Scottish Office could still say: 'Public attitudes towards sexual abuse cases are at the stage which . . . non-accidental injuries . . . [were] 15 years ago.'

Many developments in social policy are a response to the latest crisis. Maria Colwell fulfilled this trigger function (DHSS, 1974), as on a later date did the incidence of a cluster of abuse allegations in Cleveland (Butler-Sloss, 1988). This later event resulted in the publication of the first version of *Working Together* (DHSS/WO, 1988). Even in this relatively recent publication, there was no mention of the phenomenon of organised abuse.

It took a number of more high-profile cases, including Rochdale and the Orkneys, for the government to take notice. However, even at this stage, the issues were not properly recognised. Great public pressure was generated, as people wished to say that 'satanic' abuse was not taking place. This diverted energy from the questions of whether *any* form of abuse had taken place; how children could be fully protected, and how offenders could be properly convicted. Following the publication of the Clyde Report into the Orkney events (Clyde, 1992) (whose contents might lead the interested reader to believe that some sort of abuse, that was not identified, *was* taking place), the second edition of *Working Together* (DoH, 1991) was published by the government on an inter-departmental basis. This did contain sections on institutional abuse, organised abuse and 'bizarre' abuse.

Whilst individuals may disagree over whether a particular child has been abused by a particular person in a particular way, there is now little disagreement that organised abuse takes place. Few would deny that it can be very nasty, and that some horrific practices are inflicted on children.

Granted this level of awareness, I would expect acceptance of the more horrific forms of abuse to become more apparent over the next decade or so. Whether these will turn out to be ritual abuse, satanic abuse or a form of abuse that has not yet been perceived remains to be seen. Time will tell. I

hope, with the lessons of history against me, that we will be able to respond effectively when they are first identified.

Another reason why we have not been and, indeed, still are not good at dealing with organised abuse lies in our training. The basic training of all the main investigating professionals focuses on individual pathology. Medical and nursing staff are taught about responses to individual patients or even individual bones; the police generally deal with individually-notified crimes; social workers deal with individual cases or perhaps individual families. We also tend to consider 'victims' as either bringing disasters on themselves or being the random subjects of a more general phenomenon.

The message in this book is that *these 'victims' are deliberately chosen, in a sophisticated and deliberate manner*. Responses therefore need to deal with organised abuse as organised crime. The police need to treat it as they deal with other organised crime, namely with specialist teams. Health and Social Services must deal with it more on a community or large-group basis than an individual one. We are all dealing with deliberate and persistent perpetrators who are active 168 hours per week, and must respond appropriately.

Definitions

At present, there is no commonly-accepted definition or description of organised abuse. Indeed, there is no commonly-accepted title for the phenomenon. Some people believe that a number of different matters are being confused and conflated with each other. Others, including myself, believe that there is a common phenomenon, appearing in different clothes in different circumstances.

Terms that I have used include: 'organised abuse'; 'network abuse'; 'child sex rings'; 'paedophile rings', or 'webs'. Others use the terms 'pederasts' or 'multiple abusers'. Some people see institutional abuse as the same phenomenon in all circumstances; some see it as the same when there are multiple perpetrators; others do not see it as the same at all. The issues of ritual and satanic abuse are so difficult for most professionals to handle that many hope it will go away. Many are not able to discuss it without degenerating into the language of pantomime ('Oh yes it is' – 'Oh no it's not!')

This is not too surprising. At the early stage of identifying any thus far unidentified phenomenon (remember Galileo), such difficulties occur. However, it is unhelpful to children that energies are focused on battling for position rather than trying to improve performance.

One of the earliest definitions was given as recently as 1989 by N.J. Wild in *Paediatrics:*

Rings comprise an adult perpetrator (or perpetrators) and several children who

are simultaneously involved in sexual activity and aware of each others participation. Although perpetrators are not usually related to their victims, some of the children involved may have been abused by family members.

As the first definition, written after an analysis of cases in Leeds, this is seminal. It contains many truths. However, numerous professionals would now say that many children are not aware of the participation of others. Many perpetrators try to keep children isolated. Similarly, many but not all of these adults may be aware of each other. 'Simultaneously' suggests the notion of group sexual activity, which does not match the evidence. 'Contemporaneously' more accurately reflects the multi-victim situation, but it does not reflect the offender who serially abuses. This definition fails, in my view, because it does not reflect the vulnerability of the children, which is an important factor, nor the varied nature of the abusers. The above definition was not widely circulated or acknowledged outside the medical community.

The first widely-circulated definition is found two years later, in the second edition of *Working Together* (DoH, 1991):

> Organised abuse is a generic term which covers abuse, which may involve a number of abusers, a number of abused children and young people, and often encompasses different forms of abuse. It involves, to a greater or lesser extent, an element of organisation. (para. 5.26.1, p.38)

Working Together continues:

> some ... groups may use bizarre or ritualised behaviour, sometimes associated with a particular 'belief' system. (para. 5.26.2)

This statement is to be welcomed as the first official acknowledgement of organised abuse, and its more bizarre forms. It is, however, a circular definition, saying essentially that 'Organised abuse is abuse that is organised.' Whilst it is important in drawing attention for the first time to the fact that such a phenomenon exists, it goes no further in giving guidance about its nature. The definition in *Working Together* also implies that organised abuse does not occur when there is one identified perpetrator. The fact that there is a different section in *Working Together* on institutional abuse also implies that organised abuse is different from abuse in residential settings. As I shall argue later, the techniques used in all these scenarios are similar, and therefore the response should be similar.

Jean La Fontaine of the London School of Economics, and Howard Parker, Beverley Hughes and Bernard Gallagher of the University of Manchester, who carried out parallel research into the prevalence and nature of abuse (see Chapters 15 and 16), have also taken definitions further.

Jean La Fontaine, in *Child Abuse Review*, provided a lengthy analysis of

common defining characteristics, from which she derives the following definition:

> [Organised abuse is] abuse by multiple perpetrators, some or all of whom are outside the immediate household of the victim(s), and who act together to abuse the child(ren). (La Fontaine, 1993)

This is more explicit than the *Working Together* definition in stating that single perpetrators are not organised abusers. I expressed my concerns about this in a later *Child Abuse Review* (Bibby, 1994). Considering multiple abuse by a single perpetrator as a different phenomenon from multiple abuse by several perpetrators is inaccurate and dangerous. It restricts and stifles thinking about the investigation by neglecting the possibility of other abusers. Later chapters in this book show that single perpetrators use fundamentally similar methods to those used by groups of perpetrators, and can only be satisfactorily investigated by an appreciation of those methods.

In a conference in Manchester held in June 1994, on sharing knowledge on organised and ritual abuse, Professor Howard Parker and his team of Beverley Hughes and Bernard Gallagher (1994) describe four dimensions that occur in all cases of organised abuse. The balance varies in each case. The four dimensions are:

- the number of children;
- the number of perpetrators;
- the number of times of abuse;
- the amount of planning, organisation, the method of grooming and the devices and techniques used to achieve the abuse.

In April 1994, Dr David Jones of the Park Hospital, Oxford, used the construct of multiple abuse – including multiple perpetrators and multiple victims. Both he and the Manchester team feel that defining the phenomenon now is unhelpful. They feel that as we are at such an early stage of our understanding, it would narrow the way we think about it, rather than assisting us in thinking laterally.

Whilst one can sympathise with this approach and can learn from the truths contained in their models, I find that most practitioners need a definition, in order to make some sense of the problem to be tackled. To assist myself, the following definition was generated. I hope it will be of use to others.

- *Organised abuse* is the systematic abuse of children, normally by more than one male.
- It is characterised by the degree of planning in the purposeful, secret targeting, seduction, hooking and silencing of the subjects.

●   Institutional and ritual abuse are but specialised forms of organised abuse.

All previous definitions have tried to define organised abuse in terms of numbers, and relationships between perpetrators and victims. This misses the key differentiating features. They are, rather, the organised processes which the perpetrators use. Organised abuse is therefore not, in essence, a matter of numbers and systems relationships amongst the perpetrator(s) and the subject(s). It is a matter of process rather than systems. This fits in with the experience of most practitioners that the techniques used by single perpetrators are similar to those used by multiple perpetrators. The core of the definition above, therefore, is in the second item. It directs our thoughts towards the *systems* used by perpetrators.

Like many definitions at the frontiers of knowledge, I would expect that this one will have been refined and tested even in the year between writing this chapter and publication. More important, however, is to describe and test the posited core truths. This will lead to a model for practice over the next few years. If in five years' time our understanding has moved on so that this phenomenon is accepted and understood in an agreed manner, this definition will have served its purpose.

It is important to state that it is predominantly men who abuse, although some women are involved in abuse. Why this is so, and whether women are primarily predators in these scenarios or oppressed followers, must be the subject of another book.

Perpetrators may or may not be members of the nuclear family.

The research undertaken by Bernard Gallagher (Gallagher, 1994) indicates that one-third of known victims of paedophiles are female; two thirds are male. The figures are likely to be so inaccurate that they can only reliably indicate the broad finding that both straight and gay men are involved in paedophilia.

As one learns from people who deal with sexual offenders, and in particular Ray Wyre (Chapter 7 in this volume), it is apparent that vulnerable children are targeted, both consciously and unconsciously. The offence is characterised by planning, in the sense that perpetrators get themselves into positions where they can have contact with children and create opportunities to be alone with them. Secrecy is of the essence in this targeting. The abuse may be known within the closed abusing system, but it is kept secret from the outside.

The purposeful seduction of the child is normally the culmination of a lengthy period of targeting and grooming. The ensuing 'hooking' ensures that the children keep coming back as and when the perpetrator requires, similar to the way in which anglers hook and play a fish.

The children are silenced by threats, shame, and persuasion that they themselves are responsible for the acts.

From talking with many hundreds of professionals, I believe this process is common in all examples of multiple-victim abuse. It is found in institutional abuse in schools (Brannan, Jones and Murch, 1993), children's homes (Kirkwood, 1993) and daycare centres. It is found where there are allegations of rituals or bizarre events. It is also common to examples from North America and international abuse within Europe. In my view, therefore, institutional and ritual abuse are sub-sets of organised abuse.

Of course, the problem for practitioners is that, at the time the first allegations come to light, details of the process stages may well not be known. It may initially appear to be a single case of stranger abuse. It is rather like looking at a single star, unable to decide whether it is just part of an unconnected cluster or whether it is part of a yet-to-be-understood constellation. Methods of distinguishing, deciding and counteracting are to be found in Chapters 4, 9, 11 and 12.

Roger Gaspar has identified a number of features of organised abuse which, if kept in the forefront of our minds, may help us investigate abuse and support children. Just as in intra-familial abuse, the victims may feel considerable attraction and/or loyalty to the offenders. We need to establish what are the blocks to disclosure. We need to be able to differentiate between current abuse and previous abusive experiences. The forms of abuse may well be beyond the experience of the investigators. (This has great significance for staff support and training.) Initially, we may well have only scattered pieces of a jigsaw.

If any of the following special features are present in any case of abuse, then this should trigger the organised abuse procedures:

- children from more than one family;
- abuse by a person other than the father;
- information from local intelligence;
- geographical proximity of apparently disconnected abusers;
- abuse in an establishment, whether day or residential.

Wherever I have discussed the above definition, people have struggled to distinguish the characteristics from some of those found in intra-familial abuse. Quite clearly, some intra-familial abuse (in particular, roaming step-parents) definitely falls into the organised abuse category. I think that nuclear family abuse, as we understand it, starts by being more opportunist than organised abuse. On the whole, men do not marry in order to have children whom they intend to abuse at a planned stage in the future; but some *do*. Quite clearly, there are similar issues for those who are abused within the family in the next stages of seduction and silencing.

As far as the children are concerned, there are a number of differences between intra-familial and organised abuse. Children in intra-familial abuse may feel as though they are the 'property' of the father. However, the child subjected to organised abuse feels a greater degree of dehumanisation, namely that of being bought and sold or bartered as a 'commodity'. Children abused within their own family may be frightened of a person they know; children subjected to organised abuse may well be frightened of abusers or enforcers they do not know. Within the family, the hooking is explicit and sanctioned by society; for a paedophile outside the family the hooking needs to be more calculated. The one advantage staff may have to assist the subject of organised abuse is that the family could be a vital centre of support, provided we are sure they are not involved, and they are able to help.

However, the key to organised abuse is that the perpetrator sets up planned situations to arrange contact with children and maintains control over the subjects, both when they go to other caregivers and over a lengthy period of time. In intra-familial abuse, the victim is often under the day-to-day control of the abuser. Of course, this is also true in institutional abuse, and these extra pressures need to be considered when trying to release the victim from the abusers' control in both settings.

References

Bibby, P. (1994) 'Definition of organised abuse', *Child Abuse Review*, 3 (3), 163–4.

Brannan, C., Jones, J.R. and Murch, J.D. (1993) *Castle Hill Report – Practice Guide*, Shrewsbury: Shropshire County Council.

Butler-Sloss, E. (1988) *Report of the Inquiry into Child Abuse in Cleveland 1987* (The Cleveland Report), London: HMSO

Clyde, J.J. (1992) *Report of the Inquiry into the Removal of Children from Orkney in February 1991* (The Clyde Report), Edinburgh: HMSO.

Department of Health (DoH) (1991) *Working Together Under the Children Act: A Guide to Arrangements for Inter-Agency Co-operation for the Protection of Children from Abuse*, London: HMSO.

Department of Health and Social Security (DHSS) (1974) *Report of the Committee of Inquiry into the Care and Supervision Provided in Relation to Maria Colwell*, London: HMSO.

Department of Health and Social Security/Welsh Office (DHSS/WO) (1988) *Working Together for the Protection of Children*, LAC 88 (10), HMSO: London.

Gallagher, B. (1994) 'Organised and ritual sexual abuse – What we know now', paper presented to conference on 'Organised and Ritual Child Sexual Abuse: Sharing New Knowledge', University of Manchester, School of Social Work, 20/21 June.

Graves, R. (1957) *Suetonius: The Twelve Caesars, A New Translation*, London: Penguin.

Kirkwood, A. (1993) *The Leicestershire Enquiry 1992*, Leicester: Leicestershire County Council.

La Fontaine, J.S. (1993) 'Defining Organized Sexual Abuse', *Child Abuse Review*, 2 (4), 223–31.

Wild, N.J. (1989) 'Prevalence of Child Sex Rings', *Paediatrics*, 83 (4), 553–8.

2 An overview of the literature

David Gough

Introduction

Well-organised, systematic and severe abuse of children has always existed, but was formerly thought to be a rarity. There is now a growing concern that the focus upon risks to individual children and families may have obscured the organised nature of much abuse, which may require a different professional and societal response.

An initial problem is being precise about what is meant by 'organised abuse' (Bibby, 1994; see also Chapter 1 in this volume). La Fontaine (1993) provides a clear account of the issues involved in creating a definition and offers her own definition based upon multiple abusers acting together in some way to abuse the child, with at least some of these abusers not belonging to the child's household. La Fontaine's definition clarifies many of the implicit distinctions in the earlier definition provided by central government in *Working Together* (DOH, 1991) by explicitly excluding lone perpetrators, serial abuse by unconnected perpetrators and abuse that is solely intra-familial. Interestingly, most authors use the term 'organised abuse' to refer to sexual abuse, although physical and other forms of abuse might also be involved. All types of abuse, however, can be highly organised, whether this be scapegoating within a family, inter-generational physical abuse and neglect (Oliver, 1993), or abuse in institutions by peers, by individual staff (Rosenthal et al., 1991), or numbers of staff (Levy and Kahan, 1991), or child labour.

It is difficult to determine what are the critical features in defining organised abuse. Possibilities are the numbers of perpetrators and victims, the abuse of non-family members, the frequency and severity of abuse, planning or repetitive nature of the abuse, the social context in which the abuse occurs or the basis of the perpetrator's wish to carry out the abuse. Current concepts of organised abuse contain an unspecified mix of such variables.

This book is concerned primarily with sexual abuse and uses a wide definition by including single perpetrators where there is systematic abuse of children (Bibby, 1994). This broad definition is also able to include all types of ritual abuse, including ritual abuse perpetrated by single individuals. This is a working definition of abuse to help create awareness and bring attention to the organised nature of much sexual abuse. Further empirical and theoretical research is required to allow us to be clearer about the important distinguishing characteristics of organised abuse. As with all definitions of abuse, they depend upon socially-defined notions of appropriate childcare. Male circumcision, for example, is common in Western societies but could be considered a societally-sanctioned form of genital mutilation, and thus ritual abuse.

This selective review uses the categorisation of Burgess and Hartman (1987) also used by Gaspar and Bibby in Chapter 4 of this volume, although transaction and group-type cases are considered together, and ritual abuse is given a separate heading. Only sexual organised abuse is considered. General reviews of organised and ritual abuse can be found in National Resource Center on Child Sexual Abuse (NRCCSA) (1990), Hudson (1991), Faller (1994), Kelly (1993), Kelly and Scott (1993), Kelley (1993) and Burrell (1994). Vehement critiques of the 'sex abuse industry' and the search for organised abuse and recovered memories can be found in Ofshe and Watters (1994), Prendergast (1994) and the journal *Issues in Child Abuse Accusations*.

Syndicated abuse

Syndicated organised abuse is where there is a commercial basis to the abuse of the children. Commercial exploiters may not actually abuse the children themselves, though they will be involved in arranging or creating a commercial demand for the abuse to occur. The two main forms of commercial exploitation are pornography and prostitution.

Pornography

In a book describing sexual trafficking in the United States, Campagna and Poffenberger (1988) distinguish international, national, regional and local markets for pornography. Tate (1990) reports on the extent of the trade in child pornography and its links with organised crime. Hard-core child pornography used to be freely available in several countries and marketed internationally through paedophile contact magazines, but recent international concern and resultant social pressure has resulted in most countries acting to suppress the open commercial marketing of such material (Hames, 1993; see also Chapter 14 in this volume). The trade must still exist, and the

limited availability may drive up the underground market price. There may also be a bigger trade in the 'softer' child pornography, consisting of photographs of naked children, which receives less attention from law enforcement than the more hard-core material (Campagna and Poffenberger, 1988).

The most obvious purpose of pornography is for commercial profit. Campagna and Poffenberger (1988) list a number of others. Pimps controlling child prostitutes may use pornography to coerce children or their customers. Pornography may also be used by those controlling prostitutes or paedophiles to instruct the children in different sexual practices and to condition children to agree to partake in such activities.

Another common use of pornography is to provide paedophiles with a photographic record of the abuse they performed, including 'innocent', non-overtly pornographic photographic records of the children (Campagna and Poffenberger, 1988; Hames, 1993). These pornographic collections may also be shared and swapped or sold with other paedophiles. The paedophiles' attachment to these collections and their reluctance to destroy them can be very useful for law enforcement as legal evidence of sexual abuse and for tracing other paedophiles abusing children (Hames, 1993).

The conclusion of several authors is that most child pornography is generated on a local level. Some of this is produced as a 'cottage industry' for syndicated commercial use (Tate, 1990), but a large proportion is a by-product of sexual abuse by paedophiles or of child prostitution (Campagna and Poffenberger, 1988; Hames, 1993).

Prostitution

There seems to be more overt concern about intra-familial and extra-familial sexual abuse and networks of paedophiles than the equally serious issue of child prostitution. The extent and nature of child prostitution has been well documented by Sereny (1984), Campagna and Poffenberger (1988), Fassett and Walsh (1994) and, for males, by West (1992).

A simple form of child prostitution may be the exchange of victims between paedophiles on the basis of payment or in return for favours of various kinds. Most of the child prostitution described in the literature, though, is a straightforward commercial enterprise, much like adult prostitution. The important difference is that the 'workers' are children, who are being exploited by those who manage the trade and the customers that they attract. Child prostitution is thus both child labour and sexual abuse. Although the literature makes references to the prostitution of very young children, few distinctions are made between pre- and post-pubertal prostitution.

Many child prostitutes have disturbed backgrounds – including lack of affectionate or supervisory care, and sexual abuse – and become dependent on the pimps who control them. The pimps may initiate the relationship with

seduction and emotional dependency, and then manage the children with withdrawal of affection, threats, violence or addiction to drugs (Campagna and Poffenberger, 1988; Fassett and Walsh, 1994). Adult prostitutes may also introduce their own children into the trade (Campagna and Poffenberger, 1988). In all of these cases, the children's world is largely proscribed by the people who manage and principally benefit from their sexual exploitation.

There is also an international dimension, with many reports of citizens of rich, developed countries travelling to poorer countries in South America, the Indian subcontinent and South East Asia to purchase the sexual services of male and female children (Campagna and Poffenberger, 1988; Vittachi, 1989; O'Grady, 1992; Ireland, 1993; see also the reports referenced by Kelly and Scott, 1993).

Some of the children are very young, supplied for a relatively small and specialist market of foreign paodophiles A much greater number of child prostitutes are young, adolescent females, in particular demand for their youth or supposed lack of sexually transmitted diseases, or simply helping to fulfil the large internal and tourist markets' demands for prostitutes.

The commercial value of the children's bodies, the children's lack of other forms of financial support, and their few rights as children allow some adults to buy and trade in these children. In South East Asia, children are traded from poorer countries like Nepal and Burma to richer countries such as India and Thailand (Koompraphant, 1994; Upadhyaya, 1994). In the past, in poor agricultural communities, male children were more highly valued than females because of their future contribution to the household economy. With the growth of material expectations, some parents have become aware of the potential financial rewards from the prostitution of female children.

Solo abuse

Sexual abuse of an individual child by a sole perpetrator on a single occasion could fit the definition of organised abuse, but some extra criteria would probably have to be invoked. The abuse of multiple victims by a single perpetrator can be more easily seen as having an organised component, with some individuals developing elaborate strategies to target children systematically (Conte, Wolf and Smith, 1989). The sexual interest in children may start in the abusers' own childhood (NCH, 1992; Barbaree, Marshall and Hudson, 1993; Glasgow et al., 1994), resulting in lifetime abuse careers involving large numbers of children (Becker, 1994). The large numbers of children involved make the abuse predominantly extra-familial. The perpetrators who restrict themselves to intra-familial abuse may be qualitatively different, but Becker (1991) argues that this is mostly in terms of opportunity to abuse different victims, rather than there being a diagnostically different

type of paedophile. It may be that the intra-familial p
drive to search out other victims, is more fearful of be
has fewer organisational skills in achieving such furth

Another example of highly-organised solo sexual
obtaining work positions in nurseries and residential
access to potential child victims. Many of the childre
have some prior disadvantage such as disability, lack
ground, or even prior experience of abuse, all of whi
vulnerability to abuse.

Group abuse

There are many ways in which abusers might join together in their abuse of
children.

Gil (1982) defines institutional abuse as any system, programme, policy,
procedure, or individual interaction with a child in placement that exploits
or in any way is detrimental to the child's well-being or basic rights. If the
institutional abuse is socially sanctioned or is the effect of accepted practices
and policies then it equates to societal abuse. In other cases the abusive practices may be proscribed but hidden within the institution. However, in practice this distinction between sanctioned and proscribed activities is difficult
to maintain because of conflicting value bases within society. Also, society
may be more concerned about the cost of provision for very dependent or
difficult children than in providing quality care or inspection services (Jones,
1994). Such societal neglect provides perpetrators with opportunities to join
together to abuse children in institutions. For sexual abuse, the two types of
institution most discussed in the literature are daycare centres for young
children and residential care for children of all ages.

Organised abuse in the community that is not linked to an institution may
be part of a network of linked perpetrators and victims. Sometimes this network is based upon a pre-existing social or familial group. All of these types
of group-based organised abuse may have ritualistic components.

Daycare institutions

The four best-known studies of sexual abuse in daycare have been reviewed
and summarised by Faller (1994), Kelly (1993), Kelley (1994) and Kelley,
Brant and Waterman (1993).

Finkelhor, Williams and Burns (1988) conducted a national US study of
known cases of sexual abuse in daycare and identified 270 cases involving
1,639 victims, of which 13 per cent were cases of ritual abuse.

Kelley (1989) contrasted three groups of children in daycare: a group of 35

en disclosing ritual abuse in daycare, a group of 32 children disclosing
-ritual sexual abuse in daycare, and a matched comparison group of 67
hildren in daycare not reporting abuse.

Waterman et al. (1993) undertook a study of 82 children who had disclosed abuse as part of the famous McMartin pre-school case. These cases
were contrasted with 15 children disclosing non-ritual sexual abuse at a pre-
school in Nevada.

Faller (1994) and Michigan State Department of Mental Health (Bybee and
Mowbray, 1993) studied a large number of children who disclosed observing
or experiencing abuse at a pre-school in Michigan.

The daycare cases received considerable media and professional interest
and drew attention away from intra-familial abuse, although Finkelhor,
Williams and Burns (1988) calculated that children were still at greater risk of
abuse in the home than in daycare.

The daycare cases involved large numbers of children, often middle-class
children in affluent suburbs, and resulted in highly complex, lengthy and
often indeterminate legal proceedings depending largely on children's testimony. The trial in the McMartin case, for example, lasted six years, cost $15
million, and debate continues about the accuracy of an architectural report
describing filled-in tunnels under the school, where abuse may have
occurred. These cases were therefore at the forefront of awareness of organised abuse, organised ritual abuse, approaches to child interviews and children's testimony, and the polarisation that has developed between those
believing that either the children or the accused adults were victims.

Residential care institutions

Just as children are vulnerable to abuse by their family members, children in
residential care are vulnerable to abuse by other residents and by care staff
(Westcott, 1991). Surveys in America (Powers, Mooney and Nunno, 1990;
Blatt, 1992) and Britain (Westcott and Clement, 1992) indicate that such
abuse is common, though many cases are probably never identified. Abuse
in residential institutions may be by lone abusers, who then recruit others,
develop a network of abuse based on the institution, and train victims to be
perpetrators to initiate new victims into the network (Brannan et al., 1993a,
1993b). Just as with children placed in foster-care, the reasons why they are
in such care, including disability (Kelly, 1992) or physical, material or emotional abuse or deprivation (Jones, 1994), make the children more vulnerable
to abuse. In addition, if other residents have been subjected to abuse or had
other traumatic experiences, they may be physically or sexually aggressive
and abuse their fellow residents (Westcott and Clement, 1992). Abusive
members of staff may use such child difficulties to their advantage in terms
of identifying those vulnerable to abuse and those who might be potential

abusers to be recruited into a network of mutual abusers and victims. All these risks to children are compounded by deficiencies in the screening of staff (Westcott, 1991), and the closed nature of institutions leads to less overview of care activities than is usual from neighbours and visitors to families in the community.

Children in institutions can also have problems in ensuring their rights are protected. Not everyone has faith in complaints procedures in institutions, and before the era of children's rights officers, children caught running away were frequently returned to the same placement without full assessment of the reasons for their 'escape'.

The formal and legal authority of staff gives them power to exploit children in their care, but Jones (1994) argues that it is the forms of power of domination described by Weber as 'traditional' and 'charismatic' powers that allow perpetrators to abuse children in institutions and to limit the possibility of children enforcing their legal right not to be abused. The 'traditional' form of power is the legitimacy that people such as heads of residential homes for children have in the local communities. The 'charismatic' power comes from the personal charisma and almost religious power and influence of some individuals. Jones (1994) argues that improvements to legal rules and regulations will have little effect on institutional abuse if they do not tackle these non-formal methods that perpetrators use to counteract legal controls.

Community-based networks

Networks of sexual abusers are sometimes known as 'sex rings', which may involve multiple victims of one solo perpetrator, chains of overlapping perpetrators and victims or more cohesive groups of perpetrators and victims.

Burgess (1984) provided an early description of various types of sex rings, with an analysis of 60 child victims. More recently, there have been a number of high-profile cases concerning large networks of alleged abusers and victims (for example, Wild and Wynne, 1986), though cases of organised sexual abuse make up only a small proportion of all known sexual abuse cases, and most organised cases known to agencies are relatively small in scale, involving only a few perpetrators and/or victims (Creighton, 1993; La Fontaine, 1994; see also Chapter 16 in this volume). The research also shows that more female perpetrators are identified in multiple- than single-perpetrator cases (Creighton, 1993; La Fontaine, 1994; see also Chapter 15 in this volume).

In their national self-reporting survey (see Chapter 16 in this volume), Gallagher, Hughes and Parker found only 13 per cent of organised abuse cases involved families and relatives, but a more detailed search of agency records found many more such cases, suggesting that agencies tend not to consider cases based around families as organised abuse. The involvement

of families in networks of abuse has also been shown by Faller's (1991) study of poly-incestuous families. These cases involved inter-generational and lateral abuse of children, but in 60 per cent of cases there were also extra-familial victims, perpetrators, or both.

Ritual abuse

There have been an increasing number of allegations of sexual abuse involving rituals performed because of the belief-systems of the perpetrators, as part of social mechanisms to enable the abusers to carry out the abuse or as a means of intimidating the child victims. There is considerable controversy about how such ritual abuse should be defined, and the extent to which it exists according to such definitions, if at all.

Definitions

All forms of child abuse may be seen as having ritual components, but the term 'ritual abuse' is usually reserved for cases involving overt rituals, as found in religious or quasi-religious ceremonies. Although individual abusers could use rituals as part of the abuse, ritual abuse is mostly thought of as a behaviour shared by a group. Many of the alleged cases of ritual sexual abuse have been very extreme, involving extensive and prolonged sexual abuse of a large number of children by a large number of perpetrators. Some of these rituals have involved the worship of evil personified by Satan, and so are called 'satanic abuse'. Several definitions have been suggested to describe these various forms of ritual abuse.

Finkelhor, Williams and Burns (1988, p.59) have defined ritual abuse as:

> abuse that occurs in a context linked to some symbols or group activity that have a religious, magical, or supernatural connotation, and where the invocation of these symbols or activities, repeated over time, is used to frighten and intimidate the children.

Three sub-types are proposed. First, true cult-based ritual abuse, where the ritual is part of a religious or social system. Second, pseudo-ritual abuse, where there is no quasi-religious belief-system, but where rituals are used as a strategy to induce and maintain children's co-operation in sexual activities. Third, psychopathological ritualism, where the ritual arises from the psychopathological thought-systems of the perpetrator(s) (Finkelhor, Williams and Burns, 1988).

Similarly, McFadyen, Hanks and James (1993, p.37) have defined ritual abuse as:

the involvement of children in physical, psychological or sexual abuse associated with repeated activities ('ritual') which purport to relate the abuse to contexts of a religious, magical or supernatural kind.

Lloyd (1992) offers three different definitions to distinguish plain 'ritualistic child abuse' from 'cult ritualistic abuse' and 'group ritualistic abuse'. Ritualistic abuse is defined as:

the intentional physical abuse, sexual abuse, or psychological abuse of a child by a person responsible for the child's welfare, when such abuse is repeated and/or stylised and is conducted during the course of religious ceremonies, and is typified by such other acts as cruelty to animals, or threats of harm to the child, other persons, and animals. (Lloyd, 1992, p.3)

The definition for cult ritualistic abuse differs in that the abuse is by:

more than one person responsible for the child's welfare ... when such persons share spiritual beliefs and the acts are performed to reinforce the individuals' spiritual cohesion. (Lloyd, 1992, p.6)

The definition for group ritualistic abuse differs (from ritualistic abuse) in that the abuse is by:

more than one person responsible for the child's welfare [and] is performed to reinforce the group's cohesion. (Lloyd, 1992, p.6)

An earlier definition by Lloyd put more emphasis on the non-sexual abuse experienced by the child:

Physical or psychological abuse accompanying sexual abuse, performed in an intentional recurring formalised style to reinforce and implement a belief system to which the perpetrators subscribe to, religious, quasi religious, pseudo religious, or psychopathological. (Lloyd, cited in Lanning, 1990, p.29)

For Jones (1991, p.164), it is the extent of emotional or physical abuse co-existing with the sexual abuse that is important clinically. Ritual might be important, for example, in the effects on the child victim's belief-systems, but this should be evaluated according to its emotional consequences. If the extent of these co-existing abuses plus the extent to which there were multiple victims were taken into account, then it might not be necessary to invoke and then attempt to define new terms such as 'ritualistic' or 'ritual satanic abuse' (Jones, 1991).

The nature of ritual abuse

The four major studies of multiple abuse in daycare involved allegations of ritual abuse, but the literature contains numerous other clinical and personal accounts of survivors of ritual and satanic abuse (Smith and Pazder, 1980; Boyd, 1990; Snow and Sorenson, 1990; Jonker and Jonker-Bakker, 1991; Young et al., 1991; Sakheim and Devine, 1992; Scott, 1993; Coleman, 1994; Sinason, 1994).

Ritual abuse cases receive much publicity but are a small proportion of all cases known to agencies (see La Fontaine, 1994; see also Chapters 15 and 16 in this volume). The evidence for the ritual abuse of children comes primarily from the evidence of victims, either when children or as adult survivors. In some cases, the adult accounts are based on memories of abuse that had been forgotten but which were recovered during therapy initiated for some other presenting problem (Sinason, 1994; Terr, 1994). For those who believe that the children *have* been abused, the lack of corroborative evidence and the repression of memories of abuse is not surprising considering the severity of the abuse, the sophistication of the abusers and the power that they hold over the children.

The lack of independent evidence of abuse and the lack of consistent definitions makes it difficult to make definitive statements about the nature of ritual abuse or how it might differ from non-ritual organised abuse or non-organised abuse. However, the case studies of ritual abuse tend to describe abuse that is extremely severe and extensive in terms of the sexual acts performed, co-existence of severe psychological and physical abuse, duration of abuse, number of abusers, and the psychological and social significance of these abusers to the children. The co-existing physical abuse may not simply be a method to enforce obedience in the children, but may arise from the sadistic motives of the abusers (Goodwin, 1994). Where the children's families are involved in the abuse, then the network of abusers can amount to virtually all of the children's social worlds. In many reports, the child victims are also forced from a young age to perpetrate abuse on others, so furthering the children's perceived guilt and responsibility for the abusive acts. If the ritual abuse involves satanic or similar belief-systems, then the abuse could be a major component of the children's socialisation and be an assault on their concept of reality. Children might also reasonably assume that anyone that they met, including doctors, police and social workers, might be a member of such a group (Mollon, 1994). These sorts of characteristics make some argue that ritual abuse is qualitatively different from other forms of sexual abuse, however severe (Youngson, 1994).

Research has attempted to locate some of the defining characteristics of ritual abuse cases by comparing them to other non-ritual organised abuse cases. La Fontaine (1994) found that ritual abuse cases shared many of the

characteristics of family-based organised abuse, but ritual abuse cases were more likely to involve non-related and stranger perpetrators and the belief that a large number of others were involved.

Kelley (1989, 1994) compared ritual and non-ritual samples of daycare cases and found that ritual abuse was associated with a higher number of victims per daycare centre, more offenders per child, more episodes of sexual abuse, greater severity and more variation of all types of abuse, and greater child behaviour problems and internalising scores on the Child Behaviour Checklist. Very similar findings were reported by Waterman et al. in comparing the ritual McMartin cases with other non-ritual daycare cases (Waterman et al, 1993). Children from the ritual abuse cases in both studies reported greater frequencies of wearing of costumes, use of drugs, use of strange symbols and threats of magical power, as these were the types of characteristics which were used to define the cases as ritualistic.

Leavitt (1994) and Lawrence, Cozolino and Foy (1995) compared adult women reporting ritual and non-ritual sexual abuse in childhood. Leavitt (1994) found that the ritual group (satanic cases) had significantly higher scores of paranoia and of dissociative experiences. Lawrence, Cozolino and Foy (1995) reported no significant differences between groups on the rate or intensity of current post-traumatic stress, though there may have been ceiling effects from the extent of post-traumatic stress in both groups. There were also no significant group differences in current dissociative experiences. The best predictor of dissociative experiences was the intensity of the sexual abuse, which supports Jones's (1991) argument that ritual may not be the most important variable in considering the psychological effects of abuse.

Satanism and cults

Satanic abuse is a specific form of ritual abuse where the ritual is related to satanic practices. Some suggest that the concept was developed by fundamentalist Christian groups wishing to emphasise the extent of evil in our midst, but the issue has grown dramatically with a few high-profile cases, very vocal groups resisting allegations of such abuse, and the great interest shown by the professional and public media in such cases (see Clapton, 1993; Tate, 1994).

Allegations of satanic ritual abuse (SRA) raise questions of what satanic cults are and the extent to which sexual and other abuse of children is part of their belief or ritualistic system. Society embraces a wide range of religious practices which do not necessarily involve breaking the laws of a country, however strange the practices might seem to outsiders. Many argue that Satanist practices are common, and the evil practices befit that description (Hill and Goodwin, 1989; Sinason, 1994). Others argue that Satanism is rare,

and that practitioners of this and similar religions do not necessarily practise or condone sexual abuse (see discussions by Katchen, 1992; Katchen and Sakheim, 1992; Jones, 1993; Kelley, 1994).

Hill and Goodwin (1989) describe the similarities between historical accounts of satanic rituals and many of the ritual acts alleged by survivors of satanic abuse. The common features include drinking blood and semen, use of drugs, animal sacrifice, use of satanic symbols, chanting and other rituals, threats to murder the children or their loved ones, and the belief that the perpetrators have supernatural powers that the children can never escape or avoid (Kelley, 1994). Putnam (1991), however, argues that these acts have more similarity to folklore and eighteenth- and nineteenth-century occult revivals rather than any historical facts. Whatever the truth about historical accuracy, it is still unclear whether the perpetrators are really part of an organised, practising religion, are isolated individuals or small groups of self-taught practitioners (maybe with some pre-existing psychological problems), or are using satanic rituals merely to control the child victims (Finkelhor, Williams and Burns, 1988).

There is no doubt that many cults of other types exist in modern societies, some of which come to public attention through their conflict with law-enforcement agencies, recent examples being the Branch Davidians in Waco, Texas, and the Aum Shinrikyo in Japan. Hatcher (1990) has described the internal organisation and dynamics of such cults, which can destabilise to violence as the cults develop aggression in response to perceived external threats and in order to meet cult goals by supposedly significant historical dates set by cult leaders (Hatcher, 1990, p.52). It is possible that these cults commit abuse of various kinds on children of cult members, but their practices do not seem to resemble the activities described by satanic abuse survivors. This suggests that many satanic cults are either well hidden from view or are more fragmented groups of satanic abusers. Several commentators have remarked on the surprising absence of physical evidence of the satanic abuse activities reported by survivors (Lanning, 1990, 1992; Mulhern, 1990, 1991). Even if some of the more extreme acts of reported abuse, such as human sacrifices, had been illusions staged by perpetrators to deceive the children, one would expect to find at least some evidence of blood, animal or human remains or symbols used in satanic ceremonies. Preventing such concrete evidence being discovered would require immense organisational skill, internal cult stability and secrecy (Lanning, 1990, 1992).

Satanic-type cults may exist, but there are dangers in pre-defining such cults before it is even clear what is being investigated (Mulhern, 1990, 1991). Other critics are more vehement, arguing that survivor accounts are totally false and largely constructed by parents and social workers interviewing children or by therapists constructing false memories of abuse in their adult patients (Kern, 1994; Ofshe and Watters, 1994; Prendergast, 1994).

Organised abusers and their victims

There is a large and growing literature on the nature of perpetrators of child abuse (Barbaree, Marshall and Hudson, 1993; Becker, 1991, 1994) and their treatment (Morrison, Erooga and Beckett, 1994), but only limited information on the differences between perpetrators (Becker, 1991, 1994). Although there may not yet be strong grounds for distinguishing different syndromes of perpetrator abuse, there may be differences in terms of preferred sex or age of victim or in the social context in which the abuse has occurred. Finkelhor (1986) distinguishes motivation to abuse from the internal inhibitions and external resistance on the part of those protective of the children and the children themselves. Even if perpetrators are equally motivated to abuse all children, the other factors of internal and external inhibitors and resistance on the part of the child will differ, resulting in different patterns of abuse behaviour. One way forward is the analysis of the context of instances of organised abuse, such as in Cleaver and Freeman's discussion (see Chapter 17 in this volume) of the unstable kinship, low protective care, low inhibitions against sexual abuse and greater availability of single parents in organised-abuse family networks. Such research can begin to ascertain the extent and manner in which perpetrators of organised abuse differ from those of non-organised abuse.

The same issue of difference between organised and non-organised cases or their sub-types needs to be addressed for children and adult survivors of abuse. Are the people victimised by organised abuse different in any way to those victimised in non-organised ways? The research on the contexts of abuse can inform the knowledge base on who become victims, but research is also needed on the effects of organised abuse, and relationships between the type of person victimised and the type of abuse experienced.

The effects of organised abuse can result in physical effects such as injury, death, disease and pregnancy; psychological effects ranging from unhappiness to severe mental illness, and direct and indirect social effects resulting from the abuse and from child protection interventions (see, for example, the particular problems for Asians discussed in Chapter 6 in this volume). Organised abuse is typically prolonged and severe, and so is likely to be associated with poor psychological outcomes (Briere, 1992; Kendall-Tackett, Williams and Finkelhor, 1993; Putnam, 1993). The particularly severe sexual and physical abuse reported in cases of ritual abuse and the additional inversion of societal and family values in satanic abuse suggests that outcomes are likely to be even poorer for these sub-categories of organised abuse (Sinason, 1994). When the experience is too distressing for the children to deal with directly, then they may attempt to remove themselves from the experience by suppression of the memory of abuse, dissociation of feelings from experi-

ences, and the creation of multiple personalities (Briere, 1992; Putnam, 1993; see also papers in *Journal of Traumatic Stress and Dissociation*). Discussion of treatment for these effects of abuse can be found in Briere (1992), Putnam (1993) and Sinason (1994), though there is still very limited research evidence on the efficacy of sexual abuse treatment (see Gough, 1993, Chapter 11). It must also be remembered that such extreme and difficult cases have a significant emotional effect on the professionals attempting to investigate or intervene therapeutically in the cases (Youngson, 1994).

Agency responses to group-abuse cases

Investigating allegations of abuse is a difficult multi-professional and multi-agency task. These difficulties are heightened in cases of sexual abuse and heightened further in cases of organised sexual abuse. The organised nature of the abuse usually means that there are multiple perpetrators and/or victims. The agencies may not be fully aware of the extent of the relationships between these individuals or between the abusive incidents that have occurred over different periods. In many cases, the alleged abuse is centred on one or more intertwined families. Further complexity may arise from the individuals residing in different localities which are under the jurisdiction of different branches of agencies with different information available, different staff, and different working policies and practices. Co-ordination of staff and information may therefore be a major task in any investigation. Also, being organised, the perpetrators of such abuse provide a more formidable opposition to investigating agencies.

Organised perpetrators can instigate an effective legal and media-led battle against investigating agencies. Those accused of the serious charge of maltreating children must, of course, be given every opportunity to refute such allegations. The reality for the agencies, however, is that in the middle of an investigation, in addition to all the other complexities, they may have to contend with a well-orchestrated media attack (see Tate, 1994).

In order to avoid being overwhelmed by these various difficulties, agencies in the Los Angeles area of California have developed special protocols for investigating multiple-abuser or multiple-victim cases (Dickinson, 1990, pp.33–7; National Center for the Prosecution of Child Abuse (NCPCA), 1993, pp.132–40). One agency, usually law enforcement, takes charge of the investigation and co-ordination with other agencies. The strategy is to mount a large and rapid response using previously-agreed protocols, specially-designated and trained child interviewers plus other staff known to have training and experience in multiple-case investigations. Specialists not directly undertaking the investigation are also employed to advise the workforce. This co-ordinated approach includes systems for organising all the informa-

tion collected in the investigation and systems for liaising effectively with parents and the media. Different sub-teams of investigators are used, so that if a child discloses abuse and names other abused children, then the interview supervisor asks another interview team, unaware of the disclosure, to interview the other named children. This prevents cross-contamination of information and increases the integrity of the investigation and the quality of evidence presented in court (Dickinson, 1990, pp.33–7; NCPCA, 1993, pp.132–40).

Hardoon (1990, pp.37–43), a prosecutor, also reports the use of multi-agency investigative teams and specialist interviewers in Middlesex, Massachusetts. He believes that not having a prosecutor in the front-line team 'would be like having a football team without a coach' (p.40), that the prosecutors should be the lead agency responsible for taking cases to court, and would also be less likely to be in conflict with other agencies over areas of jurisdiction. The investigative process is even more critical in multiple-victim cases, because in single-victim cases the defence lawyers have a number of ways of challenging the prosecution. In the case of multiple victims disclosing abuse, given the weight of the evidence, an attack on the investigative process may be the only option available to the defence (Hardoon, 1990, p.41).

In Britain, protocols for investigation of organised abuse, including ritual abuse, are less well developed (Trowell, 1994), although many recommendations have come out of reports and inquiries such as Cleveland (Butler-Sloss, 1988), Orkney (Clyde, 1992), and Castle Hill (Brannan, Jones and Murch, 1993a, 1993b). A major issue in all investigations is the balance between clinical and law-enforcement issues, with clinical workers often emphasising the clinical priorities (Jones, 1993).

Prevalence and the polarised debate

The most controversial aspect of organised abuse is the extent to which it occurs. Arguments over child abuse in daycare, satanic and other ritual abuse and the use of repressed memories to identify cases come down to issues of case identification and prevalence.

Prevalence studies based on adults' recall of childhood abuse reveal much higher rates of sexual abuse than are known to child protection agencies, but in both types of data, it is unclear to what extent this is either solo or organised sexual abuse. Many studies only indicate whether a child was abused by multiple perpetrators, but not whether these were separate or related incidents of abuse. There are many further problems which seriously limit the extent to which incidents of abuse are identified, including the secrecy surrounding organised abuse, the current scepticism surrounding many of the

reports of abuse by survivors, and political and emotional forces surrounding the topic of sexual abuse and interventions into families to protect children. There are also factors likely to increase the possibility of false or exaggerated reports.

Factors reducing the chances that abused children will be identified

Many authors have commented on factors that limit the chances that abuse will be identified, but these factors may have a greater influence in organised abuse, and even more so in ritual and satanic ritual abuse.

A first factor is the techniques used by perpetrators to initiate and maintain victimisation, including physical or emotionally-based threats to the victim or significant others, responsibility for abuse (as victim or in victimising others), the consequences of disclosing for oneself or one's family or the perpetrator, and enmeshment in a social context or belief-system which accepts abuse (Conte, Wolf and Smith, 1989).

A second and related factor is the differential vulnerability of children. Perpetrators seek out vulnerable children. Those most vulnerable to abuse may be the least able to benefit from preventive education and least able to end the abuse. For example, children may be socially isolated, lack supervisory care, have low self-esteem, or experience physical or intellectual disabilities (see Gough, 1993, Chapter 2).

Children are extremely vulnerable if born, fostered or adopted into families or placed in residential institutions with sexual abuse perpetrators. Where the abuse is perpetrated by all or key members of the child's social existence, then the child is left with few alternative social choices. This social reality plus the psychological effects of the abuse may lead children themselves to become perpetrators.

The third factor is victims' concerns about the effects of alleging abuse on themselves and significant others, including the perpetrators. This includes lack of faith that welfare, law-enforcement and legal agencies will respond appropriately, and the fear of not being believed in a climate of alleged false memories and false accusations of abuse. A related fourth factor is survivors' lack of awareness of their right or confidence in exerting their personal right not to accept victimisation. This reinforces the importance of a fifth factor: family members', the public's, professionals' and the professional and legal systems' lack of awareness, skill or willingness to be advocates for children.

The sixth factor is the perpetrator tactic of creating confusion in the child by deception, and alcohol and drug use, so that children may be less likely to disclose, or are less likely to be believed if they do disclose (Jones, 1993).

A related seventh factor is the psychological effect of abuse, resulting in the children being confused, dissociating themselves from their experience,

or repressing the memory of abuse (Terr, 1994). This leads to the eighth factor: psychological symptoms of abuse such as repression and dissociation may make disclosure very unlikely, or inconsistent, or unclear in content (Briere, 1992; Putnam, 1993). Survivors may report false as well as accurate information about the abuse – for example creating evidence by daubing paint (Anonymous, 1994), self-injury (Hale and Sinason, 1994) and over-elaboration of details of abuse (Jones, 1993) – resulting in allegations not being believed.

Factors increasing the likelihood of false disclosures

At the polar opposite to concerns that much child sexual abuse is undetected in society is the belief that an over-emphasis on sexual abuse is resulting in the identification of many false positive cases, where allegations are made but no abuse actually took place (Johnson, 1994; Kern, 1994; Ofshe and Watters, 1994). Explanations for this phenomenon are in terms of characteristics of the process of identification by mental health or welfare practitioners, or in terms of characteristics of the alleged victims or their carers.

Many of the concerns about over-enthusiastic case identification relate to the method of interviewing children (Clyde, 1992; Home Office, 1992). Others relate to examination techniques such as physical examination for sexual abuse (Royal College of Physicians, 1991), the use of standardised indicators or scales to verify the truthfulness of disclosures about sexual abuse (Berliner and Conte, 1993) or the use of facilitated communication to interview autistic or otherwise disabled children (see special issue of *Child Abuse and Neglect*, 18 (6), 1994).

The most heated debate about the process of case identification has concerned the search for adults' repressed memories of childhood sexual assault. The high prevalence of sexual abuse in the population and the high rates of mostly previously overlooked sexual abuse histories in many psychiatrists' patients (Briere and Zaidi, 1989) have led therapists to be more vigilant in asking about abuse. Early experiences have long been thought to have had a profound effect on adult functioning, but a more modern notion of the citizen as victim has been added, so that everyone can be seen as a victim needing to search for the damage and pain experienced in childhood and still existing within their inner child (Miller, 1985). There are some who believe that, through body memory, painful experiences in our pasts are represented physically in our bodies. Such theorists and therapists search for physical manifestations of painful experiences to interpret and treat the bad memories.

One of the most fundamental attacks on the veracity of recovered memories is evidence that false memories can be implanted. In a few famous case study experiments, trusted adults have falsely 'reminded' children about

being lost in shopping centres or condominiums when they were 5 years old. The children then come to strongly believe that they can remember these experiences and in debriefing from the experiments find it difficult to believe that the experiences did not occur (Loftus and Ketcham, 1994). There are many conceptual and ethical issues raised by these studies and the use of their findings to guide judgements in individual cases or to guide social policy (see Pope, 1995), but they illustrate the possible dangers of searching for abusive experiences in childhood as an explanation for current psychological problems in adults.

In their responses to patients in therapy, therapists may unconsciously communicate the fact that abuse disclosures are 'good patient material'. Similarly, a belief in the importance of early experiences may lead therapists to continue their diagnostic search with patients until they have found some reference to a traumatic childhood experience. Others may consciously adopt repressed memory therapy (RMT), with direct questioning, imagery, age regression, hypnosis and other techniques striving to find a repressed memory of abuse. They may believe that such direct techniques will save months of therapy in finding the underlying cause of their patients' problems. Alternatively, the therapist may be confirming *a priori* assumptions about sexual abuse. This can be self-rewarding for therapists by seemingly confirming their hypotheses, their effectiveness as practitioners of RMT, and as successful warriors in the crusade against unidentified sexual, including satanic, abuse. Concern about this has resulted in worker attendance at training workshops on recovered memories being considered a possible contaminant in sexual abuse investigations, and criticisms have been made of therapists' skills and knowledge about memory and methods of eliciting recall (Yapko, 1994). There are also concerns about unscrupulous and untrained people offering survivors workshops or therapy sessions for high financial rewards.

Patient and parental characteristics are also used to explain false positives of abuse. The high prevalence and serious psychological effects of sexual abuse make it unsurprising that it should be a common explanation for psychological problems in adult life. People experiencing psychological difficulties could be vulnerable to being persuaded falsely that sexual abuse was the cause. Such misinterpretation could arise from the therapist effects already discussed, or from ideas circulating more widely in society. The book *The Courage to Heal* (Bass and Davis, 1988), for example, has been extremely influential in increasing awareness about abuse and in providing support to survivors of abuse, but has become a focus for criticism in the false memory debate because of its suggestion that readers may have been abused whether they can remember it or not (Johnson, 1994).

Furthermore, parental belief that abuse occurred can also spread like a mass sociogenic illness, where reports of illness by one or two strongly com-

plaining individuals can spread by social contagion to others (Jones, 1993), children and those who give reports of rituals possibly being informed by widely-available horror videos (Jones, 1993). There must also be a few instances where individuals knowingly make false accusations as a result of family and relationship difficulties, including divorce (Faller, Corwin and Olafson, 1993).

The polarised debate

The difficulty lies in determining in individual cases whether a report of abuse is true or false. In many allegations of sexual abuse there is no evidence beyond the testimony of the alleged victim and alleged perpetrator. Maybe only they may know the truth of what happened. In cases of recovered memories, it has been argued that if the alleged victim has been wrongly convinced by a therapist that they were abused, then only one person – the falsely accused – knows what took place. Even if there was further evidence of abuse at the time it happened, this is unlikely to still be available to substantiate memories of abuse recovered much later.

Research has shown that children are usually accurate and honest in reporting events, though they are open to social pressure from the perceived social context of the questioning (see Spencer and Flin, 1993). However, recovered memories concern adults remembering forgotten childhood events. A survey of British psychologists has found that recovered memories are commonly reported to, and mostly believed by, therapists, and the experience of having a patient recover a memory in therapy is highly associated with therapists' belief in the accuracy of recovered memories (Andrews et al., 1995). These traumatic memories are often but not exclusively about sexual abuse (Feldman-Summers and Pope, 1994; Andrews et al., 1995), and many of these memories start to be recovered before entering therapy (Andrews et al., 1995). Amnesia about sexual abuse trauma has been shown by retrospective studies (Briere and Conte, 1993) and by a single prospective study following up known abuse cases and finding that 38 per cent did not report the event to researchers 17 years later (Williams, 1992). However, errors of memory can also be in the other direction, with implanted memories becoming remembered as if they were facts (Loftus and Ketcham, 1994).

The lack of clear evidence of abuse and the serious and emotive nature of the allegations has led to a highly-polarised division between believers in extensive sexual abuse and recovered memories, and those generally not believing such reports.

'Believers' in the existence of satanic abuse are likely to be very concerned about the evil and serious damage that it causes. They can be characterised as fighting to increase awareness about the extent of sexual abuse and seeking to help victims become survivors of the abuse they have experienced.

Many argue that disclosure of abuse usually arises out of routine therapeutic work (rather than by the use of any special RMT), and they then have a responsibility to help their clients. The reality of their patients' trauma is more important than the high standards of evidence required for legal proof. Expert witnesses who testify in court on behalf of defendants accused of abuse may be seen as 'hired guns', motivated by financial greed. 'Non-believers', in general, may be characterised as undermining the work to raise consciousness and intervention against satanic and other types of sexual abuse and to be part of a 'backlash' against the revelations about the high prevalence and unacceptability of sexual abuse of children (Myers, 1994), and even of defending the views of perpetrators (see Sanderson, 1995, Ch. 5).

In contrast, the polarised 'non-believer' position can be characterised as a concern over parents being separated from their children on the basis of unwarranted and unproven allegations of abuse, made or solicited by those making careers out of the existence of child sexual abuse and those on a moral crusade against Satanism and sexual abuse. For some there is a political dimension, with child protection activity being seen as another example of the state intervening in the lives of citizens and undermining the rights and roles of parents and families, which needs to be resisted on both a case-by-case basis and by collective political action. False memories are seen as arising from the therapist conducting 'archaeological digging' to find abuse, with any disagreement by the client interpreted as 'psychological denial'. Very vocal criticism also comes from 'retractors', who have discovered repressed memories in therapy which they have subsequently decided were false. Some argue that therapists should be prosecuted for making false reports, or potentially false reports, elicited by unscientific methods.

The debate between believers and non-believers is more than a technical debate about repressed memories or evidence of abuse in individual cases. The debate is overlaid with the normal political debate between child protection and protecting parents and their families from state intervention – a debate which is even more emotive in allegations of satanic abuse. For both camps, if you are not 'part of the solution', then you are 'part of the problem'.

The two sides of the polarised debate have developed their own networking systems. Therapists and professionals and academics working in the field of child abuse have a well-developed system of journals, professional societies and associated conferences, and Internet bulletin boards. Organisations such as Survivors of Incest Anonymous produce leaflets about sexual and ritual abuse, and new specialist groups have developed such as Ritual Abuse and Information Network (RAINS), Victims of Child Abuse Laws (VOCAL) and the SAFE helpline for survivors of ritual abuse. Non-believers have also organised themselves, developing the False Memory Syndrome Foundation in the United States and the British False Memory Society. There is also the journal *Issues in Child Abuse Accusations*,

edited by Hollida Wakefield with Ralph Underwager as an associate editor, and there are several Internet bulletin boards, including 'Witchhunt'.

One effect of the 'non-believer' arguments is that they undermine belief in accusations of sexual abuse: a backlash against the increased awareness about how children's rights are infringed by abuse (Myers, 1994). Such a backlash affects society as a whole, but it also affects survivors, who may be scared of disclosing their abuse in case they are not believed or are put through aggressive questioning. Courts may also have become more sceptical about recall testimony, though they may have simply become more demanding about all evidence and about the competence of expert witnesses and their testimony. Therapist organisations have also begun to discuss more actively therapist accountability, contractual agreements between therapists and patients, and how to ensure informed consent of patients for techniques that might elicit repressed memories (see Sanderson, 1995, Ch. 5).

The challenge is for child protection, law-enforcement and mental health organisations and practitioners to deal fully with the criticisms of agency and professional practice, whilst still protecting children, believing adults and not giving sustenance to the backlash forces which would like us all to ignore and forget the realities of child sexual abuse (see Summit, 1992; Hechler, 1993).

References

Andrews, B., Morton, J., Bekerian, D.A., Brewin, C.R., Davies, G.M. and Mollon, P. (1995) 'The recovery of memories in clinical practice: Experiences and beliefs of British Psychological Society practitioners', *The Psychologist*, 8 (5), 209–14.

Anonymous (1994) 'Questions survivors and professionals ask the police' in Sinason (1994).

Barbaree, H., Marshall, W. and Hudson, S.M. (eds) (1993) *The Juvenile Sex Offender*, New York: Guildford.

Bass, E. and Davis, L. (1988) *The Courage to Heal: A Guide for Women Survivors of Child Sexual Abuse*, New York: Harper and Row.

Becker, J.V. (1991) 'Working with Perpetrators' in K. Murray and D.A. Gough (eds) *Intervening in Child Sexual Abuse*, Edinburgh: Scottish Academic Press.

Becker, J.V. (1994) 'Offenders: Characteristics and Treatment', *The Future of Children (Sexual Abuse of Children)*, 4 (2).

Berliner, L. and Conte, J.R. (1993) 'Sexual abuse evaluations: Conceptual and empirical obstacles', *Child Abuse and Neglect*, 17 (1), 111–26.

Bibby, P. (1994) 'Definition of organised abuse', *Child Abuse Review*, 3 (3), 163–4.

Blatt, E.R.I. (1992) 'Factors associated with child abuse and neglect in residential care settings', *Children and Youth Services Review*, 15, 493–517.

Boyd, A. (1990) *Blasphemous Rumours*, London: HarperCollins.

Brannan, C., Jones, J.R. and Murch, J.D. (1993a) *Castle Hill Report – Practice Guide*, Shrewsbury: Shropshire County Council.

Brannan, C., Jones, J.R. and Murch, J.D. (1993b) 'Lessons from a residential special school enquiry: Reflections on the Castle Hill Report', *Child Abuse Review*, 2, 271–5.

Briere, J. (1992) *Child Abuse Trauma*, Newbury Park, Calif: Sage.

Briere, J. and Conte, J. (1993) 'Self reported amnesia for abuse in adults molested as children', *Journal of Traumatic Stress*, 6, 21–31.

Briere, J. and Zaidi, L.Y. (1989) 'Sexual abuse histories and sequelae in female psychiatric emergency room patients', *American Journal of Psychiatry*, 146, 1,602–6.

Burgess, A. (1984) *Child Pornography and Sex Rings*, New York: Lexington Books.

Burgess, A.W. and Hartman, C.R. (1987) 'Child abuse aspects of child pornography', *Psychiatric Annals*, 7 (4), 248–53.

Burrell, S. (1994) 'A personal review of the literature' in Sinason (1994).

Butler-Sloss, E. (1988) *Report of the Inquiry into Child Abuse in Cleveland 1987* (The Cleveland Report), London: HMSO.

Bybee, D. and Mowbray, C.T. (1993) 'An analysis of allegations of sexual abuse in a multi-victim day-care center case', *Child Abuse and Neglect*, 17 (6), 767–83.

Campagna, D.S. and Poffenberger, D.L. (1988) *The Sexual Trafficking of Children: An Investigation of the Child Sex Trade*, Dover, MA: Auburn House.

Clapton, G. (1993) *The Satanic Abuse Controversy: Social Workers and the Social Work Press*, London: University of North London Press.

Clyde, J.J. (1992) *Report of the Inquiry into the Removal of Children from Orkney in February 1991* (The Clyde Report), Edinburgh: HMSO.

Coleman, J. (1994) 'Presenting features in adult victims of satanist ritual abuse', *Child Abuse Review*, 3 (2), 83–92.

Conte, J.R., Wolf, S. and Smith, T. (1989) 'What sexual offenders tell us about prevention strategies', *Child Abuse and Neglect*, 13 (2), 293–301.

Creighton, S.J. (1993) 'Organised abuse: NSPCC experience', *Child Abuse Review*, 2 (4), 232–42.

Department of Health (DOH) (1991) *Working Together Under the Children Act: A Guide to Arrangements for Inter-Agency Co-operation for the Protection of Children from Abuse*, London: HMSO.

Dickinson, B. (1990) in NRCCSA (1990), pp.33–7.

Faller, K.C. (1991) 'Poly-incestuous families: An exploratory study', *Journal of Interpersonal Violence*, 6 (3), 310–22.

Faller, K.C. (1994) 'Ritual abuse: a review of research', *The Advisor*, 7 (1), 1 and 19–27.

Faller, K.C., Corwin, D.L. and Olafson, E. (1993) 'Research on false allegations of sexual abuse in divorce', *The Advisor*, 6 (3), 1 and 7–10.

Fassett, B. and Walsh, B. (1994) 'Juvenile prostitution: An overlooked form of child sexual abuse', *The Advisor*, 7 (1), 9–10 and 30–2.

Feldman-Summers, S. and Pope, K.S. (1994) 'The experience of "forgetting" childhood abuse: a national survey of psychologists', *Journal of Consulting and Clinical Psychology*, 62, 636–9.

Finkelhor, D. (1986) *A Source-book on Child Sexual Abuse*, Newbury Park, Calif: Sage.

Finkelhor, D., Williams, L. and Burns, N. (1988) *Nursery Crimes: Sexual Abuse in Day Care*, Newbury Park, Calif: Sage.

Gil, E. (1982) 'Institutional abuse of children in out-of-home care' in R. Hanson (ed.) *Institutional Abuse of Children and Youth*, New York: Haworth Press.

Glasgow, D., Horne, L., Calam, R. and Cox, A. (1994) 'Evidence, incidence, gender and age in sexual abuse of children perpetrated by children: Towards a developmental analysis of child sexual abuse', *Child Abuse Review*, 3, 196–210.

Goodwin, J.M. (1994) 'Sadistic abuse: definition, recognition and treatment' in Sinason (1994).

Gough, D.A. (1993) *Child Abuse Interventions: A Review of the Literature*, London: HMSO.

Hale, R. and Sinason, V. (1994) 'Internal and external reality: establishing parameters' in Sinason (1994).

Hames, M. (1993) 'Child pornography: A secret web of exploitation', *Child Abuse Review*, 2 (4), 276–80.

Hardoon, L. (1990) in NRCCSA (1990), pp.37–41.

Hatcher, C. (1990) 'The investigation of allegations of ritualistic sex abuse: Contributions from cult investigations' in NRCCSA (1990).

Hechler, D. (1993) 'Damage control', *Child Abuse and Neglect*, 17 (6), 703–8.

Hill, S. and Goodwin, J. (1989) 'Satanism: similarities between patient accounts and pre-inquisition historical sources', *Dissociation*, 2 (1), 39–44.

Home Office (1992) *Memorandum of Good Practice on Video Recorded Interviews with Child Witnesses for Criminal Proceedings*, London: HMSO.

Hudson, P.S. (1991) *Ritual Child Abuse: Discovery, Diagnosis and Treatment*, Saratoga: R&E Associates.

Ireland, K. (1993) 'Sexual exploitation of children and international travel and tourism', *Child Abuse Review*, 2 (4), 263–70.

Johnson, R.C. (1994) 'Parallels between recollections of repressed childhood sexual abuse, kidnappings by space aliens, and the 1692 Salem witch hunts', *Issues in Child Abuse Accusations*, 6 (1), 41–7.

Jones, D.P.H. (1991) 'Ritualism and child sexual abuse', *Child Abuse and Neglect*, 15 (3), 163–70.

Jones, D.P.H. (1993) 'Child sexual abuse and Satanism', *ACCP Review Newsletter*, 15 (5), 207–13.

Jones, J. (1994) 'Towards an understanding of power relationships in institutional abuse', *Early Child Development*, 100, 69–76.

Jonker, F. and Jonker-Bakker, P. (1991) 'Experiences with ritualistic child sexual abuse: a case study from the Netherlands', *Child Abuse and Neglect*, 15 (3), 191–6.

Katchen, M.H. (1992) 'The history of satanic religions' in Sakheim and Devine (1992).

Katchen, M.H. and Sakheim, D.K. (1992) 'Satanic Beliefs and Practices' in Sakheim and Devine (1992).

Kelley, S.J. (1989) 'Stress responses of children to sexual abuse and ritualistic abuse in day care centers', *Journal of Interpersonal Violence*, 44 (4), 502–13.

Kelley, S.J. (1993) 'The ritualistic abuse of children', *Bailliere's Clinical Paediatrics*, 1 (1), 31–46.

Kelley, S.J. (1994) 'Abuse of children in day care centres: characteristics and consequences', *Child Abuse Review*, 3, 15–25.

Kelley, S.J., Brant, R. and Waterman, J. (1993) 'Sexual abuse of children in day care centers', *Child Abuse and Neglect*, 7 (1), 71–89.

Kelly, L. (1992) 'The connection between disability and child abuse: a review of the research evidence', *Child Abuse Review*, 1 (3), 157–67.

Kelly, L. (1993) 'Organized sexual abuse: what do we know and what do we need to know?' in CASU (Child Abuse Studies Unit), *Abuse of Women and Children: A Feminist Response*, Essential Issues in the 1990s, London: University of North London Press.

Kelly, L. and Scott, S. (1993) 'The current literature about the organized abuse of children', *Child Abuse Review*, 2, 281–7.

Kendall-Tackett, K.M., Williams, L.M. and Finkelhor, D. (1993) 'Impact of sexual abuse on children: a review and synthesis of recent empirical studies', *Psychological Bulletin*, 113, 164–80.

Kern, T.L. (1994) 'Satanic ritual abuse: how real?', *Issues in Child Abuse Accusations*, 6 (1), 32–8.

Koompraphant, S. (1994) 'How the Children become Prostitutes', paper presented at International Congress on Child Abuse and Neglect, Kuala Lumpur, September.

La Fontaine, J.S. (1993) 'Defining Organized Sexual Abuse', *Child Abuse Review*, 2 (4), 223–31.

La Fontaine, J.S. (1994) *The Extent and Nature of Organised and Ritual Abuse*, London: HMSO.

Lanning, K. (1990) in NRCCSA (1990), pp.27–30.

Lanning, K. (1992) 'A law enforcement perspective on allegations of ritual abuse' in Sakheim and Devine (1992).

Lawrence, K.J., Cozolino, L. and Foy, D.W. (1995) 'Psychological sequelae in adult females reporting childhood ritualistic abuse', *Child Abuse and Neglect*, 19 (8), 975–84.

Leavitt, F. (1994) 'Clinical correlates of alleged satanic abuse and less controversial sexual molestation', *Child Abuse and Neglect*, 18 (4), 387–92.

Levy, A. and Kahan, B. (1991) *The Pindown Experience and the Protection of Children: The Report of the Staffordshire Child Care Inquiry* (The Pindown Report), Stafford: Staffordshire County Council.

Lloyd, D.W. (1992) 'Ritual child abuse: definitions and assumptions', *Journal of Child Sexual Abuse*, 1 (3), 1–14.

Loftus, E.E. and Ketcham, K. (eds) (1994) *The Myth of Repressed Memory*, New York: St Martin's Press.

McFadyen, A., Hanks, H. and James, C. (1993) 'Ritual abuse: a definition', *Child Abuse Review*, 2 (1), 35–41.

Miller, A. (1985) *Thou Shalt Not Be Aware: Society's Betrayal of the Child*, London: Pluto Press.

Mollon, P. (1994) 'The impact of evil' in Sinason (1994).

Morrison, T., Erooga, M. and Beckett, R.C. (eds) (1994) *Sexual Offending Against Children: Assessment and Treatment of Male Abusers*, London: Routledge.

Mulhern, S. (1990) in NRCCSA (1990), pp.30–33.

Mulhern, S. (1991) 'Satanism and psychotherapy: a rumour in search of an inquisition' in J.T. Richardson, J. Best and D.G. Bromley (eds) (1991) *The Satanism Scare*, New York: Aldine de Gruyter.

Myers, J. (ed.) (1994) *The Backlash: Child Protection Under Fire*, Thousand Oaks, Calif: Sage.

National Center for the Prosecution of Child Abuse (NCPCA) (1993) *Investigation and Prosecution of Child Abuse* (2nd edn), Alexandria, Virginia: NCPCA.

National Children's Homes (NCH) (1992) *The Report of the Committee of Inquiry into Children and Young People Who Sexually Abuse Other Children*, London: NCH.

National Resource Center on Child Sexual Abuse (NRCCSA) (1990) *Think Tank Report 5: Investigation of Ritualistic Abuse Allegations*, Alabama: NRCCSA.

Ofshe, R. and Watters, E. (1994) *Making Monsters: Repressed Memories, Satanic Cult Abuse, And Sexual Hysteria*, New York: S & S Trade.

O'Grady, R. (1992) *The Child and the Tourist*, Bangkok: Epcat.

Oliver, J.E. (1993) 'Inter-generational transmission of child abuse', *American Journal of Psychiatry*, 150, 1,315–24.

Pope, K.S. (1995) 'What psychologists better know about recovered memories, research, lawsuits, and the pivotal experiment', *Clinical Psychology: Science and Practice*, 2 (3), 304–15 (review of E. Loftus and K. Ketcham (eds) (1994) *The Myth of Repressed Memory: False Memories and Allegations of Sexual Abuse*, New York: St Martin's Press).

Powers, J.L., Mooney, A. and Nunno, M. (1990) 'Institutional abuse: a review of the literature', *Journal of Child and Youth Care*, 4, 81–95.

Prendergast, M. (1994) *Victims of Memory: Incest Accusations and Shattered Lives*, Hinsburg, VT: Upper Access Books.

Putnam, F.W. (1991) 'The satanic ritual abuse controversy', *Child Abuse and Neglect*, 15 (3), 175–9.

Putnam, F.W. (1993) 'Dissociative disorders in children: behavioural profiles and problems', *Child Abuse and Neglect*, 17 (1), 39–45.

Rosenthal, J.A., Motz, J.K., Edmonson, D.A. and Groze, V. (1991) 'A descriptive study of abuse and neglect in out-of-home-placement', *Child Abuse and Neglect*, 15 (3), 249–60.

Royal College of Physicians (1991) *Physical signs of sexual abuse in children*, London: Royal College of Physicians.

Sakheim, D.K. and Devine, S.E. (eds) (1992) *Out of Darkness: Explaining Satanism and Ritual Abuse*, New York: Lexington Books.

Sanderson, C. (1995) *Counselling Adult Survivors of Child Sexual Abuse* (2nd edn), London: Jessica Kingsley.

Scott, S. (1993) 'Beyond belief: beyond help? Report on a helpline advertised after the transmission of a Channel 4 film on ritual abuse', *Child Abuse Review*, 2 (4), 243–50.

Sereny, G. (1984) *The Invisible Children: Children 'On the Game' in America, West Germany and Great Britain*, London: Pan Books.

Sinason, V. (ed.) (1994) *Treating Survivors of Satanist Abuse*, London: Routledge.

Smith, M. and Pazder, L. (1980) *Michelle Remembers*, New York: Longdon and Lattes.

Snow, B. and Sorenson, T. (1990) 'Ritualistic child abuse in a neighbourhood setting', *Journal of Interpersonal Violence*, 5 (4), 474–87.

Spencer, J.R. and Flin, R.H. (1993) *The Evidence of Children* (2nd edn), London: Blackstone.

Summit, R.C. (1992) 'Misplaced attention to delayed memory', *The Advisor*, 5 (3), 21–5.

Tate, T. (1990) *Child Pornography: An Investigation*, London: Methuen.

Tate, T. (1994) 'Press, politics and paedophilia: a practitioner's guide to the media' in Sinason (1994).

Terr, L. (1994) *Unchained Memories: True Stories of Traumatic Memories, Lost and Found*, New York: Basic Books.

Trowell, J. (1994) 'Ritual organised abuse: management issues' in Sinason (1994).

Upadhyaya, K.P. (1994) 'Child trafficking in Nepal: Problems and solutions', paper presented at International Congress on Child Abuse and Neglect, Kuala Lumpur, September.

Vittachi, A. (1989) *Stolen Childhood: In Search of the Rights of the Child*, Cambridge: Polity Press.

Waterman, J., Kelley, S.J., Oliveri, M.K. and McCord, J. (1993) *Behind the Playground Walls: Sexual Abuse in Pre-schools*, New York: Guildford.

West, D.J. (1992) *Male Prostitution*, London: Gerald Duckworth.

Westcott, H. (1991) *Institutional abuse of children – from research to policy: a review*, London: NSPCC.

Westcott, H. and Clement, M. (1992) *NSPCC Experience of Child Abuse in Residential Care and Educational Placements: Results of a Survey*, London: NSPCC.

Wild, N.J. and Wynne, J. (1986) 'Child sex rings', *British Medical Journal*, 293, 183–5.

Williams, L.M. (1992) 'Adult memories of childhood abuse: Preliminary findings from a longitudinal study', *The Advisor*, 5 (3), 19–21.

Yapko, M.D. (1994) *Suggestions of Abuse: True and False Memories of Childhood Sexual Abuse*, New York: Simon and Schuster.

Young, W.C., Sachs, R.G., Brown, B.G. and Walkins, R.T. (1991) 'Patients reporting ritual abuse in childhood: a clinical syndrome – Report of 37 cases', *Child Abuse and Neglect*, 15 (3), 181–9.

Youngson, S.C. (1994) 'Ritual abuse: consequences for professionals', *Child Abuse Review*, 2 (4), 251–62.

3   Legal issues

Maureen O'Hara

Both the civil and criminal law may be used to protect children and young people from organised forms of sexual abuse, and in many cases it will be necessary to use both civil and criminal proceedings in relation to the same child. This chapter focuses mainly on the question of children's access to justice within the arena of the criminal law. However, it begins with an outline of the main differences between criminal and civil law.

There seems to be widespread confusion about the different roles these two areas of law play in protecting children from sexual abuse. This confusion often leads to misleading reports, in which decisions not to prosecute or failure to convict in cases of alleged sexual offences against children are presented as indicators of false allegations. They are used to call into question decisions made in civil proceedings, such as care proceedings. They serve a different purpose to criminal proceedings and are based on different rules of evidence and a different standard of proof. All the references to legislation here relate to English law. English legislation is also applicable in Wales, which is not an autonomous legal jurisdiction. Much of the commentary on cross-examination and the concept of 'contamination' is also applicable to Scotland. Both jurisdictions are adversarial in nature, and both have broadly similar traditions in terms of attitudes to child witnesses, although the Scottish criminal justice system has arguably been generally more sympathetic to children than the English.

The differences between criminal and civil law

A relatively small number of reported sexual offences against children lead to criminal prosecution and conviction of the perpetrator, whilst a much larger number result in civil proceedings. For example, care proceedings

may be brought where an abuser is a member of the child's household, both in cases where he is thought to be the sole abuser and where he is thought to be a member of an organised group of abusers.

One of the main factors contributing to the small number of criminal prosecutions, and the even smaller number of criminal convictions, is the nature of the rules of evidence in criminal proceedings combined with traditional attitudes towards child witnesses. These remain deeply entrenched within the criminal justice system despite very significant reforms which have been taking place since the late 1980s. Whilst civil proceedings are not free of traditional, negative judicial attitudes towards children (the nature of which I discuss in more detail below), they are, by their nature, more flexible and more focused on children's welfare.

The main purpose of criminal proceedings, in addition to their symbolic and deterrent purposes, is the punishment of convicted offenders. To convict a defendant, it must be proved *beyond reasonable doubt* not only that the offence was committed but that it was the defendant who committed it. With some exceptions, hearsay evidence, in which a witness repeats a statement allegedly made to him or her outside court, is not admissible at criminal trials, so a child's testimony cannot be presented to the court by anyone except the child. (Video-taped recordings of children's evidence are technically a form of hearsay, and their admissibility is one of the exceptions to the hearsay rule.)

The defence has the right to cross-examine all witnesses for the prosecution, although in the case of child witnesses giving evidence about alleged sexual or violent offences, the defendant cannot now carry out cross-examination in person.

The main purpose of civil proceedings involving allegations of child sexual abuse is the protection of the child, and the role of the court is to make decisions about the child's upbringing in accordance with the principle that the *child's welfare* must be the paramount consideration in all civil proceedings concerning that child. As civil proceedings are not concerned with convicting and punishing offenders, the rules of evidence which apply to them are less stringent than those applying to criminal trials. For example, hearsay evidence is admitted in principle in civil proceedings, with certain safeguards, and children are not cross-examined and do not have to present evidence directly to the court. For a civil court to make a finding that a child has been abused, the standard of proof is the *balance of probabilities*. In cases where a civil court makes no clear finding of abuse, it may still take action to safeguard the welfare of a child, such as restricting or preventing a particular adult's contact with that child.

Because of the differences in the purposes and nature of civil and criminal law, it is not unusual for action to be taken in civil proceedings to protect children from sexual abuse in cases where there has been no criminal prose-

cution or where a defendant has been found not guilty at a criminal trial, although a 'not guilty' finding may influence the outcome of civil proceedings in some cases. The absence of a criminal conviction for alleged sexual abuse is not, therefore, a categorical indication, as some media reports would suggest, that the children concerned have not been sexually abused and that no further intervention by child protection agencies is necessary.

The criminal law

There are a number of criminal offences – such as those relating to the production, distribution and possession of child pornography, and to organised child prostitution – which deal specifically with organised forms of child sexual abuse. Such offences are tried within essentially the same legal framework as all other types of sexual offences against children, whether committed by organised groups or individuals. However, the difficulties of bringing successful criminal prosecutions which are common to all sexual offences are in many ways exacerbated in relation to organised sexual abuse.

Child witnesses giving evidence about their own experiences of sexual abuse or those of other children face enormous distress, and sometimes trauma. Unambiguous corroborating evidence of sexual abuse is relatively rare, and many actual and potential prosecutions hinge on the child's evidence alone. Traditional attitudes towards both adult and child complainants at trials for sexual offences, and attitudes to child witnesses in general, make it relatively easy for defence counsel to discredit child witnesses, who often find it particularly difficult to withstand cross-examination techniques. In cases involving organised sexual abuse – where there may be several child witnesses and several defendants, all represented by different barristers, each of whom may separately cross-examine any child giving evidence against their client – the distress experienced by children is magnified enormously, often to an unbearable degree. In many cases, child witnesses break down during cross-examination, and the trial is halted because they are unable to continue giving evidence; in other cases, the Crown Prosecution Service (CPS) decides not to bring cases to trial at all for fear that the case will be lost because child witnesses will not be able to withstand the distress involved. This may happen particularly in cases where there is no evidence which could corroborate the child's account, where the child is very young, or where the child has a communication, learning or other form of disability which is unlikely to be appropriately accommodated by the trial process.

Attitudes towards child witnesses

Underlying many of the problems faced by children in gaining access to justice is a well-elaborated mythology about children's capacities as witnesses, frequently expressed in the comments of lawyers and judges, and summarised in the following quotation from a text on the law of evidence published as recently as 1984:

> First, a child's powers of observation and memory are less reliable than an adult's. Secondly, children are prone to live in a make-believe world, so that they magnify incidents which happen to them or invent them completely. Thirdly, they are also very egocentric, so that details seemingly unrelated to their own world are quickly forgotten by them. Fourthly, because of their immaturity they are very suggestible and can easily be influenced by adults and other children. One lying child may influence others to lie; anxious parents may take a child through a story again and again so that it becomes drilled in untruths. A fifth danger is that children often have little notion of the duty to speak the truth, and they may fail to realise how important their evidence is in a case and how important it is for it to be accurate. Finally, children sometimes behave in a way evil beyond their years. They may consent to sexual offences against themselves and then deny consent. They may completely invent sexual offences. (Heydon, 1984, p.84)

As knowledge about the extent and nature of the sexual abuse of children has increased, there has been widespread criticism of the attitudes expressed above and the judicial practices and rules of evidence which flow from these attitudes. Criticisms of the way in which the criminal justice system deals with cases where sexual offences against children are alleged have, in many respects, echoed criticisms of judicial treatment of allegations of sexual offences against adult women.

There is now a growing body of research evidence which refutes traditional judicial assumptions about the nature and extent of sexual offences (Rush, 1980; Finkelhor, 1984; Russell, 1986; Kelly et al., 1991) and about children's reliability as witnesses (Goodman, 1984, 1990; Spencer and Flin, 1990).

Partly as a result of this evidence, as well as of lobbying by feminist and child welfare organisations, in recent years there have been many significant reforms of law and practice relating to the prosecution of sexual offences, and a number of provisions aimed at protecting the welfare of child witnesses at criminal trials have been introduced.

The *Report of the Advisory Group on Video Evidence* (Pigot, 1989) was of crucial importance in the development of recent reforms. The Pigot Report was the result of consultation with the voluntary and statutory sectors, as well as representatives of a wide range of professional groups involved in child protection and the criminal justice system. It concluded that:

all the evidence which we received suggests that the stress, trauma and public humiliation so often experienced by the victims of sexual offences in court, and the intimidation to which they are sometimes subjected out of court, deter many from testifying at all and certainly militate strongly against the bringing of false evidence. (p.56)

The central recommendation of the Pigot Report was that in all criminal cases involving child witnesses, the prosecution should be able, as of right, to apply for the child witness to be examined and cross-examined at a pre-trial out-of-court hearing which would be video-recorded and later shown to the trial jury. The report emphasised that:

children . . . ought never to be required to appear in public as witnesses . . . whether in open court or protected by screens or closed circuit television, unless they wish to do so. This principle, we believe, is not only absolutely necessary for their welfare, but is also essential in overcoming the reluctance of children and their parents to assist the authorities. It would create a certainty which, we suggest, would enable many more prosecutions to be pursued successfully and therefore enhance the protection afforded to the very young by the courts. (pp.21–2)

The Pigot Report also recommended that the proposed pre-trial hearings should be as informal as possible, and that no one should be present in the room with the child apart from the judge, prosecuting and defending counsel, and a parent, guardian or other supporter for the child. The defendant(s) should not be in the same room as the child, but would be able to view the proceedings through a two-way mirror or closed-circuit television, and instruct their legal representatives through an audio link.

A majority of the advisory group also recommended that, at the judge's discretion, special arrangements should be made at the pre-trial hearing for particularly vulnerable children, such as children who are very young or very disturbed, so that questions from counsel could be relayed to the child through a paediatrician, child psychiatrist, social worker or other adult trusted by the child. In such cases, no one but the trusted adult would be visible to the child, but other adults involved in the hearing would be able to communicate with the child through the trusted adult acting as interlocutor.

During the passage through parliament of the Criminal Justice Act 1991, which resulted in partial implementation of the Pigot Report scheme, amendments were put forward aimed at introducing the scheme in full and extending the special provisions for particularly vulnerable children to children with certain disabilities such as, for example, autism, which make communication with more than one person especially difficult in stressful situations. However, these amendments were not successful.

The 1991 Act introduced a scheme whereby a video tape of a child's statement could be admissible in court as evidence-in-chief – the evidence given

by a witness on behalf of whichever party is calling him or her as a witness, which in the cases under discussion here would be the prosecution. However, such a video tape is admissible only if the child will be available during the trial to be cross-examined by the defence in cases where the defendant pleads 'not guilty'. To ensure that children do not have to see the defendants while they give evidence at the trial, they may be cross-examined from behind a screen or by means of a live television link. These provisions are used at the judge's discretion.

Video-taped interviews of children for possible use in criminal proceedings are generally carried out by joint police/Social Services teams. Guidelines on the conduct of such interviews are contained in the *Memorandum of Good Practice on Video Recorded Interviews with Child Witnesses for Criminal Proceedings* (Home Office/Department of Health, 1992). A recent study of the implementation of the memorandum, carried out by the Social Services Inspectorate (SSI), concluded that:

> The study has shown that social services and police authorities have responded to the Memorandum of Good Practice by training staff, equipping video suites and interviewing a large number of abused children on video. However, when the study was completed very few videos had been used in court to present the children's evidence (although more were coming through the system as this report was being prepared). It is also a matter of concern to those working with abused children that very few convictions have resulted from the cases where video evidence has been used . . . Social workers and police officers trained in video interviewing, and their managers, are feeling very frustrated that their time, efforts and financial resources have often seemed to be worthless, when an alleged perpetrator is free to abuse again, and the child is left bewildered and possibly damaged by the experience. (SSI, 1994, p.55)

The system of video-taped evidence which was introduced by the 1991 Act was an attempt to make the experience of giving evidence less stressful for child witnesses and to make it easier to prosecute and convict perpetrators of sexual offences against children. However, the low rates of prosecution and conviction found in the SSI's study indicate that the Act's reforms have not generally had the effect of significantly increasing conviction rates.

Whilst these reforms have probably succeeded in making the process of giving evidence less stressful for many children, their failure to increase conviction rates significantly suggests that reform has not gone far enough. Arguably, the reforms introduced to date have failed to bring about the kind of fundamental changes in attitudes towards child witnesses which would be necessary to effect significant changes in practice. They have also failed to address adequately the question of what kinds of modifications to Britain's adversarial traditions of criminal justice are necessary if children are not to be excluded from access to justice.

There are a number of aspects of the present system which contribute to the difficulties in bringing successful prosecutions. Two aspects which are particularly significant in cases of organised abuse are the way in which the concept of 'contamination' of evidence is applied to child witnesses, and the ways in which cross-examination techniques may be used to discredit their evidence. These two aspects are linked, and both are at least partly rooted in the continuation of the traditional judicial attitudes to child witnesses discussed above.

The concept of 'contamination' of evidence

One meaning of 'contamination' is 'the blending into one of several stories, legends or plots'. It is this meaning which is applied to witness testimony – for example in cases where two witnesses are thought to have rehearsed their evidence together before trial in order to present it in a way which will seem consistent to the court. In some instances, guarding against the possibility of such rehearsal is essential to the maintenance of justice. However, the concept of 'contamination' is applied much more loosely and widely to child witnesses than it is to adults, and is used successfully to discredit the integrity of children's evidence in a variety of situations which would not be countenanced if the witnesses concerned were adults.

The assumption that children, as a group, are extremely susceptible to 'contamination', not only in relation to their accounts of events but also in relation to their subjective experience and interpretation of events, still shapes every stage of the investigation and trial process, even though there is now extensive research evidence refuting it (Goodman, 1984, 1990; Spencer and Flin, 1990).

The memorandum emphasises the importance of trying to obtain all the child's evidence in one interview, essentially because, if there is more than one interview, the defence counsel is likely to suggest in court that the child has been 'coached' or pressurised between interviews to provide the later accounts. This is despite widespread knowledge among child protection professionals that children who have been sexually abused rarely communicate everything about their experiences in the early stages of investigation, and that they are much more likely to give their accounts gradually over a period of time as they establish more trust in the investigator(s). The SSI study comments that:

> The single most frequently and strongly criticised aspect of the Memorandum was the suggestion that most children could be expected to disclose abuse to strangers in a single interview, lasting at most an hour. Most authorities believe this to be naïve and unrealistic, and that it contradicted all experiences of disclosures, of children testing and waiting for responses and reassurance before they disclose more.

One comment was:

> The Memorandum is too rigid, we need time and space for the child to talk. It may well take a number of sessions, but then we are told that this is evidentially diminishing. (SSI, 1994, p.49)

After a decision has been made to prosecute, children who are to be called as witnesses may be prevented from receiving therapy until after the trial, in case the defence tries to present the therapy as a form of 'contamination'. The memorandum recommends that the CPS be informed if a prospective child witness is to receive therapy before trial. It does not require Social Services Departments to seek the permission of the CPS before arranging therapy, and the CPS does not have any authority to make decisions about whether children should receive therapy. However, some Social Services Departments do, in effect, seek the permission of the CPS before arranging therapy, and in some areas the CPS takes the view that child witnesses should not receive therapy before trial. Others take the view that individual therapy for the child is appropriate before trial, but that any form of group therapy should be avoided, because of the particular scope it might give the defence for accusations of contamination.

In cases of organised abuse, where several children will have been abused by the same adults and where, in some cases, each child will have witnessed the abuse of some or all of the other children, the concept of contamination may be used to discredit children's testimony by implying that the children have conspired against the defendants and/or rehearsed the evidence against them. So amorphous and pervasive is the concept of contamination in its application to children that their capacity to corroborate each other's evidence may, in practice, be turned against them and used to the advantage of their abusers. Children who have been abused in a ritualised context may be particularly vulnerable to assertions of contamination of each other's evidence. There have been successful prosecutions of adults involved in ritualised abuse of children, both in the United States (Finkelhor et al., 1988) and in Britain (Dawson and Johnstone, 1989), in which the courts explicitly acknowledged that the ritual elements of the abuse described by the children had, in fact, taken place. However, traditional assumptions about children's supposed tendencies to fantasise and to encourage the elaborations of each other's 'fantasies', along with the general incredulity of adults in the face of accounts of ritualised abuse, combine to make it relatively easy to discredit children's testimony in such contexts. There are indications that some abusers deliberately include ritualistic or bizarre elements in their abuse of children in order to reduce the children's credibility if they report the abuse (Thoth and Walen, 1987, cited in Spencer and Flin, 1990, pp.259–60).

Attempts to prevent contamination of children's evidence often extend to

preventing children discussing their experiences of abuse with anyone before the trial, and non-abusing parents may be asked to avoid any discussion with their children about the children's experiences of abuse, even when such discussions are initiated by a child. Such practices make it very difficult for children to make sense of their experiences of abuse and can have a very negative effect on their relationships with those adults who may be best equipped to support them.

The different ways in which adult and child witnesses are treated are prejudicial to the interests of children and are a cause of serious concern. The extremes to which safeguards against contamination are taken with children are illustrated in the following example from the SSI study:

> A child, cross-examined for over two days, had to be accommodated on two consecutive nights in a foster home, since it was believed that if he returned to his own home the evidence might be contaminated. (1994, p.25)

Cross-examination

The experience of cross-examination is usually an ordeal in and of itself for both children and adults, and in many ways is intended to be so. Most adults would find the experience of being cross-examined for two days, while at the same time being removed from their home and everything familiar to them, extremely stressful. Some would find it unendurable.

Spencer and Flin, on whose work my discussion of cross-examination here draws substantially, point out that:

> the experience of an adversarial cross-examination is often especially stressful for children. Adults may (or may not!) be mature enough to see the need for their evidence to be tested by a defence lawyer 'putting it to them' that they are telling lies. For a young child it is often confusing and distressing; confusing, because she thought the adult world was on her side when the authorities at first believed her, and she now thinks the adult world has turned to disbelief; distressing, particularly for the truthful child, because for a child to be falsely accused of telling lies is one of the more stressful things that can happen to her. (1990, p.72)

As Spencer and Flin note, most of the techniques used in cross-examination run counter to what is known from psychological research about the most effective ways of obtaining accurate and truthful accounts of events, as well as running counter to traditional judicial thinking about how to obtain accurate accounts in every situation except cross-examination. When examining witnesses-in-chief – that is, examining 'their own' witnesses – lawyers are forbidden to use leading questions, and they will challenge leading questions used by the other side. However, leading questions are one of the core

techniques of cross-examination, as the following quote from a book about cross-examination illustrates:

> Leading questions, i.e., those which suggest the answer, are the normal form in cross-examination; in effect, the advocate asserts the facts, and the witness agrees or disagrees . . . One form of cross-examination is to lead the witness forcefully on one point after another, keeping maximum control over him and his testimony with a view to excluding harmful statements. Any deviation from the point of the question, or evasiveness, may be countered by warnings, reminders, repetition of questions, and insistence on proper answers . . . The cross-examiner would avoid open-ended questions, e.g. 'How?; Why? . . . He would avoid general questions seeking explanations or reasons which would open the door to wide and harmful statements . . . Alternatively, a comprehensive leading statement covering a whole incident may be put for acceptance or denial, which prevents the witness from disputing the details, one by one . . . But any kind of forceful leading will be less effective if it gives the impression that the evidence is coming from the cross-examiner, not the witness. Thus, it is desirable to conceal the extent of control and leading, so far as possible, while maintaining it to the necessary extent. (Stone, 1988, cited in Spencer and Flin, 1990, pp.223–4)

Clearly, the purpose here is not to get at the truth, but to conceal it if it is to the disadvantage of the cross-examiner's client, and to distort it as far as possible to that client's advantage.

A frequent method of confusing witnesses during cross-examination, and of distorting their evidence, is the use of questions about peripheral details of an event, often phrased in a leading form. Research indicates that it is more difficult to use leading questions to elicit inaccurate answers from children (or adults) if the questions relate to aspects of an event which are perceived as central by the child rather than those the child perceives as unimportant. Yet cross-examining children about peripheral and irrelevant detail, such as the type or colour of an item of clothing worn by a defendant, is treated as legitimate; and inaccurate answers to such questions may be used by counsel to call into question the credibility of a child's evidence as a whole.

Rapid shifts of question topics, often from central to peripheral matters, are also used to confuse witnesses and try to discredit their evidence. Mark and Roslin Brennan examined this technique in their Australian study of cross-examination transcripts, in which they found rapid shifts from topic to topic to be a frequent feature:

> In everyday interactions the unspoken conventions for changing topics of conversation are accepted. There is generally an obvious link between what has just been discussed and the new item of conversation on the agenda . . . In court there is no provision within the language to establish these linkages. The cross-examiner jumps from topic to topic and the child witness is expected to keep pace. The juxtaposition of questions seems inexplicable as topics are jostled randomly. The

effects of this are most critical when intimate details of the child's alleged sexual assault are questioned, and juxtaposed with general and more objective questions . . . The technique of juxtaposing unrelated topics excludes the possibility of any transition time. Without this . . . it is likely that the child will become disorientated, confused and unclear about the general line of questioning. The greater the frequency of these shifts from the personal to the objective, the greater the cumulative effect of the confusion will be. (1988, cited in Spencer and Flin, 1990, p.226)

Many other common features of cross-examination combine with those discussed above to confuse and intimidate child witnesses. These include the use of long, circuitous sentences, often phrased in language inappropriate to the child's understanding and vocabulary. Children with communication or learning difficulties are at a particular disadvantage when faced with such cross-examination techniques, and for this reason the CPS may decide not to put cases involving the abuse of children with certain disabilities forward for prosecution. This has serious implications in relation to organised sexual abuse, since children with disabilities are often targeted for abuse precisely because of the difficulties they face in giving evidence. Children who are living in institutions, or who are particularly dependent on institutional settings such as special day schools, may also be targeted.

Frequently, but not always, the counsel's attitude during cross-examination may be aggressive and confrontational. However, many cross-examination techniques may be used with varying degrees of forcefulness, ranging from aggressive styles of questioning to more gentle styles which convey an impression of sympathy to the child while controlling and leading the child's testimony in the manner described by Stone above.

Aggressive styles of cross-examination are particularly traumatic for many children. However, the experience of cross-examination is distressing and often traumatic for children even where the barrister takes a relatively conciliatory approach, because its essential purpose is to confuse the child and discredit the child's evidence wherever possible.

At trials involving organised abuse where there are several defendants, each separately represented, a child witness may be cross-examined by several barristers, and each will be using variations of the techniques described above. In such circumstances, the cross-examination is likely to last for several hours and possibly for days, and the degree of disorientation and distress caused to the child is incalculable. This is particularly so where the child is, in effect, being kept in a kind of 'quarantine' to prevent the possibility of contamination. Many child witnesses break down during the trial and are unable to continue giving evidence, with the consequence that their abusers walk free.

Conclusion

Despite the difficulties, some children do withstand cross-examination and the range of other ordeals which are often involved in giving evidence at criminal trials, and succeed in giving coherent accounts of their experiences of sexual abuse which lead to the conviction of their abusers. This has included children abused by organised networks who have been cross-examined by numerous barristers over periods of several days, as well as children with communication difficulties who would be dismissed out of hand as potential witnesses by some lawyers.

However, many children are prevented from giving evidence at all by the nature of the current system, and many of those who do give evidence are profoundly traumatised by the experience.

In England, it now seems to be increasingly accepted that the reforms of the Criminal Justice Acts 1988 and 1991, significant as they were, have not succeeded in creating a system which gives children who have been abused access to justice. An Inter-Departmental Steering Group on Child Evidence has recently been established to examine all aspects of the policies and practices used in criminal cases involving child witnesses, and to consider whether further reforms are necessary.

If any future reforms are to bring about fundamental changes, they will need to address ways of changing the assumptions about child witnesses on which much judicial thinking about contamination is based and to examine seriously whether cross-examination of child witnesses is genuinely in the interests of justice. Modifications to the adversarial system of criminal justice, of which the practice of cross-examination is viewed as a central plank, have been made in the past in response to particular circumstances; and no system of justice is exclusively either adversarial or inquisitorial in nature.

At the very least, consideration needs to be given to bringing about firmer and more consistent control by judges of the oppressive styles of questioning which are currently a common feature of cross-examination of children and to ending the practices of preventing child witnesses receiving therapy before trial and putting them in 'quarantine' during it.

References

Dawson, J. and Johnstone, C. (1989) 'When the truth hurts', *Community Care*, 30 March, 11–13.

Finkelhor, D. (1984) *Child Sexual Abuse: New Theory and Research*, London: Collier Macmillan.

Finkelhor, D., Williams, L. and Burns, N. (1988) *Nursery Crimes: Sexual Abuse in Day Care*, Newbury Park, Calif: Sage.

Goodman, G. (1984) 'Children's Testimony in Historical Perspective', *Journal of Social Issues*, 40, 9–31.

Goodman, G. (1990) 'On stress and accuracy in research on children's testimony' in Doris, J. (ed.) *The Suggestibility of Children's Recollections*, Washington, DC: American Psychological Association.

Heydon, J. (1984) *Evidence: Cases and Materials* (2nd edn), London: Butterworths.

Home Office/Department of Health (1992) *Memorandum of Good Practice on Video Recorded Interviews with Child Witnesses for Criminal Proceedings*, London: HMSO.

Kelly, L., Regan, L. and Burton, S. (1991) *An Exploratory Study of the Prevalence of Sexual Abuse in a Sample of 16–21 Year Olds*, London: Child Abuse Studies Unit, The Polytechnic of North London.

O'Hara, M. (1992) *Child Sexual Abuse: A Guide to the Law*, London: Children's Legal Centre.

O'Hara, M. (1994) *Supporting the Child Witness*, London: Children's Legal Centre.

Pigot, T. (1989) *Report of the Advisory Group on Video Evidence* (The Pigot Report), London: HMSO.

Rush, F. (1980) *The Best Kept Secret: Sexual Abuse of Children*, Englewood Cliffs, NJ: Basic Books.

Russell, D. (1986) *The Secret Trauma: Incest in the Lives of Girls and Women*, New York: Basic Books.

Social Services Inspectorate (SSI) (1994) *The Child, the Court and the Video: A study of the implementation of the Memorandum of Good Practice in video interviewing of child witnesses*, London: Department of Health.

Spencer, J.R. and Flin, R. (1990) *The Evidence of Children: The Law and the Psychology*, London: Blackstone.

4 How rings work

Roger Gaspar and Peter Bibby

A common problem when dealing with a paedophile ring is being out of one's depth. With certain approaches, investigators may fail to realise what is going on and deal with abuse as a mistakenly single offence. An alternative approach is to proceed by trial and error, in hope rather than expectation. This is the approach we adopted when we became aware, in 1987, that two connected groups of men were abusing children from the Kilburn area of Brent.

We realised that the models we had been trained to use, which were sufficient for dealing with intra-familial abuse, were inadequate in this case. The existing procedures were soon seen as being positively dangerous for children as we tried to achieve a successful separation of the children from the paedophiles. The historical model within which most child protection investigators work is that of abuse in a particular family. Allegations may be supported by medical evidence. Statements from victims or confessions from fathers may be forthcoming. A protective adult may be found, or some other form of protective action takes place. It was apparent that a different paradigm was needed to help in dealing with the phenomenon that was being newly unearthed.

We had difficulty in understanding why a child who had undergone the following experience did not say anything about it:

He walked up to me very quickly and put his right hand on my left shoulder and grabbed it very hard . . . the more I pushed away, the harder he gripped my shoulder . . . his whole manner changed. I kept shouting for him to get off.

He used both hands to turn me face down on the bed. He kept telling me to be quiet. I was really frightened and I thought I was going to get hurt so I gave in to him.

He had his right arm across my chest pinning my body against him. He then undid my trousers and pulled them down around my ankles . . . I was pinned to

the bed . . . he smeared Vaseline on my body . . . I felt his erection enter my bum. I was crying and telling him to get off. He kept pumping away. I was in terrible pain. He told me to bite the pillow to stop me making a noise.
When he had finished, he left me on the bed crying.

It is also difficult to understand why children keep going back to be abused, sometimes in the most degrading manner, and why, when away from the offender, they do not disclose.

If you observe relationships between offenders and their victims it becomes apparent that the perpetrators exercise control in a variety of ways that extend beyond the physical limits of the abusers' property. Their territory of control often extends into all aspects of the victims' lives. Most insidiously, it extends into silencing.

Unless we understand how organised abusers work, we will continue to respond in the time-honoured, *ad hoc* manner that has characterised our responses to date. This has resulted in some successes, but many failures.

In the rest of this chapter we look at:

● who these offenders are;
● how they work and set about abusing;
● how they survive in the community and avoid detection.

Who are they?

We have found it helpful to draw on the work of Burgess and Hartman (1987) in categorising the various offenders into four types. The common features are the process outlined in the definition on page 5 and the fact that they have multiple victims.

Solo multiple offender

The solo multiple offender is an individual who recruits and abuses alone. This type of offender is included in this description of organised abuse because of the system he will use to recruit, dominate, abuse and control victims. As we will see in Chapter 9, such processes used by the paedophile are unlikely to be penetrated by a traditional, reactive investigation and will need special attention.

Control of victims will be marked. There may be no family connections in the abuse. This category will be typified by individuals who either work with children or who have created substantial opportunities to spend time with them. This type of offender is found in schools, children's homes, nurseries or in lone occupations that allow for access to children on a one-to-one basis, such as religious ministers, youth leaders, etc. It also frequently

includes individuals who have no such 'work' opportunities, but who have created purely social opportunities, as described later in this chapter.

The fact that they are solo offenders does not mean there are no support networks. There may be connections with other offenders and links with past victims.

The group ring offender

In many ways, this is the stereotypical paedophile, who is mainly involved with other adults in abusing a particular group of children. Children are recruited by, and generally for the benefit of, the whole group. Members of the group will know some of the other members, but may not know them all. The family/friendship abusing groups outlined by Cleaver and Freeman in Chapter 17 often fall into this category, as did the subjects of the untested allegations in the Orkney case.

The transition ring offender

In many ways, this type of offending is a development of the solo offender. The abuse takes place in a similar way, but there are links with other people for the purpose of exchange of child pornography. The existence of pornographic photos, videos or electronic images of identifiable children is a significant influence in the silencing and hooking of children. Links between these abusers are limited to exchange of pornography, but not of children.

The syndicated ring offender

These are the more commercialised abusers who have as a major objective the entrepreneurial aspects of the child sex trade. They will use children for the commercial production of pornography, the provision of direct sexual services and the development of a customer network. These people will not necessarily be abusers themselves but may see it as a commercial venture. They will be actively involved in ensuring the security of the operation and continuity of supply.

Common features

It will generally be possible for most paedophile activities to be put into one of these categories. However, this does not necessarily mean that any offender will remain in one category for all time, nor that the original classification will remain accurate.

There are a number of common features across all types of offender. The evidence tends to suggest that each paedophile has a preferred age group.

Once victims are no longer within this age group, the physical act of abusing may cease, but the control will be maintained.

There is limited research concerning the extent of creation and usage of pornography in child abuse, but there is great concern about its prevalence and nature. Photographs of children, obscene or not, are used to eroticise offenders and teenage victims, desensitise children and silence its subjects (see Chapter 13).

How offenders work and set about abusing

Having described different structural models, it is necessary to look at the process of abuse. In the preferred definition found in Chapter 1, three necessary stages in the abusive process are mentioned. These are: (1) the targeting and seduction, (2) the hooking and (3) the silencing of the children. In addition, to be successful, paedophiles need to make sure that their co-offenders and other adult contacts either do not inform on them or, like the children, that they are not credible witnesses. In addition, adults who might be in a position to appreciate what they are witnessing need to be desensitised.

As mentioned above, a recurring question nagged us: if what these boys are telling us is true and they disliked it so much, why did they return again and again? This was obviously a fundamental question which each boy would face at the trial, since it reflected on their credibility as truthful witnesses. After all, no free-minded, willing person deliberately puts themselves into a position where something unpleasant happens to them.

In testing the credibility of the boys and looking for an explanation to this question, we looked in some depth at what each was saying. What emerged was a clear pattern to the abusing by the offenders, where the subjects' control of the situation and their ability to make rational choices was eroded or removed.

The process of abuse

The first stage was a recruitment or seduction phase: not a seduction in the sexual sense, but a process where the boy's defences were eroded and the paedophile gradually became more important to the boy than his parents or carers. The process began with devices to gain the attention of the boy: sweets, toys, computer games, trips to the seaside or the fairground for the young; beer, money, cigarettes, drugs or pornography for the older boy.

Once sure of their attention, the paedophile's natural ability with children got to work and ensured their retention. A feature was the amount of time each paedophile was prepared to spend with each boy: talking, listening and encouraging their participation in whatever was the appropriate attraction.

Each paedophile appeared to have a natural talent at talking to children in their favoured age group. They were good at it because they were interested in the children. Their motives were, of course, entirely self-centred, although they would argue otherwise.

We might ask ourselves, as investigators, how long we spend listening and talking to children about what is important to *them* rather than what is important to *us*. The paedophile will do the former, and he will spend hours at it because, typically, it's his hobby, his sole interest. It has been said that most fathers know more about the inside of their car than they do about their children. The paedophile is obsessed with improving his practice 24 hours a day, seven days a week. In response, we have a 40-hour week of only five days. We may well have other responsibilities as well.

Some examples of the seduction or recruitment phase may assist:

He had a large train set laid out, dishes and packets of sweets laid out on the shelves which he told us we could have. He told us we could come back any time and he would have some more toys for us.

He gave us a cigarette each and a cup of tea and a biscuit. I started going down there regularly when I wanted a fag or when I needed money.

There was a train set on the table, Scalextric on the floor and a TV game in the corner. In the bedroom were other toys, cars, lorries, aeroplanes, games, CB radios. He told me I could come and play anytime I wanted.

He made me sandwiches, gave me a choc ice and a cake. He said I could come back anytime.

After this initial recruitment phase, a build-up began towards the actual act of abuse. Typically, there were three methods used to offend:

● objective coercion;
● emotional coercion;
● physical control.

Each of these methods appeared to be linked to the way in which the seduction phase had developed. If a boy was particularly attracted by the toys or other rewards on offer, this was developed into abuse through objective coercion:

I knew he'd bought me a digital watch. I don't know why. He said, he would give me the watch if I took my trousers and pants down.

He asked me what I would like, pointing to the toys around the room. I asked for a remote controlled car. He said, 'you can have it if I can have you.'

He said, 'you can have it [a transistor radio] as long as you give me your bum.'

The emotional coercion was less clear in the accounts of others, but nevertheless present:

He said, 'I can trust you, you're my friend.' The more I visited the more his conversation would become involved with me. He would say things like, 'I love you.' When it started, he said, 'remember what I've been telling you these last few weeks.'

There were parties and trips to the fair. He said, 'if you want to be one of my lads, you'll have to let me bum you.'

With certain victims, this bargaining or coercion was not used. Instead, the children were subjected to outright physical force or placed in circumstances where they felt escape was hopeless:

On the first night I stayed, I had to sleep on a mattress in his bedroom. I didn't understand why he didn't wear anything. He told me to take off my pyjamas. When I refused, he forced me down over a chair.

I tried to think of ways to escape him but he had a metal pole with two metal balls, one at each end. Also he had an air rifle. I thought if I tried to run, he would hurt me.

He used to ask the other children to go so we'd be alone. Then he'd take me into the bedroom.

Even reading these extracts from various children talking about different offenders, it is difficult for an adult to understand why the children said nothing to caregivers. However, the next phase was a controlling period, starting with the trauma of the abusing act, compounded by blocking tactics introduced by the paedophiles to ensure silence:

I had no sexual experience then. I was very frightened. I was scared and confused about it all. I didn't know if something was wrong with me.

This was the first time my willy went stiff. Now I know what that means. I didn't tell my Mum because I was too frightened.

I was so frightened. I couldn't comprehend what was going on. I was so confused. It was the most frightening thing that had ever happened to me.

I was subdued. I knew what was going to happen but was powerless to do anything about it. I was in such a state of shock.

The blocks which compounded this trauma were linked to the method of

offending. Boys who had succumbed through objective coercion found themselves further entrapped:

Afterwards he would be nice to me and give me small presents or money. He used to say I shouldn't tell anyone.

I didn't tell anyone because I was worried about what people might think. Everytime he bummed me, he gave me between £7 and £10.

Boys who had defied parental rules about visiting strange places or who visited with parental permission found themselves in an equally difficult position:

I went without the knowledge of my mother. He said, 'it was our little secret.'

I did as I was told to stop my mother finding out what was going on. If I stopped going round there she would want to know why or what was wrong.

Others thought that they were to blame for what had occurred:

I never told my family or anyone about the bumming because I was scared about what I had done, and he told me not to.

If you tell anyone, they won't believe you, so let's keep it our little secret.

I let this happen mainly because of the things he would give me; fags, sweets and sometimes games.

Many of the blocks built in at this stage are major hurdles for the interviewer. The paedophile will have spent considerable time on the victim of the abuse, who may now fear an interview more than the abuse occurring again. Indeed, some victims had realised the commercial value of their bodies and were prepared to earn money once they had rationalised the nature of the act.

Since the paedophile has spent time on the children to get them into this position, the interviewer must be prepared for a similar commitment. One attempt at interviewing, restricted to the length of a video tape, is unlikely to be fruitful. Similarly, some thought needs to be given to warnings the paedophile might have given the child: does an interview at the police station reinforce the paedophile's warning that the child will be the one in trouble? Is the video suite or clinic room really a place where the child feels safe, or is this, to him or her, the first step to being put into care? Are the children's homes really places where they can talk – was that where they could not tell

their parents what happened? Do the children want to talk in front of their parents, whom they could not tell previously? How do they tell their parents why they could not tell them? Does a child have a choice about the gender of the interviewer? (It does not necessarily follow that a child will want an interviewer of their own gender, or a female.)

These are not difficult ideas to appreciate. Indeed, in our training we often get workers to develop strategies which reproduce a paedophile ring. The four questions they are asked to answer are:

1   How would you set about seducing children?
2   How would you hook the children to ensure that they keep on returning?
3   How would you make sure that the children did not tell?
4   How would you set up and control a network of abusers so that it was secure?

One group of workers undertaking the University of Leicester's Post Qualifying Course in Child Protection came up with the answers given below in just 15 minutes.

In what ways would you set about seducing children?

- activities;
- natural hobbies – child-centred, swimming, amusement arcades;
- 'image'

  - part of the family;
  - 'uncle', 'aunt' figure;
  - helper, authority;
  - friend, 'responsible';

- develop relationship with child – be patient;
- treats;
- general childhood needs;
- usually needy children;
- vulnerable;
- 'deepening' of relationship;
- physical contact – increase;
- testing out – hugging, 'comforting';
- make child feel responsible;
- dependence of child – emotional;
- special relationship;
- make child feel good;
- introduce child into 'area' of abuse, special place, den;
- spin-offs, rewards.

In what ways would you hook children you had seduced to ensure they would come back?

- child pornography – 'It's normal for children to be sexual', therefore OK to engage in sexual activity;
- video/photograph activity – ensure that the perpetrator's face is not shown;
- use photographic material to entrap victim – threat of disclosure to peers; adult induces fear in child; ensures power;
- reward – child goodies – feelings of affection – money – holidays, etc.;
- physical threat – fear – peer pressure;
- use deprived areas, e.g. as in Romania; use wealth to hook children then make pornography to sell through paedophile group;
- use ritual, e.g. 'Satanism' – 'secret society' (masonic, 'church', 'witch-craft') – 'armed forces';
- make links with family as 'good person' to help with children.

In what ways would you silence children so they do not tell anyone?

- threats;
- bribery;
- rewards – punishment;
- treats;
- coercion;
- peer pressure;
- consequences;
- taken to the police station; into care – away from home; publicity;
- fear;
- take responsibility or blame;
- making it special.

How would you set up and control a network of abusers so that it was secure?

- rituals and rules;
- stringent gate-keeping;
- high level of contact;
- support strong public image for each member;
- no one allowed on the periphery, all must participate;
- generate and maintain a level of fear of consequences – photos, videos;
- core group, but not everyone knows everyone else in the ring;
- conspiratorial;
- pooling resources;
- communication – coded language, verbal communication.

If these theoretical strategies, which can be developed in 15-minute buzz-groups, were to be put into effect, they would produce a formidable paedophile ring. This shows that planning such offences is not a very complex exercise. It only requires the will to carry it out. It also shows that the thought processes of offenders are not so different from our own. It also brings staff, for the first time, into contact with the sordidness of this abusing world. This can lead to problems when dealing with a real case. Staff must be alerted to the issues at this stage, rather than in the middle of an investigation, when management support and possibly counselling will be required.

Avoiding detection

How do offenders make sure that they are kept secure? We have indicated above why it is that victims do not tell. In this section, we look at ways in which perpetrators ensure their own survival.

There are innumerable examples of abusers supporting each other. When one is arrested, his colleagues will endeavour to clear his premises of incriminating evidence. They will support each other through attendance and note-taking in court. They will endeavour to undermine credibility of the case by approaching credible witnesses, their friends or their family with threats about giving evidence, leaving only the children, who would be assumed to be less credible, to give evidence in court. We have examples of abusers approaching apparently unconnected people in a completely different part of the country to undertake these tasks.

The list above gives an indication of the security control methods that are used in many rings. Their members are as supportive of each other as any secret organisation you might think of, and provide information and guidance that would put any specialist hobby group to shame.

Our problem in dealing with this 100 per cent commitment is a combination of innocence, incredulity and comparative lack of commitment, with some professionals choosing to take time out to undertake other activities. Much of this book is an attempt to increase our knowledge and commitment, so that we may approach the issue from an equal standing.

References

Burgess, A.W. and Hartman, C.R. (1987) 'Child abuse aspects of child pornography', *Psychiatric Annals*, 7 (4), 248–53.

5 The effect on children and their families

Arnon Bentovim and Marianne Bentovim

The child's perspective in organised abuse

Research in the United Kingdom (Wild and Wynne, 1986; Pooley and Wood, 1994) and the United States (Belanger, Belcher and Birnhard, 1984; Burgess, Groth and McCausland, 1981; Burgess et al., 1984) has demonstrated the various patterns characteristic of the organised abuse of children. It is possible to distinguish different contexts in which this might occur, and these are covered elsewhere in this volume.

Police research, in particular the work of the Obscene Publications Branch at Scotland Yard, has shown that in some cases, highly-complex paedophile rings are operating in the UK, linking paedophiles together through the exchange of pornographic materials, sharing and recruiting victims, and even forging links with paedophile organisations in Europe and the Far East. At the other end of the scale, there may be one lone paedophile operating within an area or institution, but who nevertheless may have abused hundreds of children during a career of offending behaviour. One of the common features of organised abuse is the systematic targeting, grooming and induction into perverse sexual practices which encourages today's victims to become tomorrow's perpetrators. The Frank Beck trial in Leicester in 1992 highlighted this process and is a salutary example of the mechanisms of induction and victimisation, followed by perpetrating behaviour, within an institutional setting.

In 1990, the Department of Health sponsored the training in England and Wales of key members of the Area Child Protection Committees (ACPCs) to assist them in developing specific policies and strategies for dealing with organised abuse within their areas. Similar initiatives were later taken by the Welsh, Northern Ireland and Scottish Offices. Careful assessment is required to identify, investigate and manage the effects of organised abuse of chil-

dren, and careful treatment strategies then need to be put in place to provide ongoing support for victims and their families.

The child's perception

To understand the child's perspective in being involved in an organised ring requires an understanding of the effects of sexual abuse itself, and also the effects of being inducted into an organised ring. The majority of clinical accounts of the effects of sexual abuse indicate that for most victims, there are a variety of negative consequences of abuse, often lasting for many years (Beitchman et al., 1992). These include emotional disturbances such as somatic complaints, sleep difficulties, nightmares and self-destructive behaviour, and also aggression, sometimes associated with sexual activities, and a detrimental effect on the sexuality of the children involved. What may feel emotionally satisfying at one stage, for example being involved in a ring which purports to give support and belonging, may be felt as an abuse at a later stage, for example if eroticised needs have been created which are at variance with those of peers. The following perspectives will be considered:

1   effects on sexualisation;
2   emotional effects;
3   depressed mood;
4   anxiety;
5   the specific effects associated with rings.

Sexualisation

The most specific response to being involved in sexual abuse is the heightening of sexual activities, both during childhood and later on in adult life. Children and young people are sensual beings, and intense sexual stimulation results in the reinforcement of basic responses and the re-enactment in dreams, thoughts and activities of previous stimulation. Children are thus eroticised by abuse and, as a result, children may show sexual behaviour, may initiate sexual contact with adults, or with younger children, become involved in sexual play with others and can behave in a provocative way towards adults. Thus, being abused heightens the sexuality of children and inevitably fosters its growth, even if it is subsequently repressed.

Younger children tend to re-enact sexual activities, through play or behaviour activities, in an overt way, for example masturbation, but a number of studies (Watkins and Bentovim, 1992) have shown that being involved in sexual activities has a profound organising effect on the growing sexuality of adolescents, and that a cycle of deviant fantasies, masturbation and sexual activities can be shaped by inappropriate early experiences into a variety of

behaviours. Conversely, there can be a marked inhibiting effect on the development of sexual activities and sexual responses. Abused boys commonly show confusion and anxiety over their sexual identity. They become very concerned over why they were chosen as victims, they fear that homosexual qualities must have been recognised in them by the abuser, or that their inadequate resistance to abuse means that there is a likelihood of them having some homosexual orientation. Finding a younger victim who can be induced into sexual activities, perhaps within a ring, particularly when there is financial reward, can serve to quell the doubts over their sexual identity of older adolescents or young people who have themselves been involved in abuse over a prolonged period.

Emotional effects

A sense of guilt and responsibility for abusive experiences is reported by many victims. It appears that this often arises in older children, because they believe they should or could have stopped the abuse if they had wished to. If there was some positive physical response, or enjoyment of increased attention or warmth, if they were rewarded financially for introducing other children, or for their own actions, then there may be a sense of far greater responsibility. Statements made by abusers attributing the responsibility for abuse to the child and their desire for financial or other rewards may lead to confusion about the origins of abuse, making the child feel responsible, absolving the adult, but at the same time evoking a sense of rage towards the adult who abused them.

The sense of powerlessness in being unable to stop repeated episodes of abuse or to control what happens is frequently expressed by abused children. Many victims describe a sense of loss and isolation. Being involved in a ring gives a sense of identity and belonging, and there may be intense loyalty to the group and a fear of loss of what is perceived as emotional support. Because of the secrecy induced out of threats or fear, there may be intense isolation from siblings, peer group and family. If the young person has initially turned to the abuser because of their own sense of privation, being victimised makes them realise that they have been used for the adult's sexual or financial gain. This may lead to difficulty in trusting, with major concerns about relating to the opposite sex, or prematurely clinging to partners who may be unsuitable. There are also concerns about photographs in which the young person fears they may be recognised, with very major negative emotional effects (see 'Specific effects of rings and ritual abuse' below).

Depressed mood

Depressed mood, often associated with anger, is also described as associated with helplessness and hopelessness, with a pervasive sense of anger directed towards those the young person feels has let them down – the abuser, family members, Social Services or other agencies. There is an impression that such anger has different gender effects. Girls tend to direct anger towards themselves, with suicidal gestures, self-harming behaviours and depression, whereas boys seem to express their feelings outwards in destructive antisocial responses, conduct disorders, possible identification with the abuser, and the development of abusive behaviour.

Anxiety effects

Anxiety is expressed through increased fearfulness, somatic complaints, change in sleep patterns, and nightmares. Such symptoms are frequently associated with post-traumatic stress, flashbacks or visualisations of experiences, or re-enactments associated with reminders of the context of abuse or of the individuals who perpetrated it. There may be withdrawal from situations or contexts where abuse has occurred, startled reactions and hyper-vigilance, associated with hyper-arousal. Such effects can last into adult life and can have serious and damaging long-term effects, including the development of anxiety states, phobic responses and obsessional compulsive disorders.

Specific effects of rings and ritual abuse

The effects and feelings of responsibility for being involved in a ring can be widespread and highly confusing for young people's sense of identity. There are often conflicts, because there may be criminal proceedings, and the outcomes of such proceedings have to be awaited before therapeutic work can be offered. Burgess et al. (1984) found that those involved for over a year, and those involved in pornography, had the most negative perception of themselves. Their knowledge that there may be a permanent record of their activities, and that pictures may appear in magazines and be seen by people they know, may be a cause of continuing high levels of anxiety, even after exploitation has stopped.

Thus there may be a pervasive high level of anxiety, associated with general withdrawal and avoidance, or there may be the effect of identification with the aggressor, taking on in a forceful way the role of the abuser and perpetuating the process, particularly when it is financially rewarding. Thus when, in addition, there are ritualistic elements, child sexual abuse is embedded within a powerful belief-system. If the system is a deviant one, such as

the Satanism (Pooley and Wood, 1994) already referred to, this can create significant long-standing distortion of the young persons' perspectives, their beliefs, their allegiances, and their fundamental personality structure to such a degree that adaptive recovery is very difficult indeed. Furthermore, the combination of child sexual abuse with premeditated and sadistic activities appears to result in more serious psychological effects. When child sexual abuse is accompanied by extreme degradation and demeaning of the victim, this has the most devastating consequences for the victim's self-esteem. Thus, in assessing the effects of abuse and what has happened to a young person, it may be preferable to define the context of abuse very clearly, whether there are one or more perpetrators, and whether, in addition to sexual abuse, there is extensive physical or emotional abuse.

Assessment

It is important to consider the source of referral of a suspected case of organised abuse and note whether:

- concerns come from within the professional network and may have been raised by a teacher, social worker or police officer;

or

- information has been given by a friend or peer (possibly another child victim);

or

- the information has been given by an offender, perhaps during police investigation.

As with cases of intra-familial sexual abuse or non-accidental injury or emotional abuse, it is the duty of the local authority Social Services Department (or the NSPCC), on receipt of alerting information concerning a child, to plan and co-ordinate an appropriate investigation. This should be done by constructing an 'index of suspicion' based on alerting factors, for example the child's behaviour, the child's emotional state, the child's physical state, the status of the referral information, and its source. Family factors should be noted, including whether or not they have concerns or whether the family context itself may present some risk to the child. Also to be considered are relevant social factors, including, for example, whether or not the child has new friends currently, either older or the same age; whether the child has become secretive about social activities; whether the child appears to have extra money, and whether the child has been 'befriended' by an

adult who offers treats including sweets, rewards or outings, ostensibly out of kindness or concern for the child's welfare.

Preliminary concerns should be discussed within the relevant professional network at a strategy meeting and a plan made to gather other relevant information in respect of the child, family and relevant others. It is crucial that there is good liaison between police and Social Services personnel in order to maximise sensitive, effective evaluation of potential victims, but also to achieve effective investigations of alleged offenders.

It is obviously very important to arrange to interview the child or children concerned.

Individual assessment interview

This should take place in a neutral, safe setting and be conducted by specially-trained police and social work teams. It is likely that the *Memorandum of Good Practice* guidelines issued by the Home Office (DoH/HO, 1992) will assist the interviewers in their task of eliciting whether anything untoward has happened to the child, and also provide the child with an opportunity to speak to independent but concerned professionals.

In exploring whether or not the child may have been the victim of sexual abuse, it is clearly important to establish who else was involved, both children and adults, and whether in a victim role or perpetrating role. Careful information needs to be elicited about the time and place where any alleged sexual offence took place, as well as to explore the nature of the alleged offences committed. If information begins to emerge which suggests that this is not a case of intra-familial abuse, but rather of abuse committed outside the family, possibly within an organised group, it may be important to ask how and by whom the child was approached or recruited. The child may show some confusion or difficulty in understanding that an adult who may have befriended them and shown kindness to them was also responsible for abusing them or others.

If the child victim was then used to recruit others, the child may feel similarly confused about their role in the process and feel torn between their loyalty to their 'friend'/perpetrator and their fellow victims. If a reward or financial incentive was offered and accepted, the child may feel extremely guilty, and may view that as evidence of having tacitly consented to sexual activities or to recruit others to do so. It will be important to establish whether threats or coercion were used in order to induce compliance of the victim by the perpetrator, and whether or not the victim was urged to begin to abuse younger children. If so, the victim may be very unsure about the boundaries of their responsibility and about whether they were or were not responsible for these victim experiences, or were or were not responsible for the perpetrating behaviour. In perpetrating offences and recreating their vic-

timisation experiences, it is as though the young person is 'formalised' into a subculture of sexually abusive behaviour.

It is important to establish whether any members of the child's family or other known social networks were involved, and whether or not the child was involved in pornography or prostitution. In establishing whether the child was threatened or silenced, information may be forthcoming about particularly sadistic forms of abuse or torture having taken place, the effects of which are likely to have been deeply traumatising.

Assessment of the family

Assuming that no member of the child's immediate family has been implicated by them in the abuse, it is important to meet with the child and family to establish the quality of parent/child relationships and to understand the family's views and feelings about what has occurred. It is important to consider any factors which may have contributed to the vulnerability of the child in the family, for example whether there have been any tensions in parent/child relationships which have led the child to seek an 'understanding' adult elsewhere; whether there is any history of physical, sexual or emotional abuse or neglect in the family which may have rendered the child more vulnerable to re-victimisation. It is generally worth exploring how the parents view the child, whether there have been any difficulties from their point of view in managing the child or the child's behaviour, whether or not the parents themselves had had any recent concerns. Exploring the parents' own experiences of childhood is important, as is establishing whether any members of the extended family may have been involved in any way in the abuse. There may be links between family members and the abuser network, even if the child's immediate family and parents are not aware of this. There may, however, be a multi-generational culture of abuse, involving either extended family members exclusively, or including some outsiders.

In family-led networks, it is important to establish which family members participated in or knew of the abuse and consider whether there was some failure on their part to offer appropriate protection to the child. Identifying a potentially protective parent at this stage is very important, as, after disclosure, the child will require a great deal of support (as indeed will the parents). Establishing whether any siblings were involved is important and implies seeing them separately for assessment. Exploring whether abuse may have been present in the family as well as within the network is important. Some children may have been involved by their families in pornography, prostitution, sex, bestiality or other sexualised behaviours, and there may be discrepancies between the child's accounts of events and those of their family. Trying to establish the relative validity of statements is important, as is considering whether or not silencing strategies were used.

Management

If no family member has been involved in the abuse, it is often perfectly feasible for the child to remain at home in the care of their parents, provided that a satisfactory child protection programme can be worked out with their carers. The child may well need careful support and monitoring to prevent re-abuse of themselves or others, and support in coming to terms with often ambivalent feelings about their abusers. Consideration should be given to providing both individual therapeutic help to the child and family support, as appropriate. It may be the case that some group work is deemed to be appropriate, for example where a ring has operated in a small community or school, although there may be contra-indications to this, perhaps where the children's therapeutic needs may be mutually exclusive or contrary to the requirements for giving evidence in court proceedings.

There are a number of dilemmas for the victims of organised sex rings; a vulnerable child may have become significantly attached to their abuser and feel loyalty towards him and emotionally dependent on him. By disclosing inappropriate sexual activities within the relationship, the child may face acute feelings of loss on being denied contact with their abuser, sometimes pointing out that that person paid more attention to them than members of their own family. If rewarded or paid, the child often feels guilty and responsible for what has occurred and feels that, having accepted money, they had in effect consented to the transaction, and by not refusing the money, had received some secondary gain from it. If the child was used to recruit others, they may feel coerced by the abuser but also allied to him through the execution of the important role assigned to them. On the other hand, the victim may feel a sense of obligation to other children they had recruited, and will sometimes deny or minimise knowledge of the other children's involvement in explicit sexual activities as a defence against feeling responsible for them.

Some victims who are encouraged to abuse younger children identify with their abuser, and abusing others may serve as some sort of rationalisation to justify their own victim experiences. Thus acting out and subjecting others to similar acts can be seen as a way of externalising feelings and responses to their own victim experiences.

Abuse within a ring or defined network may, of course, represent a re-victimisation for some children who had previously been abused, perhaps within their families, and this may then lead to significant re-traumatisation. It is known that the effects of trauma or repeated traumas are accumulative, and therefore there are very real concerns for the psychological recovery of some children who have been multiply abused. Perverse sexualisation and an abuse of power and trust may sadly become 'normalised' for some children and make it very difficult for them to form normal attachment relationships based on mutual respect and consent. The role of sexuality in such relation-

ships is also distorted and may lead to significant and chronic psychosexual problems in future. So too may identification with abusive, sadistic behaviour, which may come to characterise future relationships, with a wish to abuse or humiliate being used as a defensive strategy against remembering humiliating and confusing victim experiences. Victimisation may lead to excessive passivity in future relationships or to a preoccupation with homosexuality, which may be dealt with either by seeking repeated homosexual liaisons or indulging in promiscuous sexual relationships with women in an attempt to ward off fears or fantasies about a homosexual orientation.

Case example – Stuart

This case example demonstrates the process of uncovering a case of organised abuse.

Stuart, aged 14, had begun spending weekends at the home of Bill, a single man aged 50, together with a friend, Simon, also aged 14. Bill was a helper at a youth group attended by both boys, and in addition he invited boys in ones or twos to go out with him for trips. One favoured activity was to go trainspotting, and this was what had initially appealed to Stuart and Simon. Both boys were noted to have more money to spend than usual, and boasted at school that they had access to adult videos and computer games.

The mother of another boy who went to the group became suspicious about activities taking place at Bill's flat and contacted the local Social Services Department. A preliminary strategy meeting was held, at which it was revealed by Stuart's teacher that there had been several concerns about him in recent months, with a deterioration in his school performance and attendance and a change in his behaviour so that he had become verbally abusive to staff. He was noted to be a confused, unhappy boy who had difficulties in his relationships with his peers and was often called 'gay' and 'pervert' at school. The social worker, who had made a preliminary assessment of Stuart's family, revealed that there was a history of long-standing marital difficulties and frequent violent arguments between Stuart's parents, with Stuart often absenting himself from the family home. Stuart's relationship with his father appeared to be poor, and they did not enjoy time together. Stuart's mother was busy looking after his younger brother and sister, and Stuart was aware that she did not have a lot of time for him either. Thus he appeared to have enjoyed the interest which Bill showed in him, particularly the treats and outings he provided. Stuart seemed to have developed quite a significant attachment to Bill, and because of Bill's status as a youth worker, Stuart's parents did not suspect any ulterior motive in the interest he showed in their son. A preliminary investigation by the Police Protection Team revealed that Bill was a Schedule I offender. Stuart and Simon were both sub-

sequently interviewed separately, and Stuart disclosed, with considerable difficulty, that they had participated in various sexual activities which had taken place at Bill's flat, and had at various times involved himself, Simon, Bill and other boys whom he named. Sexual activities had begun by the boys being allowed to watch explicit videos with Bill, and had then led into him fondling their genitals, engaging them in acts of mutual masturbation, and had progressed to oral sex and buggery.

When further assessed by a child psychiatrist and psychotherapist, Stuart was noted to have strong ambivalent feelings about Bill, feeling very remorseful and sad that Bill had been remanded in custody awaiting trial, but on the other hand feeling furious and enraged and utterly betrayed by him. He felt Bill provided attention and time which his parents did not have for him, and felt that the pocket-money and treats he received were reasonable rewards for sexual favours. In accepting them, Stuart further thought that this must have meant he consented to engage in sexual activities with Bill, and he had even begun recruiting other boys. He had in some ways begun to identify with Bill as a role model, and there was real concern about the possibility that he might develop a pattern of offending behaviour himself.

He had profound misgivings about his sexual identity, fearing the boys at school must have noticed he was 'gay', and assumed that he must have been so, and that was why Bill targeted him. Nevertheless, he wanted to have a girlfriend.

Stuart was referred for individual psychotherapy on a time-limited basis, followed by group therapy. His parents were offered counselling, and family meetings were arranged, although Stuart's father never attended these.

Therapeutic work with the child and family

It is usual to think of therapeutic work as occurring over a period of time and in a sequence of stages:

1 a period of disclosure;
2 work during a period of separation, when the abused child needs to be separated from the abuser in a protective context, where appropriate;
3 a phase of rehabilitation;
4 a phase of working together to find a new family for those children where rehabilitation is not possible.

The disclosure phase

As already indicated, the disclosure phase is highly complex because not

only does abuse and its impact on the child have to be recognised, but in addition, assessment of whether the family or non-abusive parent can give adequate protection is necessary, as well as an assessment of the offender. Extensive consultation is necessary, and decisions have to be made about where the child should live safely; particularly when there is a ring and there is an extensive assessment of a number of children and families, turmoil can occur, with a danger of confusion for children, families and professionals.

Breaking the taboo of secrecy is essential throughout this phase, and the ability of an offender to acknowledge responsibility may be helpful in beginning to reverse the child's sense of guilt and self-blame. Unfortunately, particularly where sex rings occur, there may be major criminal proceedings, denial by offenders is common, and children and families may be confused and extremely anxious. For children who have to give evidence in court, there is likely to be additional stress, and evidential considerations may lead to a delay in starting treatment, even though this should commence as soon as possible.

Work during separation from abuse

To deal with the effects of sexualisation, emotional ill effects, depression, anxiety and behavioural problems, a variety of approaches are necessary, for example the use of cognitive approaches, behavioural approaches, psychodynamic approaches and systemic approaches. What is essential is the processing of the emotional and cognitive effects of abuse.

Emotional processing

This means that the child victim must be expected to talk about their experiences in therapeutic work, either individually or in groups. Repeated exposure to memories in a safe and supportive milieu deconditions the effect of abusive associations. It is necessary to recollect all aspects of the experience to identify the stimuli that evoke abusive associations. This is particularly complicated where there has been multiple abuse over an extended period. Episodes may be forgotten or repressed, or the elements of different experiences mixed up and confused.

Strategies to manage fear and anxiety are necessary to increase the child's sense of self-efficacy, and the use of relaxation, controlled breathing and thought-stopping are all necessary to help cope with deleterious experiences. This needs to be linked with work on the expression of anger. There are a variety of group techniques to help children express their feelings.

There are some issues to take into consideration about the relationship of group work to the criminal proceedings. It is essential that accurate notes are kept of topics and subjects discussed, so that claims that children are being

coached in what to say can be countered. It is advisable to inform the police or Crown Prosecution Service of the content of any proposed therapy, whether group or individual, to prevent allegations that therapists or others have 'taught' what should be said in court proceedings.

Cognitive processing

This is to do with the way the child understands and 'processes' abusive experiences. There needs to be direct attribution of responsibility to whoever is responsible for both the abusive acts or any failure to protect the child. This issue needs to be explored and reinforced a number of times in various contexts.

Self-blame needs to be addressed and corrective explanations given about the behaviour of paedophiles, how offenders groom and target their victims, the compulsive nature of their abusive behaviour and about the working of the ring. The teaching of self-assertiveness and social skills is important, as is training in communication skills, to help develop an approach which counters the pervasive effects of negative beliefs.

Dealing with sexualisation and sexualised behaviour

There needs to be educational work, both individually and in groups, to deal with repetitive masturbatory fantasies and enactments. Basic sexual knowledge needs to be imparted, because these young people are often very active but may have a very low level of understanding. It is important to reduce the intensity of sexualisation and sexualised behaviour which occurs as a result of being involved in extensive sexual activities.

There may be young people with profound mood disturbances, suicidal behaviour, self-mutilation or serious anorexic symptoms which require inpatient or longer-term community therapeutic placements. When seriously abusive behaviour has been triggered, this again may need both group and residential care in a safe context to reduce the risk to other children posed by the young person who has developed an abusive orientation as a result of being involved in a ring.

Family work

This is often helpful once the victimised child has received some individual or group therapy. Group work may be particularly helpful in enabling parents to share the sense of loss and bereavement associated with the discovery that their children may have been involved in long-standing abusive acts in their community. Siblings often need support, and the deep sense of anger and rage towards people who may have been trusted, or appear to have been

giving the children rewards and even apparently supporting abusive parents, all need to be confronted and dealt with through individual, family and parent group meetings. Protective parents need a good deal of help to cope with and understand the emotional responses, the sexualisation and the behavioural patterns of children who have been involved in extensive abusive activities. Parents may blame themselves for entrusting their child to the care of an offender and feel terribly guilty.

Parents themselves may have been abused, and this may have played an important role in inhibiting an accurate preventative perception of the behaviour of their children. Above all, secrecy needs to be addressed and replaced with openness, and there needs to be a sharing between social work professionals, therapeutic professionals and those providing support in the community.

Foster-carers or residential care workers also need guidance and support in managing and helping abused children. Great skill and sensitivity may be required to look after children who were abused within a paedophile ring operating within a school or residential home, and placement in a similar institution may well lead to a degree of re-traumatisation for the child. The child may have felt overwhelmed by fear, with a feeling there was no one safe to turn to, and this may have a serious long-term effect on their capacity to form trusting relationships.

Case example – Imogen

A case example which illustrates some of the serious psychological sequelae of sexual abuse by a paedophile is that of Imogen, 17 years old, who was an in-patient in a specialist eating disorders unit within a psychiatric hospital. She had previously been an in-patient for nine months in another hospital for treatment of anorexia nervosa, but management of her eating disorder was extremely difficult.

At the specialist unit, Imogen received individual psychotherapy and took part in the daily meetings on the ward where young people were encouraged to talk about themselves and their problems. Imogen presented as a deeply unhappy, traumatised girl who was fearful, uncommunicative and expressed suicidal ideation and intent. She engaged in self-mutilation, cutting her arms, and took very little care of herself. She was extremely reluctant to see her family when they visited, and gave a history of never having felt close to either of her parents.

Gradually, within the context of her psychotherapy, Imogen began to reveal having been sexually abused by a so-called 'family friend' for several years. This man, whom she called 'Uncle John', had often baby-sat her when she was a young child and had shown an interest in her which extended to

taking her out, paying for horse-riding lessons, etc. Gradually, Imogen would visit Uncle John at his house more frequently, and it was here that he began to sexually molest her. The abuse became more serious over time, and finally included sexual intercourse. Uncle John gave Imogen money, new clothes and took her out, and she would visit him on a regular basis.

She revealed to her therapist the belief that, since she had accepted John's money and treats and had continued to visit him, even though she was being abused, she was basically responsible for that abuse. The fact that she did not tell anyone about it compounded her sense of guilt and shame, her determination to starve herself and mutilate herself seemed to represent an attempt to assuage her feelings of guilt and remorse, and she felt she deserved punishment. She did not feel she deserved to be alive, and hence wished to die.

It seemed that the lack of emotional care and nurturing of Imogen by her parents, particularly her mother, had contributed to her feeling vulnerable and isolated within her family, and she had welcomed Uncle John's attention. In some ways, he was meeting her attachment needs, and emotional closeness was what she appeared to be seeking.

Imogen had become extremely upset on discovering that she was not the only child befriended by Uncle John, and he suggested on several occasions that she should bring some of her friends round, but her jealousy towards any other potential 'favourites' prevented her from becoming a recruiting victim.

Imogen has already suffered some severe debilitating and chronic emotional and psychiatric disorders as a result of her experience of abuse. She has not yet reached the point where she dare reveal her perpetrator's full name or feel ready to make a statement to the police, although she will be given every support in doing so. She is also being helped to face the prospect of sharing this information with her parents, with the assistance of her psychotherapist and a family therapist.

Meanwhile, who has become Uncle John's latest victim?

References

Beitchman, J.H., Zucker, K.J., Hood, J.E., DaCosta, G.A., Akman, D. and Cassavia, E. (1992) 'A review of the long term effects of child sexual abuse', *Child Abuse and Neglect*, 16 (1), 101–18.

Belanger, A.J., Belcher, L.B. and Birnhard, L. (1984) 'Typology of Sex Rings Exploiting Children' in Burgess, A.W. (ed.) *Child Pornography and Sex Rings*, Lexington, MA: Lexington Books.

Burgess, A.W., Groth, A.N. and McCausland, M.P. (1981) 'Child Sex Initiation Rings', *American Journal of Orthopsychiatry*, 51, 110–19.

Burgess, A.W., Hartman, C.R., McCausland, M.P. and Powers, P. (1984) 'Children and Adolescents Exploited Through Sex Rings and Pornography', *American Journal of Psychiatry*, 141, 656–62.

Department of Health/Home Office (DoH/HO) (1992) *Memorandum of Good Practice on Video Recorded Interviews with Child Witnesses for Criminal Proceedings*, London: HMSO.

Pooley, J. and Wood, W. (1994) 'Rituals – The Power to Damage and the Power to Heal' in V. Sinason (ed.) *Treating Survivors of Satanist Abuse*, London: Routledge.

Watkins, W. and Bentovim, A. (1992) 'The sexual abuse of male children and adolescents: A review of recent research', *Journal of Child Psychology and Psychiatry*, 33, 197–248.

Wild, N.J. and Wynne, J.M. (1986) 'Child Sex Rings', *British Medical Journal*, 293, 183–5.

6 Organised abuse and Asian communities

Perdeep Gill

This chapter is a first step into the barely-begun debate on organised child sexual abuse and the Asian communities. The Asian population of Britain does not seem to appear in the recent debate. This may be for our supposed protection from such a subject, or may be another example of our minimalisation, dressed up as respect for our cultural identity. Some of us, mainly women, are now struggling to end this isolation of Asian children, whose abuse at the hands of organised perpetrators is as damaging as that of any other child. This chapter is written as part of the process of our communities giving permission to heal our children of the effects of organised sexual abuse and protect them from it.

Research, investigation and speculation concerning organised child sexual abuse has hardly touched the Asian community. There is one exception, Tower Hamlets, upon which I will comment later.

Specific conditions for abuse and silence in Asian communities

For seven years, I have been working with children and adult female survivors of child sexual abuse. To borrow from Freud, I can say that I have tested the reality of organised abuse within and upon the Asian communities 'on the couch'. For those of you who need statistics, research may flow from the raising of voices such as this, but suffice it to say that we already know enough about why (almost exclusively) men sexually abuse. My aim is to provoke thought amongst those now dealing with or likely to come across organised abuse. I wish to illustrate that Asian communities are no less likely than white British communities to face child sexual abuse, both opportunistic and organised. Indeed, I will point out features of minority culture,

under both physical and ideological attack, which may increase the incidence of abuse and/or its chances of remaining undetected. For this purpose, I shall compare elements of the emigrant experience with a theoretical model of the indicators of abuse derived from the dominant Western culture.

First, though, some definitions: by 'Asian communities' I refer to groupings of people born in the Indian subcontinent (or descendants of those who emigrated to East Africa and the UK) and who hold a cultural affinity for the subcontinent (for example a first language of Urdu, Punjabi, Bengali or Hindi, etc. and religious beliefs or a symbolic life derived from Sikhism, Islam or Hinduism, etc.). From within, such communities would recognise their individuation by language and religion. From without, we might simply be seen as 'Asian' and recognised by our dress, our food or our physical differences to the majority population.

By 'organised abuse' I refer to the definition in *Working Together* (DoH, 1991):

> a generic term which covers abuse which may involve a number of abusers, a number of abused children and young people, and often encompasses different forms of abuse. It involves, to a greater or lesser extent, an element of organisation.

I will be considering specifically the links between the impact of emigration on a culture and the preconditions for organised child sexual abuse. Emigration has been a traumatic experience for the Asian communities, who initially arrived in Britain with fantasies and dreams of a 'better life'. The harsh reality was that of poorly-paid employment, poor housing and tidal waves of institutional and personal discrimination and racism.

The new world that had appeared so welcoming was, in fact, insistent that the Asian communities were 'aliens', outsiders. The experience of emigration is typified by a sense of not belonging and of being on the periphery of society. This is particularly traumatising to people whose understanding of being is so connected with belonging to a community. Attachments have been broken from one's country, community and family. Over a period of time, families and communities are partly rejoined; however, attachments remain fragile. There remains a fog of isolation for the group, family and individual. In the face of alienation and discrimination, the Asian communities experience great anxiety and are communities under siege. Immigration laws create a culture of fear and defensiveness, necessitating a web of secrecy with regard to legal status, family relationships and even people's ages. Survival techniques have necessarily become characterised by secrecy. An emigrant Asian community not only defends itself against the hammering of discrimination but also fears being colonised by the dominant culture. The Asian communities have responded by rigidifying. The organic process whereby a culture continually develops is fiercely resisted by the main body of the communities.

The reactive ideology of the family and strict adherence to an entrenched patriarchal system becomes the coercive force in defining the survival of the community and the individual. Questioning and challenging are perceived as cultural betrayal. Most importantly, the identity of women and children is swallowed by the concept of community, the survival of which becomes synonymous with our moral purity. There is extreme suppression of sex and sexuality, as they become defined as the essence of impurity and the symbol of Western culture.

However, the host culture is the dominant culture, and our communities cannot escape that fact. Asian communities suffer the tragedy of internalised racism, whereby the Western culture is felt to be superior. The threat to the community is then perceived as coming from within *and* from without. Defence takes the form of the projection back onto the dominant culture of internalised, negative beliefs. Our own cultures are then uncritically held to be morally superior, and all badness and decadence become the property of Western culture.

Patriarchal communities use sex as the touchstone of their moral purity and daughters as the bearers of this cultural icon. So Asian girls carry the double burden of the projection of cultural purity, literally, upon their bodies and of having to keep silent if this very purity is despoiled, for fear it would damage their community which has so heavily invested its self-image in them.

The impact of emigration and a community coping with psychological and physical discrimination leads to the solidifying of idealised and behavioural norms that also mark out cultural preconditions for child sexual abuse.

Finkelhor (1984) has identified these as:

- social isolation, erosion of networks;
- an ideology of family sanctity and patriarchal prerogatives for fathers, interlinked with a masculine requirement to be dominant and powerful in relationships;
- barriers to women's equality;
- social powerlessness of children and the unavailability of sex education.

These preconditions feature clearly in Asian communities following the impact of emigration, leaving children particularly vulnerable to intra-familial and organised child sexual abuse. The impact of emigration is only a part of the experience of the Asian communities, and developmental processes may differ sharply between communities.

The variables here are the length of time that has passed since emigration, acceptance into the host community, employment rewards and standard of

living. If a community feels secure in its new form, this lessens the dynamics of siege and the secrecy and male power hegemony that accompany it.

The state of contradiction in which Asian communities exist with regard to the host culture is damaging for our children, who fall victim to organised sexual abuse. Its discovery within our communities pushes people into denial. The typical response to its discovery – as in Tower Hamlets (Lucas, 1991) – is blanket denial: 'It doesn't happen "back home", it is proscribed by religion and so it cannot be happening.'

Acceptance may be forthcoming if the perpetrators are from outside the community, as this horrifically confirms the decadence of Western culture. But this denial of abuse from within and acceptance of it from without only serves to prolong the siege mentality and reinforces the preconditions for abuse within the Asian communities. Where the possibility of organised abuse within the community is rigidly upheld as unacceptable, other reasons for the allegations have to be sought. Children are accused of lying and of betraying their culture for having such thoughts. The pressure from the host culture to become 'Western' is easily blamed.

In Asian communities under the pressure of investigation into organised abuse, I have found patterns emerging as follows:

- Perpetrators demand that the allegations be treated confidentially and kept secret from their community. Paedophiles who are known, though perhaps not openly identified as such, may be ostracised as generally undesirable by their communities. Yet, at least on a superficial level, relationships remain as before; the offender maintains his social involvement in the community. The community upholds a front of secrecy and so minimalises the reality of abuse.
- On engaging women of Asian communities, they are able to track memories of whispers, in the older generations or 'back home', of insinuations related to sexual abuse by certain males within their sphere. Such men may be sent away from the area in which they have 'been discovered', for example back to the subcontinent, or to the UK from the subcontinent.
- Other women have reconsidered the unbelievability of organised child sexual abuse and raised questions about the strict rules in their community with regard to relationships between girls, women and the men in their families and communities. For instance, in the communities that represent the greatest patriarchal rigidity and the greatest denial, there appear to be the strictest rules about protecting the purity of daughters. They must accompany their mothers and must not be left alone with their fathers or uncles.

Such rules highlight a perceived sexual danger from within our communi-

ties. The inescapable evidence of the growth of Asian adult and child pornography undermines the ability to deny organised abuse within our communities. Denial based on the reasoning that something could not occur because it breaks a rule (religious, etc.) is inherently flawed. Rules are established as a consequence of awareness of what could (and does) happen. In further exploring the vulnerability of Asian children to organised child sexual abuse from either outside or within the community, we recognise the process of victimisation.

Summit's 'accommodation syndrome' (Summit, 1983) can be applied to understanding the impact of emigration on the child as well as the experience of sexual abuse. Summit suggests that five factors characterise the process of victimisation which explains how children are forced into accepting their sexual abuse. These are:

- secrecy;
- helplessness;
- entrapment and accommodation;
- delayed conflict;
- retraction of complaint.

These are also essential elements of the Asian community's coping mechanisms against the organised abuse of racial discrimination. To understand and detect organised abuse in our communities, it is vital to understand how children from the Asian communities have been introduced and familiarised into a process of victimisation generally. Organised child sexual abuse slots into an established pattern of 'accommodating' to abuse.

We need to begin thinking about the Asian paedophile. It is difficult to pinpoint documented, general characteristics of paedophiles within Asian communities, as the cultural ethos enables the paedophile to hide or blend characteristics so they are not so distinguishable as their counterparts in the dominant culture. Paedophiles are not a homogeneous group, and the qualitative differences in operating must, in part, be influenced by their cultural backgrounds. Whilst paedophiles universally have in common the systematic abuse of children, each culture produces, as it were, its own style of abuse. Organised abuse within our communities sadly reflects dominant traits within the culture.

Abuse and professional silence

There is a dearth of studies of ethnic minorities and child sexual abuse (let alone organised child sexual abuse). Those that do exist (for example the excellent research on false negatives by Lawson (1992) which focused on

Puerto Rican families and the comparison of Afro-American and white American victims in Wyatt and Powell (1988)) do not consider the particularities of the cultural context.

On organised child sexual abuse, one looks to, say, *Child Pornography* by Tim Tate (1990) or *Satanist Abuse* by Sinason (1994) in vain for references to such abuse being part of the Asian experience too. I do not pick these works out to denigrate them but to illustrate my point. In particular, Sinason's book contains contributions from professionals across the UK. The only reference to ethnicity is made by Trowell (1994), who suggests it is an important issue to be considered. In the chapter on 'The Leeds Experience' by Hobbs and Wynne (1994), again there is no mention of ethnicity as a factor in the abuse. Yet Leeds is a multi-cultural city on the doorstep of Bradford, a city now renowned for its Asian communities.

I want to suggest three reasons for this blindness to the Asian population:

● racism, which would make us invisible or undeserving generally;
● professional fear of intervention being labelled 'racist';
● Asian workers' mistrust of white colleagues' intervention.

This may be expanded further into:

● 'Positive racism' – the stereotype of the Asian culture as mutually supportive and beneficial to all members of the community. This is the alienated Western fantasy of pre-industrial societies. There is an investment in not wanting to believe that organised child sexual abuse could occur in supposedly idyllic communities.
● 'Negative racism' – the fear of being labelled racist. There is much confusion and anxiety amongst professionals about the detection of organised child sexual abuse within the Asian communities. It seems to be related to a dual concern regarding the communities' reaction of feeling persecuted and the wish to desperately avoid labelling or pathologising a community. Paralysis and shortcomings in intervention were succinctly mirrored in the conclusions reached following the Tower Hamlets case (Lucas, 1991). Here, 'Western' models of intervention were considered inappropriate when responding to organised child sexual abuse and its impact on Asian families.

In my view, this is not only a nonsensical but a dangerously neglectful analysis. The notion of a Western approach suggests an accepted concept of an Eastern/non-Western intervention, the meaning of which is not established. I suggest that such terminology is mystifying. Such a mechanism permits the avoidance of the statutory duty to intervene.

Organised child sexual abuse is not a homogeneous problem, but is mani-

fested in different ways in a culturally diverse society. Therefore, qualitative issues such as an Asian child's culture need to be incorporated in order to ensure an effective assessment and treatment service. It is unacceptable that the issues of race and culture are not even on the agenda of those expert professionals working in the field of child protection and treatment. Even in 1994, I heard issues of ethnicity or being 'coloured' described as 'a red herring'. Such blindly racist attitudes on the part of those at the top of the child protection and treatment professions mean that children from Asian communities are not being protected against organised child sexual abuse. It is the lack of thought-out intervention – not intervention itself – that is dangerous. To leave Asian children unprotected is racist.

Asian workers mistrust their white colleagues' intervention, because we share our communities' experience of siege, and we too have to struggle with our received ideas that organised abuse is not an Asian phenomenon. But Asian professionals are not encouraged to give up these ideas when white professionals talk of us as 'coloured' and tell us that ethnicity or culture are peripheral issues in organised abuse. Each culture produces its own style of deviancy, and in a culture based on the importance of the extended family network, we should not be surprised that this is reflected in the minds and behaviours of paedophiles. The organisation of child sexual abuse within the Asian communities is grounded in the male family members' network. This should not surprise us, yet who can say this without the fear that white professionals will simply view abuse in Asian communities in some formulaic way, such as: 'Closed communities are breeding grounds for abuse, and so all Asian communities are suspect.' The thought fills us with dread and explains why some Asian professionals drift into blunder and inaction while trying to justify the protection of our communities, ignoring the need to protect the most vulnerable within a vulnerable community.

This mistrust of white colleagues is illustrated in the following case of organised abuse from outside the Asian community. It happened in 1992, in a local authority with a large Asian population.

Case example: Avoidance of duty as cultural sensitivity

A white male paedophile with previous convictions had been employed, using connections and faked references, in a junior school, teaching a predominantly Asian class. One child told a friend that she was being abused by the teacher. The friend told her mother, who contacted the police. A joint police and Social Services investigation took place. During the interview, the Asian child alleged that the teacher had 'bummed her'. She further added that this also happened to other children in her class. A medical examination

supported her allegations of anal interference. The teacher was quickly found to be HIV-positive. A case conference was convened, where a decision was made to withhold the issue of the perpetrator's HIV status from the child's parent. The rationale was that there was little chance of contamination and that, furthermore, the tests required a longer period than the family's holiday visa allowed. In respect of further investigation, it was decided · that it was unlikely that other children would make allegations. There was much discussion of the possible political repercussions.

The issue of responsibility for further investigation was fudged and inaction justified as the school catchment area crossed several boroughs. Astonishingly, a member of this conference was the head of the school, against whom, several years previously, allegations of sexual abuse had been made by another Asian child. Child protection officers at that time had labelled the child's mother as 'hysterical', despite a psychiatric opinion supporting the child's allegations. Therefore, it was perhaps not surprising that he argued strongly for curtailment of further investigations in this later case.

As for the other members of the conference, they were all white professionals, with the exception of one Asian social worker. She found the issue of child sexual abuse within her community unbearable and coped through minimalisation and denial. Once again, it was not surprising that this Asian professional wished the issue to be left alone; what was amazing was that the conference members argued that they sought guidance from their Asian colleague. Her words were treated as 'The Truth' and as a rationale for straying from child protection procedures on the basis of cultural sensitivity!

I wish now to turn to abuse that is organised within Asian communities. A recent case example shows (a) the organisation of abuse along family lines and (b) the impossibility of white professionals understanding the nature of the abuse.

Case example: Cultural sensitivity informing duty

In a small town in the country with few Asian families, a teenage girl from a large Asian family with many younger siblings runs away. She has told a friend that she was sexually abused by her father. On being jointly interviewed by the police and a social worker, she makes vague allegations of sexual abuse. She is accommodated in another town and subsequently refuses even to confirm her story. All the professionals are white.

The father claims that the girl is making up a story because he has forbidden her to have boyfriends, which she resists in order to be Westernised. The Social Services Department consider planning to reunite the child and her family. An Asian female professional is called in to help the process. The girl

now confirms in detail the allegations of abuse and talks of her fears regarding her siblings. Eventually, this worker sees most of the siblings, who disclose (even the 5-year-old) sexual abuse at the hands of their father, uncle and adult cousins, and seeing sexual acts between all these adults.

There are further references to many other children in the extended family network also being abused. Abuse took place in their home and the various relatives' towns throughout the UK and in their country of origin. The older girl openly confirmed that she could only now speak about the extent of her abuse, as for her, telling an Asian professional meant not 'selling out' her community to the dominant white culture. Without the Asian intervention, she would have protected her abusers in order to protect her wider culture from assault. Another hallmark of organised abuse here was that the girls in this extended family had marriages arranged at extremely young ages, either to perpetrating cousins or non-related men who, however, maintained the 'culture' of sexual abuse.

This is a pattern I have seen elsewhere in our communities, and it is something to which non-Asian professionals are, in the main, blind.

Understanding the pattern of abuse within Asian communities

In working with survivors of sexual abuse, I became aware of a significant number of women and children who were re-abused. At first glance, the sexual abuses appeared unrelated, and I sought understanding in the theories regarding patterns of victimisation. Yet there was a pattern emerging of the perpetrators knowing each other. Again, I rationalised this as not surprising, as the communities are small and tight-knit, and everyone knows each other. Yet, on closer examination of the survivors' abuse and re-abuse, there were often more substantial links between the offenders than just loosely belonging to the same community.

The initial perpetrator tended to be a close member of the family – a father, brother, cousin or uncle – and lived in the same house and had easy access to the child(ren) without arousing suspicion. The other offenders were either members of the extended family not living in the same house or friends given access to the children by the first perpetrator. It was not necessarily openly acknowledged to the child that the relative/friend was to have contact for the purpose of abuse, but the strict cultural boundaries regarding contact between men outside the home and girls are often actively shifted by perpetrators involved in organised abuse. Again, at first glance the notion of several perpetrators in a family fits the theory of the 'dysfunctional' and enmeshed family. However, I argue that this is in fact a group of people organised to abuse children under the cover of family networks. The concept

of 'family' is very different within Asian communities from that of the host community, and 'family' may extend to include all those who have emigrated from the same geographical area. This concept of 'family' is not dysfunctional but is vulnerable to abusers organising along its complex support networks.

The child is given the culturally-accepted message from a significant (abusing) adult that you must obey the adult you are introduced to, and respect and do as this elder tells you as you would a father. The hidden and imprisoning message is the instruction and threat that you will be abused, and you will offend this male elder if you do not do as you are told. That is to say, organised abuse within Asian communities uses the patriarchal organisation of the community in order to systematically abuse children. This underlying message is very powerful as part of the process of victimisation, acting to confuse and disorientate the child. Welding the abuse to the dynamics of a retrenched culture mystifies in order to protect the organised abusers.

The cultural preconditions that provide an environment for sexual abuse to flourish within the Asian communities have already been established in the application of Finkelhor's theory. Yet it cannot be emphasised enough that in cultures that adhere to (male) elders having to be obeyed without question, challenging is viewed as betrayal. Furthermore, their sanction on sex education leaves children vulnerable to sexual abuse. Children are groomed by reference to cultural rules, and there is great threat of punishment for not adhering to the rules. This appears to be much more the case regarding the first perpetrator/the significant adult who asserts and demands his right to be obeyed.

Other perpetrators that are 'introduced' to the child appear to combine this with other means of hooking children: much attention is focused on the child; there is an unspoken promise of liberalism in the relationship, a glimpse of the Western world, with much talk of being in love with the young person and promises of marriage and a different lifestyle, the price, of course, being sexual abuse. Yet the hooking process is a method of confusing: blurring the nature of abuse, it becomes a means of instilling in the child the notion of the child wanting the sexual relationship, and the supposed Western freedoms that follow. The child is then ready to be instructed to prepare other children and introduce them to the perpetrator. The distorted allegiance to the perpetrator as liberator is solidified by the threat of the perpetrator loving another child more.

Competition and conflict with other abused children is administered as a way of reinforcing the distorted attachments. A perpetrator may suggest a resolution to such conflict by introducing another adult who could marry one of the girls – a subtle process of widening the organised abuse.

Organised abuse not only reflects but also effectively uses the commu-

nity's system of organisation. For example, in some Asian communities the cultural structure deems girls as a marriageable commodity, and hence ready for sex, from the age of 13 years. Hence a paedophile may marry in order to hide his activity of abusing. Of course, marrying someone very young and from 'back home' means she is isolated and totally dependent on her husband. This reinforces a patriarchal archetype of the submissive wife and sets the scene for unopposed abuse of children in the future.

More alarmingly, I have been struck by accounts regarding women who, as girls, were the victims of organised abuse and whose husbands have abused their children – the point being that these women's marriages were arranged by significant members of the family (abusers). The question arises: is this really just coincidence, or is the institution of marriage being manipulated by paedophiles to maintain their organised activity?

This is a tentative understanding of a pattern of organised abuse, based on the testimony of Asian survivors. Little is known of the real relationships and communications between the perpetrators that organise sexual abuse within the Asian communities. I hope that my counterparts working with offenders take note of the desperate need to explore the operations of paedophiles within cultural contexts, and that the testimony of young girls is heard by professionals who would rather forget.

References

Department of Health (DoH) (1991) *Working Together Under the Children Act: A Guide to Arrangements for Inter-Agency Co-operation for the Protection of Children from Abuse*, London: HMSO.

Finkelhor, D. (1984) *Child Sexual Abuse: New Theory and Research*, New York: Free Press.

Hobbs, C. and Wynne, J. (1994) 'The Leeds Experience' in Sinason (1994).

Lawson, L. (1992) 'False Negatives in Child Sexual Abuse Disclosure Interviews', *Journal of Interpersonal Violence*, 7 (4), 532–42.

Lucas, D. (1991) 'Height of Confusion', *Social Work Today*, 22 (28), 9.

Sinason, V. (ed.) (1994) *Treating Survivors of Satanist Abuse*, London: Routledge.

Summit, R. (1983) 'The Child Abuse Accommodation Syndrome', *Child Abuse and Neglect*, 7 (2), 177–93.

Tate, T. (1990) *Child Pornography: An Investigation*, London: Methuen.

Trowell, J. (1994) 'Ritual Organised Abuse: Management Issues' in Sinason (1994).

Wyatt, G.E. and Powell, C.J. (eds) (1988) *Lasting Effects of Child Sexual Abuse*, London: Sage.

7 The mind of the paedophile

Ray Wyre

In this chapter, I place the 'fixated paedophile' in context and expand on implications for practice. Over the years, the term 'paedophile' has taken on various meanings. The word means literally 'child love'. It has been used to describe men (and some women) who exhibit sexual arousal and attraction towards pre-pubertal children. When there is sexual arousal towards post-pubertal children who are below the age of consent, the term that has been used is 'hebephilia'. Sometimes, where men abuse boys, the term 'homosexual paedophile' is used. This is unhelpful, as it confuses paedophiles with members of the homosexual community.

The fact that a person has paedophile tendencies does not necessarily mean that he has sexually abused a child or is going to abuse a child. Conversely, not everybody who sexually abuses a child can be described as being a paedophile. Other terms have come into being. The word 'child molester' is often preferred. 'Molestation' also suggests a wider concept of abuse rather than just sexual.

A person who has paedophile desires might be able to control his behaviour if he recognises that the abuse of a child is wrong. A person may have high levels of desire and fantasy about a child sexually, but if he is also going to abuse, he will necessarily exhibit high levels of distorted thinking, and have to overcome his internal inhibitors.

Disinhibitors can give permission to the offender to carry out the abuse. They appear to be: certain emotional states like loneliness, depression and anger; drugs and alcohol; adult and child pornography; fantasy and masturbation to thoughts of children (here the orgasm acts as a reinforcer), and peer pressure.

The typology of sex offenders who abuse children will always be controversial. We need to be aware that there are different types of child molesters in order to understand their patterns of behaviour. This is particularly

important when we have to prioritise suspects in an investigation. Certain behaviours can indicate certain motivations for the abuse. Identifying the needs that are met through any sexual offending behaviour can help prioritise suspects. However, it must be remembered that although there are abusive 'types', individuals who abuse can come from all walks of life and all social, class and ethnic backgrounds. There is no such thing as an out-of-character offender.

In this chapter, I intend to talk about those child molesters who have been called 'fixated paedophiles'.

Characteristics of fixated paedophiles

They tend to have the following main characteristics.

Their main arousal and orientation is towards children

Many men are sexually aroused by children but control their behaviour or get adult women to play the roles of children. They do not have to be sexually aroused towards children to abuse them. They may be aroused by a specific sexual practice and can manipulate the child to satisfy this desire (flagellation, oral abuse and behaviour involving urinating are examples of this). The offender might be motivated by anger to a level where the object of this anger is irrelevant. (I have worked with men who have raped their daughters in order to 'get back at' their partner).

They may engage in highly addictive behaviour

Paedophiles can be very highly addicted to their behaviour. This is similar to a gambling or a drug addiction. An understanding of the devices of deceit used by these other types of addict helps explain why there are some paedophile offenders who really do want to stop but find it impossible.

Despite appearances, they may feel inadequate

Fixated paedophiles in positions of power, in prominent positions within our society, may not initially appear to have inadequate personalities. However, if you scratch the surface, these men will usually feel inadequate compared to their peers.

They may molest large numbers of children

Of all sex offenders, fixated paedophiles are most likely to abuse again, and

they can abuse hundreds of children during their criminal career. Some will stay with one child for many years and then move on to another child. Other paedophiles move quickly from one child to another, and some abuse more than one child at the same time.

However, we must always be careful in accepting the numbers of children a paedophile claims he has abused. I have little doubt that some paedophiles in treatment begin to exaggerate the scale of their abuse. There are a number of reasons for this. The most common is their desire to please the therapist; the second is that, if you wish to be seen as 'getting better', it can be an advantage to make it seem as though you were very bad.

We may never know the full extent of abuse, because children who are victims of paedophiles seldom reveal it.

They may adopt pseudo-parental roles or may deliberately set out to gain the trust of ('seduce') the parents or other caregivers

In the relationships they create prior to the abuse, fixated paedophiles often relate to the children as a father might do to his child. For this reason, I would argue that men should retain a role in childcare, even though there have been recent debates about whether men should work with children because certain men have used their positions within care situations to abuse children. Children who have no fathers or other adult male figures in their lives are susceptible to men who give them attention, whether for good or bad motives.

Paedophiles need children's caregivers to trust them. They can be excellent at persuading parents to accept that their relationship with children is acceptable and in the children's interests. Some such men actually become part of the family. They are invited round at weekends and are allowed to baby-sit. This is very common within certain types of religious groups. The single man attending a service on his own will often find himself invited back for dinner by a family. The relationship may deepen, and the time he spends with the family will probably increase, especially if he demonstrates a willingness to help out with the family, either practically or financially.

They may be seductive in their approach

The normal approach to a child by a paedophile is one of seduction. The process is very similar to the seduction process within adult relationships, but this should not be compared to the 'chat-up' line within an adult/adult relationship. This seduction can go to the very being of the child, and their identity, beliefs and fantasies will be affected by it.

Because of the secrecy and control involved in abuse, children often have

only the offenders to give them information. The 'hands-on' abuse by the paedophile is often felt to be congruent by the child, because the offender has prepared the child in a psychological way to accept the abuse and has created the emotional dependency to keep the child trapped.

The seduction process can often be as arousing for the paedophile as the abuse itself. It often outwardly resembles the actions of someone who cares and loves children appropriately. Investigating paedophilia is extremely difficult because of this. What is it that makes one expression of affection towards a child acceptable, and when is it abusive? If the behaviour moved into genital touching, for example, the earlier affection should also be considered part of the abuse.

They take time to form relationships with children

Paedophiles can devote many days, weeks, months and sometimes years to targeting and seducing children. One paedophile said to me that the reason it was so easy to abuse children was because most fathers knew more about their cars than they did about their children. During this period, the offender may be targeting and testing certain children and will be careful before he moves into 'hands-on' abusing. If a child discloses the abuse during this testing period, it is unlikely that anything will happen to remedy the situation, because the paedophile may claim that the activity was 'play-fighting', 'accidental touching' or that the child has misconstrued something that was said. Anyone making enquiries might think that a fuss is being made over nothing. However, if the child does not disclose during the testing period, the offender will see this as a green light to proceed with 'hands-on' abuse.

Parents should ask: 'Why does this person want to spend all this time with my child?' Parents might be happy for their child to be taken off their hands for a while. The more parents are aware, the more questions they may ask. This does not mean that children should not be with other adults or that adults should not take children away from their families for short periods. But I am concerned about how easy it has been for men to gain access to children with their parents' permission.

Paedophiles will be able to relate to children. They will often be seen as 'nice men'. Monsters do not get close to children, but 'nice men' do. They can stop being strangers two seconds after meeting a child. Children's definitions of 'a stranger' are often very different to what adults call 'a stranger'. Strangers, to children, are often 'dirty, horrible men', or 'men who make you feel uncomfortable'. Outsiders will often say of an offender that 'he really liked children', that 'he really enjoyed their company, and children enjoyed his'.

They may use child erotic material and sometimes child or adult pornography to lower the inhibitions of children

The use of pornography has a number of purposes. It may arouse children, depending on their age. It can lead to sexual discussion. It helps target certain children, depending on their response. It can be used to create a collusive secret behind adults' backs, but with the offender offering reassurance about the secret. It sexualises the environment for children. They may become sexual with each other. It can be used in the corruption of children. It contains within it myths and fantasies concerning women and children, and it portrays people as sexual objects. It also makes it difficult for children to be witnesses, as their evidence may be presented as being contaminated by exposure to pornography, in which they have appeared to collude, rather than reflecting actual abuse.

They may seek to portray their behaviour as 'normal'

Paedophiles usually wish their behaviour to be seen as 'normal' and encourage political debate as to how normal 'sex with children' is. Some paedophiles emphasise how common it is in order to try to make the public believe that it *is* normal. Cases in the media where young girls are described as being 'seductive', being 'promiscuous' and 'wanting to be involved with men' may be used to legitimise the behaviour, as well as some high-profile cases, like Mandy Smith's relationship, at 13, with the Rolling Stone Bill Wyman.

Various organisations, like NAMBLA (North American Man Boy Love Association), Paidika, the former England-based Paedophile Information Exchange and Magpie, could all be described as promoting 'inter-generational sex'. They suggest that the taboo against child sex abuse is part of 'ageism'.

Their friends and associates are probably paedophiles and share information and a common language

Owing to their need to have their views validated, paedophiles will relate best to others who share their beliefs. We should be concerned about who their friends are. Contact with other paedophiles can commence or be enhanced in prison. Offenders who have met inside have ended up running sex rings together. There are also subtle ways of letting others know that you have an interest in children – 'He's past the sell-by date', if spoken about a teenager, will be enough to give the message.

They may have strong cognitive distortions and beliefs

Their beliefs can easily be seen in the magazines distributed by the organisations mentioned above. At times, it is hard to credit the arguments that they will use to justify their behaviour. Some paedophiles use their own childhood experiences to support their present behaviour. Some men will say that they enjoyed being touched as boys, that they were not victims, that they enjoyed it and wanted it. Because of the way their abusers abused them, they might even think that they were the cause of their own abuse. If the paedophiles believe that children want this activity, they are unlikely to believe that what they are doing is wrong and causes damage.

They are usually over 25 years of age yet may have no dating pattern with men or women

Our work has shown that many paedophiles start to abuse when they are still teenagers. However, paedophiles are not normally identified until they are over 25. It might also be that the behaviour of the paedophile takes some time to develop. If a younger person is accused of sexual abuse, it is unusual to identify him at that stage as a fixated paedophile. Most non-sexual offenders grow out of their offending by their early twenties. However, this does not appear to be the case for fixated paedophiles. It has been said that they 'grow into it'. The older the offenders are before being caught, the harder it is to intervene successfully in their lives.

By intuition and design, they may select vulnerable children, who may be physically and/or emotionally neglected

The paedophile's ability to target the 'right' child is well known. Out of a group of children, he will sense which child to go for, which one to test out. He does not want the child to tell, he wants the child to be dependent upon him, thereby reducing the likelihood of anyone finding out. If he can meet other needs that a vulnerable child has, then this will reduce the likelihood of the child disclosing, because the child will 'accommodate' the abuse.

They do not usually marry, but may be in a marriage of convenience

The increasing numbers of single-parent families have been an advantage to paedophiles. Often, adult women might see covert paedophiles as non-threatening and would see their desire to care for children as something positive. They may even fall in love with them and marry them. The fact that the fixated paedophile may have a sexual relationship with a woman does not

automatically contradict the characteristic of being aroused by children. Some paedophiles are aroused by adults; some hardly ever have sex, and other paedophiles have explained how, when they are having sex with their partners, they think of children to achieve orgasm.

They may belong to children's organisations

It is important that organisations where individuals are working with children look at how they recruit staff and volunteers. There must be supervision structures set up in all organisations so that worrying behaviour or attitudes can quickly be addressed. The staff must know the difference between an unaware and an aware culture, and seek to make sure that they operate an aware culture. If such structures are not in place, then staff will feel that they cannot express their concerns about an individual's behaviour, and it will also be easier for the paedophile to control the environment he is working in.

They may have a preference for children of a particular age range – the older the child, the more likely they are to select one gender

The stereotypical victim age group for paedophiles is 8–12 years. As body hair appears, the fixated paedophile may give the child up. However, whilst individuals are still known to have an interest in this age range, we know that some offenders will abuse children from birth. Once children have moved from the abusers' preferred age range, they may be passed on to other abusers who have a liking for that particular age range.

In a recent case, the paedophile was accused of being sexually aroused by boys and girls. Within interview, his main target group was girls of 8–10 years old. Within the privacy of his masturbation life, he was adamant that he did not think of a boy sexually. However, he had been charged with offences against boys. As the discussion continued, I discovered that his primary fantasy was girls, but that he enjoyed girls and boys touching each other while he watched. This not only fed his fantasy life but also reinforced his beliefs that children 'liked it' and that 'they would not do it to each other if they did not like it'. He failed to see the corruption involved and that the behaviour he was encouraging could lead to the children believing that they were sex offenders.

If the fixated paedophile is abusing very young children, then it is unlikely that it will matter to him what gender the child is. If the motive for abuse is other than primarily sexual, then either gender might be abused. Further, if the abuse takes the form of oral sex, then the gender of the victim may matter even less to the paedophile.

Their use of language about children may give a clue – 'clean, pure, innocent rosebuds'

Paedophiles' use of language is revealing. The sorts of questions they ask, the tones of their voices, the way they see children can sometimes be recognised. A man may say to a boy in a sweet shop 'It's really nice to meet a boy who is as polite as you' in all innocence. However the context of that statement, the tone of voice used could alter its significance.

They may prefer limited sexual involvement

Some paedophiles are content with touching. Some may not even touch the child's genitals but may wish to cuddle and be close. Such behaviour may not be seen as offending. The masturbatory fantasies associated with this cuddling are, however, abusive in nature.

They may enjoy photographing children

Paedophiles may have many photos of children and enjoy taking photos. They may be seen on the beach taking photos or using a video camera to film children they do not know. Photos of clothed children may concentrate on 'crutch shots'.

Child sex rings

Paedophiles who begin to sexually abuse children in collusion with others increase the possibility of their being caught. Despite this, there are many men who have been involved in this group activity. They can either abuse and share the children, or having abused a child, pass the child on to another abuser. It must be remembered that not all offenders in a sex ring will know all the children being abused, nor all the abusers. An interesting aspect of sex rings in comparison to other large-scale offending is that, if many children are involved with lots of adults, and especially if the offending is carried out in a bizarre context, it is unlikely that a successful prosecution will follow. Or if initial convictions are successful, an appeal will normally reverse the verdict. This is partly due to the suggestion of contamination mentioned by Maureen O'Hara in Chapter 3.

Patterns of behaviour

I now look at typical behaviour patterns of paedophiles as they seek to abuse children.

There are two patterns of behaviour, that of the fixated paedophile and that of the professional paedophile. Each has a common core that can be summarised in the following way:

Motivation – fantasy – distorted thinking/beliefs – overcoming internal inhibitors – targeting, initiating contact – overcoming external controls – overcoming victim's resistance – redefining victim's behaviour.

The two patterns of behaviour of paedophiles are outlined in more detail in the appendix to this chapter. The first is typical of many fixated paedophiles. The second shows how a pattern of behaviour can involve other adults.

'Non-predatory' and 'predatory' paedophiles

When paedophiles describe how they go about abusing, they often talk about 'non-predatory' and 'predatory' paedophiles. Both types of behaviour are abusive. Although the former type would like to minimise what they are doing, I believe their abuse of children can even be more insidious.

'Non-predatory' paedophiles

'Non-predatory' paedophiles are individuals who believe that children can give consent to sexual acts. They believe that children are sexual, would enjoy sex, and can give consent. An extreme example of this would be the paedophile who believes that even a baby can give consent. The rationale is based on such beliefs as: 'If you throw a baby up into the air and it shouts blue murder, you know that it does not like it. If, however, it gurgles and laughs, you know it does.' This may lead the paedophile to say: 'You know that a baby likes sexual activity because it will thrust its genitals towards you.'

Such reasoning clearly reflects distorted thinking and beliefs with which the paedophile needs to surround himself. The particular danger of fixated, non-predatory paedophiles is that their actions are in fact *predatory*, but they do not want to accept this. They fail to see how their use of influence, power and control, and the way that they form the relationship, gives the child no choice. How does a child deal with a person who can offer what most chil-

dren want (money, toys, gifts, attention, apparent love)?

Anything that will attract children to paedophiles' homes will be used. One offender had 20 amusement machines in his garage. Children from the local school and housing estate were always there. They needed money to play on the machines. This created dependency on the offender, which led eventually to gifts being given for 'favours'. This corruption of children is an important part of the paedophile's behaviour: not just because of the sexual abuse, but because of the behaviour the offender engages in to entrap the children.

How do children cope when the offender turns the attention into sexual attention, especially when we have a society that often says to children 'grow up', and where sex is about being 'grown-up'? For many children, the first introduction to sexual touch and behaviour is at the hands of an abuser. Much of the child protection training that goes on in schools does not give children a sense of what it is offenders want to do. One of our staff asked his 8-year-old son following a session on child protection why was it that he should not take a sweet from a stranger. The child said that it was probably because the sweet would be poisonous.

In some cases, the offender becomes involved with a child who has already been sexualised by an earlier abuser. In these cases, the offender may not see that he is re-victimising a victim. Instead, his beliefs about children being sexual partners may be reinforced by his perception of the behaviour of the child. Any accommodating behaviour (the child not disclosing, the child appearing orgasmic) will be interpreted in a way that makes the offender feel better.

'Predatory' paedophiles

'Predatory' paedophiles sexually abuse within a context of abduction, or may express immediate anger in a sexual way – for example the rapist within the home, or the stranger rapist of children. In these contexts, the abuser is not seeking to obtain consent (even if a child could be said to be able to give it). The offender is expressing other needs in a sexual way.

They are willing to abuse and to abduct. They are willing to grab a child, to abuse and manipulate, to threaten and to ignore the hurt and the pain the child is expressing. Despite this, they will still seek to justify their behaviour. When Robert Black, the murderer of Susan Maxwell, Caroline Hogg and Sarah Harper, abducted a little 6-year-old girl, he said that his actions were not violent. He said this, having abducted a little girl, tied her hands behind her back, taken off her shoes and socks, put sticky tape over her mouth, put her head into a cushion cover and pulled the draw-string, put her into a sleeping bag, zipped it up, and thrown her into the back of his van. This was not, according to Black, a violent act. Violence was hitting. Had he not been

apprehended, the child would have died. He would no doubt have said it was 'an accident' and that he had not intended it to happen.

Why don't children disclose abuse?

As one looks at the non-predatory, fixated paedophile and his pattern of behaviour, one can see why I have called it a 'phantom offence'. This is because victims do not disclose. If victims do not disclose, then the authorities will not prioritise and investigate. The reasons why children do not disclose are easily understood if we overcome our ignorance of how the offenders operate and how they control – it is heroic that any victim ever discloses. However, it *is* helpful to look in detail at how children respond to this type of abuser and what it *is* like to be the victim of a paedophile.

As we have seen, the targeting of a child is not random. Because of the relationship the paedophile is forming, the child may have no sense at all of his ulterior motive. The child will therefore see a man who is giving them attention, maybe giving them practical things and making them feel special. If the child were to say anything during the exploratory stages, nothing illegal would have happened. Any investigation would be unlikely to reveal any offending behaviour. In fact, people might say that a lot of fuss is being made about nothing.

If workers with survivors speak angrily about 'monster perverts', they fail to address what the child may be thinking about the abuser. This may also prevent children being able to reveal how they may have acted out the abuse on other children. Offences of gross indecency, for example when the offender gets the child to touch him, can be interpreted by children as though *they* are the abusers of the adult.

However, if we look closely, we will find that although the child might not make any comments to others, they will make it clear that they are unhappy in their dealings with the man. Protection may be achieved by the child saying 'no', although it is more likely to be achieved by the child avoiding this person, because they might not be clear as to his real intent. They pull away from him, or if they remain in some relationship with him, he may sense that there is no way forward. The paedophile will normally become fed up with that child and will start to move away towards 'easier' children.

All children should learn assertiveness. In saying this, I am not placing all the responsibility for being abused onto the victim. I am, however, making the point that offenders do target vulnerable and available children. Such children are easier to seduce into an abusing relationship than others. Of course, with very young children, their protection is very much left to their carers, and any child is susceptible to the predatory abuser.

If the offender finds that the child does not pull away and does not disclose, he will probably move into the next phases. This may involve direct touching. This can be achieved in a variety of ways. At some point, he will need to isolate the child. Usually, if the child has parents or a parent, the paedophile is also relating at some level to them. He may even have the permission of a parent for the child to stay with him overnight.

There are no limits to the ideas and suggestions that an offender may use to sexualise the child. The profile of the professional paedophile described later in this chapter shows how easy it is to move into the different phases of abuse. At each stage of abuse, the offender may even be working out with the child what they should be saying to the parents. Children have secrets all the time. The clever abuser is someone who makes abuse another secret, but in collusion with the paedophile. This will make it even more difficult for the child to say anything in the future. Threats may also be made, and they can be varied; however, threats imply that the behaviour is wrong. Suggesting to a child that 'I won't tell your parents if you don't' makes out to the child that it is an equal relationship and a joint secret.

Offenders use many controls to overcome the victims' resistance. Power and control is clearly part of the motivation involved. This may be expressed in ways other than abusing the child. The abuser will often have authority over the child and enjoy expressing it. He may offer advice and express concern about many aspects of the child's life. Some will even describe how they 'kept the child on the straight and narrow'. Offenders who have used the so-called 'rent boy' scene have often boasted that the boy is still alive because they took him off the streets and let him share their home.

It is easy for young children to be confused, which makes it difficult for the child to be believed. It is important that workers with children have a thorough knowledge of sex offenders. They will then be able to empower children more effectively, as they may hear the 'offender within the child'. You may think you are talking to an 8-year-old child, but you might be talking to a 30-year-old in the child's head. It is in this process that we see the corruption of children. The abusers may get the children to commit offences. They may give alcohol and drugs. This has a number of objectives, in that the children will be unable to tell because the abusers have made them offenders. They also become suspicious of authority, so that again they will not tell. Even if they did, their testimony would be suspect because they were involved in illegal behaviour. Too many cases are thrown out of court due to the fact that the children giving evidence have been in trouble with the law. It is as though such children are disqualified from giving evidence of being abused. More worrying is the failure of the legal system to understand how abusers get children to sexually abuse other children and make them into sex offenders. This makes it incredibly difficult to disclose. Courts have always wanted 'pure' witnesses. Corruption of children, which is one consequence

of sexual abuse, does not tend to produce the witnesses that courts are looking for.

Why do some victims become abusers, whilst others do not?

The clever abuser will get children to recruit other children: 'They knew they could trust me, I had been having sex with a group of men since I was 6 and they had no come-back. If I wanted a boy, I would even write on the toilet wall at the school that X [giving his full name] was gay.' This, in a homophobic society, would lead to this boy being ridiculed, he might not want to go to school and would be likely to be bullied: 'I would then befriend him; remember I am only a couple of years older. I would then take him to my friends, paedophiles, who would give him attention, and turn this into abuse.'

This type of behaviour does not draw attention to the paedophile. Until we recognise that sex abuse is a relationship that is corrupting and violating, we will never understand paedophilia.

I believe this should inform our understanding of why some victims of abuse grow up to abuse others, and why some do not. If you look at a group of children to see why some offended and others didn't, the key lies in the type of abuser and in the relationship he forms with the child. The controls on the relationship appear to have more bearing on this than the type of abuse.

To address this problem, I believe it is necessary to identify the following:

- What relationship does the offender have with the child?
- Is he a primary carer, and is he substituting for someone else who should be in that role?
- What was the age of the child, not just at the onset of the 'hands-on' abuse but when they came under the influence of the offender?
- What were the distorted thought processes and beliefs of the offender, and how much of this has been transferred to the child?
- What were the fantasies of the offender, both sexual and non-sexual, and how were these expressed to the child?
- How long did this offender spend with the child? How many days, weeks, months, years?
- Was he seduction- or anger-motivated in his abuse?
- What were the psychological, emotional, physical and/or social controls used to overcome the victim's resistance?
- What was the pattern of behaviour carried out by the abuser?
- What emotional needs were attached to the abuse? Did the offender

meet other needs in the child? And were any of these needs anchored to the abuse?

- Did sex, anger, power, control or fear motivate the offending?
- Did his mood change within the offending?
- What did the victim do to survive?
- Was the child at the age of developing sexual fantasies? How did the abuse affect their fantasy life?
- What behaviours did the child adopt to regain some power over their life? Did the child negotiate with the offender: 'Look, I will come to you on Friday night', instead of lying awake every night wondering if he is going to visit?
- Did the offender involve other children, and did he get the child to abuse other children?
- Did the child, having been sexualised, act this behaviour out on sisters, brothers, other children, etc.?
- What was the type of abuse, what was its range, and what was its frequency?
- What non-abusing carers did the child have contact with, and were other emotional needs met appropriately?
- Were there bizarre elements in the sexual abuse?
- Were these bizarre elements used to control the child?

The type of relationship with the abuser will often determine the nature of the experience for the child and whether or not the child is likely to continue. Some of the above issues demonstrate why treating all survivors the same or saying that their experience is the same is unhelpful. The offender must, by definition, cause confusion in the victim, and some children are more likely to go on to abuse than others. A child being attacked in the street by a predatory paedophile will develop a different set of beliefs about their abuse than someone who is abused by a paedophile who takes time in forming the relationship. To be successful in the treatment of these children, we must identify the type of abuse the child has suffered.

References

Wyre, R. (1995) *The Murder of Childhood*, Harmondsworth: Penguin.

Appendix

Typical pattern of behaviour of a fixated paedophile

Stage 1

- fantasises and masturbates to previous sexual contacts;
- fantasises over anticipated contacts;
- gets to know a boy informally (either at a club or in the street);
- gets to know the parents first to develop trust;
- continues to get to know the boy socially;
- takes the boy to the cinema, theatre;
- accompanies the boy home;
- develops further trust with parents;
- gains boy's trust.

Stage 2

- finds out what is troubling the boy at school;
- finds out what is troubling the boy at home;
- becomes the 'counsellor';
- develops a 'friendship';
- sometimes targets neglected boys;
- 'counselling' takes place in the car.

Stage 3

- boy begins to come to the house at the paedophile's invitation;
- encourages the boy to tell his parents;
- when the boy leaves or arrives, some form of physical contact takes place, for example wrestling;
- teaches the boy to play games, for example chess;
- they watch television together;
- begins to put arm around boy; if any resistance, he withdraws;
- tries physical contact again a couple of meetings later;
- if physical contact is accepted, there is a dramatic increase in fantasy and expectation, reinforced by masturbation as he looks forward to the boy becoming a sexual partner;
- touches the boy sexually outside his clothing;
- if boy resists, he stops and tries again later; if he is reported, there is nothing that could easily lead to a conviction;
- having touched the boy sexually outside his clothing, he waits and then moves on to greater intimacy;

- mutual masturbation; carries on for quite a while (ejaculation);
- not much talking takes place;
- finds out if boy or his friends have done it before;
- warns boy that he had better not tell anyone;
- moves on to mutual oral sex;
- buggery on the boy first;
- buggery on offender.

Covert pattern of a professional paedophile

This example concerns a man who was an active member of the Paedophile Information Exchange. He boasted that he was employed to make 'straight' kids 'bent'. He was paid for photographs he took of children.

Stage 1

- He has intuitive feelings about a boy in the street as a likely victim.
- He follows him.
- He identifies the boy's school.
- He finds out where he lives.
- He identifies his leisure activities, for example where he plays football.
- He finds out where the boy usually goes to play.
- He finds out how late the boy can stay out.
- He assesses parental influence and control.
- He tries to find out the boy's hobbies.
- He finds out which sweet shop the boy frequents.
- He finds out whether the boy hangs around outside.
- He establishes whether or not the boy is a loner.

Stage 2

- He decides intuitively when to make an approach. It could be at the sweet shop: 'Do you need a little more money? Let me pay.'
- He has a casual chat. If the boy accepts payment, he leaves the shop on his own: 'I'm seen as a nice man' (that is, he is not seen as a stranger). He does not appear to be a risk. The whole scene and pursuit gives a feeling of power and encouragement to the offender. The final outcome is abuse. Monetary gain is secondary.
- He meets the boy again and starts a conversation – very informal.
- He finds out how much pocket-money the boy gets, and undermines his parents.
- He asks what the boy's interests are. If he already knows, he talks as though he does not know.

- He finds out what the boy's mother or father do not let him do, who controls the home.
- He may be introduced to mum and dad; he is very happy for this to happen.
- He has sometimes used a false name.
- He may begin to take the boy out. He is a fairground specialist, takes children to the fairground and offers them free rides: 'Children will do anything to get free rides on a fairground.'
- At some stage, he introduces the boy to the fact that he is a photographer.
- He asks the boy if he can take innocuous photos.
- He starts to invite the boy home. He leaves magazines like *Health and Efficiency* lying around.
- He asks the boy: 'How would you like me to take one of you in your underpants?'
- He pays for the picture, and they go to a place where the money can be spent.
- Later, he offers more money for a 'natural pose'.
- He leaves pornographic child pictures lying around.
- He offers more money; the boy is trapped.
- Another boy is introduced. Mutual masturbation takes place.
- He is willing to stop at an earlier stage as the photos are distributed through various sources to Holland, Belgium, then to America, then back to this country and Europe.
- Once boy accepts mutual masturbation, the breaking-in process has begun.
- Buggery is introduced next.
- He may introduce a girl.
- The boy's name and address are passed around on computer lists. He may get the boy involved in prostitution. Some paedophiles have 'safe houses' they go to for sex.

8 The HIV/AIDS issue

Angela Thomas

In this chapter, we examine the links between general child sexual abuse and HIV/AIDS. We look then at issues that may be related specifically to organised abuse.

However, it is difficult to determine whether the particular nature of organised abuse poses increased risks for children. Several factors contribute to this difficulty at the present time. There is still limited research relating to child sexual abuse and HIV/AIDS, none of which focuses specifically upon the link between organised abuse and HIV/AIDS.

The lack of agreement on the definition of organised abuse complicates the issue! Full and useful definitions of organised abuse are found in Chapter 1 which will illuminate these matters further. However, such definitions do not specify any type of abusive activity as characteristic of organised abuse. This is of particular relevance when considering the issue of HIV/AIDS. It is more useful, therefore, to examine specific abusive acts which are known to occur in cases of child sexual abuse, regardless of the definition or label attached to them, and to assess these activities in terms of the risk of HIV transmission.

Child sexual abuse as a transmission route of HIV

We need to acknowledge the potential for the transmission of the HIV virus in all cases where the exchange of bodily fluids takes place and the abuser is infected with HIV. This means, for example, that children may be infected following penile anal or vaginal penetration, through blood-to-blood contact, or through participation in oral sex.

Adults are offered guidance by the Health Education Authority in respect of high-risk behaviours related to the transmission of HIV. The transmission

routes mentioned above, with the exception of oral–genital sex, put adults at high risk of infection. Where unprotected penetrative sexual intercourse occurs (either anal or vaginal), physically immature young people are likely to be at similar if not increased risk of infection, given the physical trauma which can result. Multiple episodes of abuse can only increase these risks, as can the involvement of large numbers of abusers. With very young children, the risk of infection is increased because of the greater probability of lesions. Abuse involving the use of syringes to administer drugs, where no regard is paid to hygiene or safety, is also a high-risk area.

Oral–genital sex is also reported as being a feature in many cases of organised abuse. This activity is classed as very low-risk in terms of HIV transmission, although the risk increases when cuts or sores are present in the mouth.

Specific evidence relating to sexually abused children and HIV is detailed by Gellert et al. (1993). This research in the USA assessed the situational and socio-demographic characteristics of children infected with HIV as a result of sexual abuse. Out of a total of 113,198 sex abuse assessments, 5,622 HIV antibody tests were conducted. These tests revealed 28 HIV-positive children who lacked any transmission route other than sexual abuse.

The duration and forms of abuse these victims suffered were reported as being variable. Three victims reported a single episode of abuse, and 13 victims six or more episodes. Penile vaginal and/or rectal penetration was reported in 50 per cent of cases. Other types of abuse were not detailed.

The authors argued for the education of Health and Social Service professionals providing care to children about the risk of sexual abuse as a transmission route of HIV. They acknowledged HIV infection as a 'low-incidence problem' but felt the increasing reporting of both HIV and child sexual abuse could result in increased evidence of transmission by this route.

A study by Gutman et al. (1991) indicated that at least 4 (4.2 per cent) of 96 children with HIV and 4 (29 per cent) of 14 sexually abused children with HIV acquired the infection through child sexual abuse. This study undoubtedly established that children can be infected with HIV as a result of sexual abuse. Child sexual abuse, in the terms of this study, was said to include rape, paedophilia, child prostitution, child pornography, child sex rings and incest.

During a recent study in Britain, the author became aware of two HIV-positive abusers, both of whom had abused many young children (Thomas, 1994). It was not possible to establish whether they had, in fact, infected any of the children they abused. The available data, though limited, establish that transmission of HIV as a result of child sexual abuse can and does occur. It remains impossible to quantify the level of risk on the basis of the information currently available. Several variables may influence the outcome, most especially prevalence rates of HIV in a particular area. Where organised abuse is known to involve the exchange of bodily fluids, professionals would

do well to consider the possibility of infection with HIV. This is particularly so where the abuser is known to engage in HIV-high-risk behaviours.

HIV as a concern for young people who have been sexually abused

Professionals may well find that young people themselves will be the first to express concerns about HIV following abusive experiences. There are certainly many references to HIV/AIDS in the media, and such references are frequently sensational and emotive in nature. It should perhaps come as no surprise that young people listen to this information and then make the link between their abuse and the possibility of HIV infection.

Data from ChildLine appears to support this premise. They confirmed that in a monitoring period between 1 January and 11 July 1991:

> ChildLine counselled a significant number of children who had been sexually abused and for whom AIDS was a particular concern.

Many of these young people are now phoning in with HIV/AIDS-related concerns, indicating an increasing awareness of the disease. However, ChildLine also acknowledged that fears may prevent some young people from seeking help:

> ChildLine counsellors often speak to children who feel unable to talk about their problems to anyone they know, but this seems particularly true in the context of AIDS and HIV, when being open and understanding is not only desirable but could be a matter of life or death.

They spoke of the feelings of fear and uncertainty surrounding the issue, and the degree of ignorance which appears to exist.

A recent study in Britain (Thomas, 1994), commissioned by Barnardos, a large children's agency, and Wakefield Healthcare, the healthcare commissioners for the district, examined the links between child sexual abuse and HIV. The decision to implement research was largely prompted by the discovery of a sex ring in which a minimum of 22 young people were found to have been sexually abused by a single abuser. The abuser was known to be an injecting drug-user, although little was known about his drug-using practices. This knowledge provoked sufficient concern, however, for some of the children to ask: 'Will I have caught AIDS?' This in turn highlighted the need for an adequate response from the workers involved.

In other cases, fear of having acquired HIV as a result of sexual abuse had been the catalyst which had led to disclosure of the abuse. A Wakefield genito-urinary medicine clinic reported a small number of young people pre-

senting in such a manner. Other workers reported that such concerns were more likely to occur where the incident was one of abuse perpetrated by a male upon a male. Unfortunately, this may reflect the stereotypical view of AIDS as being largely the concern of the gay community, despite statistics indicating the rise in heterosexual transmission rates.

What connection might there be between these facts and organised abuse?

It may well be that for some children, the greater fear of HIV/AIDS will help them to break the fear-induced silence surrounding their abuse and thus prompt them to seek advice and help.

Many professionals, however, have noted the intensity of fear which often characterises certain forms of organised abuse (Finkelhor, Williams and Burns, 1988). For these children, fear of HIV may be an additional burden which they feel unable to voice. Indeed, the impact of a life-threatening illness, namely HIV, upon children who may already have been subjected to threats of death is perhaps too overwhelming to consider.

It seems that workers not only have to be sensitive to and responsive to concerns which young people may express following abusive events but, where children have not verbalised their concern, workers may need to question, very carefully, how a child's best interests may be served. Should the unspeakable be voiced – the risk of HIV infection – or is this introducing yet another traumatic and potentially overwhelming concern into the equation?

Parental concerns about HIV following child sexual abuse

In many cases, it is the parents of young children who express the concerns. A limited number of workers in Wakefield reported much concern about HIV being an additional and traumatic consideration which parents appeared to be reluctant to address. For one particular mother, HIV was still said to be a worry three years after the abusive event.

In Cornwall, where a counselling service is available for young people with concerns about HIV following sexual abuse, the counsellor reported differences of opinion between some children and parents (Bennetts, Brown and Sloan, 1992). In these cases, pressure for testing to establish HIV antibody status came from parents, in opposition to the views of the young people. It is perhaps interesting to note that approximately 50 per cent of those counselled proceeded to testing.

The links between child sexual abuse and the adoption of high-risk behaviours in adulthood

For many victims of child sexual abuse, the experience can result in long-term effects which are harmful to health (Beitchman et al., 1992). This is not to deny the resilience and courage with which many survivors of child sexual abuse surmount their difficulties and successfully overcome their negative experiences. Where organised abuse has taken place, there is a strong possibility that the level of trauma may have been intensified. The degree of trauma can have a corresponding effect upon behaviour (Finkelhor, Williams and Burns, 1988). It is therefore not unreasonable to anticipate an increase in negative outcomes for the subjects of organised abuse.

Several studies have shown a link between child sexual abuse and later involvement in prostitution (James and Meyerding, 1977; Zierler et al., 1991). Sexual abuse is increasingly cited as a factor amongst young runaways. Many young people leave home to avoid abusive situations, only to find themselves at increased risk of abuse and exploitation, commercially or sexually. Many of these young people are then said to engage in 'survival sex' – the exchange of sexual favours in return for food, drugs, and shelter (Dibblin, 1991).

A study in the USA by Zierler et al. (1991) examined the health-related consequences of child sexual abuse and sought to establish whether sexual abuse was a risk factor for subsequent HIV infection in adulthood.

The study revealed that:

Men who had a history of sexual abuse had a twofold increase in prevalence of HIV infection, relative to unabused men.

Other findings were that:

People who reported childhood rape compared with people who did not were four times more likely to be working as prostitutes.

Behaviours were noted which had potential implications for HIV transmission. To quote:

Sexually abused women and men were more likely to change sexual partners frequently and to engage in sexual activities with casual acquaintances than people who were never sexually abused.

The study certainly points out some of the effects upon later behaviour which may result from child sexual abuse, and which may then have adverse effects upon appropriate disease-preventing behaviours in adulthood. The individuals in this study were defined as 'exposed to sexual abuse' if they

reported a history of rape or forced sex at least once during childhood or as a teenager.

These studies do not differentiate between the types of abuse involved and do not indicate whether victims of organised abuse are more or less likely to display the behaviours detailed above. However, it does seem reasonable to assume that later behaviour will be as determined by the trauma of their earlier paedophilic abusive sexual experiences as that of other victims of sexual abuse.

Minority ethnic and cultural issues

Some cases of abuse may be further complicated by racial and cultural differences. A case in Tower Hamlets, London, illustrated this (Redding, 1991). A large number of boys and young men were found to have been sexually abused. It emerged that the abuser was in fact HIV-positive, with the risk of infection that this implied. Many of these young people were of Bengali origin.

Communication issues were highlighted in this case. It proved difficult, in the time available, to identify a Bengali-speaking social worker with the necessary child protection experience who could offer support and guidance in a culturally acceptable manner. The target of same-sex counselling was not achieved.

This case undoubtedly highlighted particular aspects for consideration. It is obviously important that people are able to receive counselling, if needed, in their first language and from people who are sensitive to and aware of their particular culture. This is especially so when sensitive and intimate subjects, such as child sexual abuse and HIV, are the topics for discussion. Development of strategic plans to deal with transracial abuse might well avoid some of the difficulties encountered in Tower Hamlets.

Issues for consideration

In summary, there is enough evidence to confirm that HIV is an issue for consideration in all cases of child sexual abuse. The type of activity undertaken is much more significant than the setting of the abuse, in terms of infection with HIV.

Certain types of organised abuse may provoke particular concern. We must therefore accept the challenge of how to respond in a balanced manner.

When to respond: Should we be reactive or proactive?

There are those who believe that professionals should only respond to those children who are already verbalising their concerns about HIV following abusive experiences. To make children aware of the possibility of an incurable, life-threatening illness when so little help can be offered in the pre-symptomatic stage of the illness is seen as adding a further unnecessary burden of suffering upon the victim.

It may also be felt that the abuse suffered by the victim has been such that the victim may not have the resources to deal with such knowledge. On the other hand, by not making children and/or parents aware of the possibility of infection, they are denied any choices they might have in the matter. It is further argued that articulating the risk of infection in this manner enables fears to be voiced which might otherwise be too alarming. These fears may then be addressed in a supportive and rational atmosphere.

Some workers worry about the possibility of abuse victims being infected with HIV and unwittingly transmitting the infection to future sexual partners once of an age to engage in consensual sex.

When considering these particular issues, it is important that workers ultimately make an informed and sensitive judgement based upon an assessment of the child's best interests.

Should victims of abuse be tested to establish HIV antibody status?

The question of testing to establish HIV antibody status is one which inevitably arises when children are known to have been at risk of HIV infection. The social and emotional implications of testing are such that it is not a matter to be undertaken lightly. The advantages/disadvantages of testing need to be weighed carefully before any decision to proceed is taken. Uncertainties will still exist even after testing.

The advantages of testing include the possible reduction of anxiety should the test prove negative. Should the test prove positive, the young person will have access to supportive counselling and ongoing monitoring of condition, with access to prophylactic treatment at an early stage. They may also be made aware, at the appropriate time, of the need for safer sexual practices and the implications for future pregnancy.

The disadvantages of testing include possible stigmatisation and isolation, should the HIV-positive diagnosis become known. This can lead to exclusion from life insurance schemes, and possible difficulties in obtaining a mortgage and finding a job in later life. There are also implications for travel, with some countries restricting entry for those who are HIV-positive. Some workers also query whether parents and/or children would be able to deal with

the implications of an HIV-positive diagnosis. Even where the test proves negative, young people, in later life, may be subject to further questions about 'lifestyle' when applying for life insurance and subsequently incur financial penalties.

The complexity of these considerations indicates that they must be discussed and understood fully by those taking the decision. Adequate counselling, if it is to be fully appreciated, must be a matter of appropriate and sensitive timing and conducted by someone skilled in communicating with young people. These factors may be especially relevant in cases of organised abuse, where workers feel that levels of fear and trauma are high.

Children and young people's participation in the decision-making process

The rights of young people are nowadays gaining increased recognition. In Britain, the Children Act 1989 emphasises the participation of children in decisions affecting their future and states that children should be kept informed about matters relevant to them.

The Department of Health has issued guidelines on the subject of consent to testing (DoH, 1992). These guidelines state that children of 16 and over must give consent before an HIV test is undertaken. In the case of children under 16, it must be established who has sufficient authority to consent to a test. It is also stated: 'if the child is of sufficient age and understanding to be capable of giving consent, this permission must be sought'.

These guidelines clearly state children's right to be involved in decisions which relate to them and acknowledges their right to information pertaining to them. They do not deal with a conflict of view between the child and their parent or guardian.

Issues relating to the abuser

Many people question whether only the victim should undergo an HIV test. They feel it is more appropriate for the abuser to undergo such a test. The issue is far from being straightforward. At present, abusers cannot be compelled to take a test to establish HIV antibody status, and their voluntary agreement to the proposal, in the majority of cases, seems unlikely. Compulsory testing raises many issues of civil liberties which have implications for us all as citizens. Does an offender lose certain rights, and if so, which are they? Can we justify the loss of certain rights, in this case the right of refusal to HIV testing, on the grounds of helping the victim?

Staff working with abusers may well point to the fact that, often, the abusers have themselves been abused and that differentiating between abused and abusers is not always straightforward. The issue of culpability is

often far from simple where the age of the abuser is close to that of the abused. An inquiry by the National Children's Homes (1992) found that as many as 1 in 3 sexual abusers were under 18 and noted that, because child sexual abuse is under-reported, the actual number of young abusers is likely to be much higher.

Knowing the HIV status of the abuser does not indicate the HIV status of the abused. This uncertainty will still remain and will need to be addressed.

Confidentiality

The possible consequences for children outlined above indicate the need for confidentiality, both regarding the test procedure and the result. Where child protection issues are also involved, policy needs to define clearly who may have access to this information, and when. Such information belongs essentially to the child. It should only be given on a 'need-to-know' basis, where the child's need for protection is involved.

Workers may become aware that an abuser is HIV-positive. The tension between their responsibility towards the particular child/children involved and the duty of confidentiality to the perpetrator is raised. Those working in the statutory agencies have an obligation to protect children which overrides the duty of confidentiality, although instances causing concern may not always be clear-cut. This particular issue may well need careful debate if staff are to receive appropriate guidance and support. Legal guidance may be necessary. Tower Hamlets received helpful guidance on this matter (Redding, 1991).

Implications for policy and procedure

Organised abuse is an emotive and anxiety-provoking issue. Concerns about HIV/AIDS add to the intensity of concern. The need for a balanced approach and a cool, rational response is therefore of great importance. The local ACPC's policy must provide workers with the necessary strategic guidance but still allow for a response based upon individual need.

The development of a multi-agency response would ensure that children's concerns were dealt with in a consistent manner. Such an approach would ensure adequate training for staff, giving them an awareness of and sensitivity to the issue, and also giving them the confidence to respond.

Conclusion

This chapter has highlighted some of the issues over HIV/AIDS which must now be considered. The emotive and sensitive nature of both organised

abuse and HIV/AIDS indicates that organisations must consider the implications, both for them and their workers' practice.

References

Beitchman, J.H., Zucker, K.J., Hood, J.E., DaCosta, G.A., Akman, D. and Cassavia, E. (1992) 'A review of the long term effects of child sexual abuse', *Child Abuse and Neglect*, 16 (1), 101–18.

Bennetts, C., Brown, M. and Sloan, J. (1992) *Aids: The hidden agenda in child sexual abuse*, Harlow: Longman.

Department of Health (DoH) (1992) *Children and HIV: Guidance for Local Authorities*, London: HMSO.

Dibblin, J. (1991) *Wherever I lay my hat: Young women and homelessness*, London: Shelter.

Finkelhor, D., Williams, L. and Burns, N. (1988) *Nursery Crimes: Sexual Abuse in Day Care*, Newbury Park, Calif: Sage.

Gellert, G.A., Durfee, M.J., Berkowitz, C.D., Higgins, K.V. and Tubiolo, V.C. (1993) 'Situational and socio-demographic characteristics of children infected with human immuno-deficiency virus from paediatric sexual abuse', *Paediatrics*, 91 (1), 39–44.

Gutman, L.T., St Claire, K., Weedy, C., Niemeyer, J.G. and McKinney, R.E. (1991) 'Human immuno-deficiency virus transmission by child sexual abuse', *American Journal of the Diseases of Children*, 145, 137–41.

James, J. and Meyerding, J. (1977) 'Early sexual experiences and prostitution', *American Journal of Psychiatry*, 134, 1,381–5.

National Children's Homes (1992) *The Report of the Committee of Inquiry into Children and Young People who Sexually Abuse Other Children*, London: NCH.

Redding, D. (1991) 'Sexual abuse of nine children in Tower Hamlets by an HIV + man', *Community Care*, January/February.

Thomas, A. (1994) *A health and social needs assessment: Child sexual abuse and HIV/AIDS*, Wakefield: Barnardos/Wakefield Healthcare.

Zierler, S., Feingold, L., Laufer, D., Valentgas, P., Kantrowitz-Gordon, I. and Mayer, K. (1991) 'Adult survivors of childhood sexual abuse and subsequent risk of HIV infection', *American Journal of Public Health*, 81 (5), 572–5.

9 Organising a response

Roger Gaspar

Irrespective of the allegation of crime under investigation, the investigator is limited in the approaches which may be used. The first principle, however, is that the investigator is an enquirer after the truth. As indicated in the Clyde Report (Clyde, 1992), the investigator must not confuse concern – treating the victim with care and sympathy and taking each allegation seriously – with an assumption that what is being said is necessarily true.

The second principle is to identify with clarity the sources of information and to cross-check wherever possible with other sources to test what has been said or indicated by items found.

Choice of approach

If we draw from general investigation theory, there are typically four choices of approach:

- reactive, or offence-based;
- crime reduction;
- location-based;
- offender-based.

In deciding the approach to be followed, the reactive, or offence-based, approach is the key. The use of the other three approaches depends on information derived from it.

The reactive, or offence-based, approach

The reactive approach is used in the majority of investigations. It works sim-

ply: a victim makes an allegation, and the investigation which follows focuses either on the victim (if it is an offence against the individual) or on the crime scene (if the offence is against property). Forensic science would regard the victim as a 'scene' in assault or sexual cases, in addition to the location or locations at which the victim met the assailant.

The reactive approach has three key activities: the search for witnesses, the search for physical evidence and the search for crime-solving data peculiar to that crime (see Figure 9.1).

The investigator cannot expect all the *witnesses* to come forward automatically. By definition, the first witness will be the victim, although in cases involving the loss of property, the evidence from the victim may be confined to formal data about property last being seen on one occasion and found missing on another. Other witnesses may have a variety of agendas to which the investigator must direct some thought. The witness may be unaware that any inquiry is taking place; the classic remedy for this is a house-to-house inquiry in a defined area. The witness may be unaware that what they saw was, in fact, part of the commission of a crime; this is remedied by careful thought regarding areas in which potential witnesses might be found and painstaking questioning of individuals to identify and link relevant facts. The witness may be too frightened to volunteer information or respond to

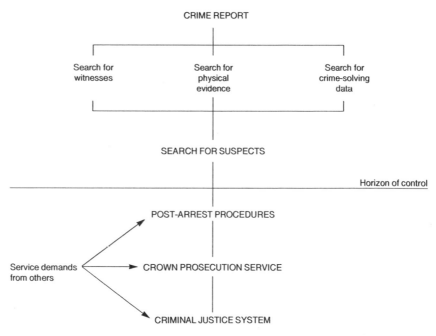

Figure 9.1   The reactive approach

inquiries such as these, or simply disinclined to assist; appropriate remedies in such cases are generally based on a patient, tactful and persistent approach.

The search for *physical evidence* typically involves the assistance of a trained forensic officer – generally either a fingerprint officer or scenes-of-crime officer – in the discovery and handling of objects. Other experts such as pathologists and forensic scientists will be available on appropriate occasions. 'Physical evidence' prompts an image of a search for fingerprints, blood, fibres, instrument marks and so on. In cases involving physical violence or assault, a trained doctor will be used to identify injuries and take the appropriate samples. Each of these specialists will be highly trained and work to exacting standards. Investigators will be able to, or will have to, delegate many of the search functions to the specialists, but should always remember that they maintain control of the inquiry and are responsible for all aspects of quality control and ensuring that all necessary tasks are completed.

Investigators must also bear in mind that the search for physical evidence is not confined to forensic inquiry but includes the search for items left by the offender or property traced to the possession of the suspect which are relevant to the inquiry. This includes stolen property or items of clothing which match the description given by the victim or witnesses.

The search for *crime-solving data* differs from the previous two activities in that it is about *information* rather than *evidence*. It is similar to the other activities in that the object is to identify a suspect, but it has no role in the other important aspect of the other activities – to assist the investigator in determining whether a crime has been committed. The nature of the data will vary from crime to crime. For example, in a burglary inquiry, an unusual type of entry to the premises might enable investigators to check whether such a method has been used before by a particular individual or individuals. In an armed robbery, an informant might be active and be able to provide details of the identity of those responsible.

Crime-solving data is that information which is used by the investigator to identify the suspect other than by formal evidential means. This method requires caution and is only the first step in applying the evidence. Such is the caution that needs to be applied that some of the dangers are best illustrated by specific examples.

Informants are, almost by definition, individuals who are involved in crime themselves: how else would they be positioned to provide the information required? Their motives for passing on information can be varied: revenge, money, envy or the desire to eliminate a rival. Some have been known to provide information as a smoke-screen for their own criminal activities. All information received from an informant must therefore be treated with great care.

The use of a method index to suggest the identity of persons who have

been known to use a particular method also requires caution. The fact that an identical method has been used previously by a known offender provides no guarantee of uniqueness. Is the suspected person in prison? Does the description match? Is it likely he or she would operate in the locality?

These three activities are the core of the reactive investigation. Once the preliminary activity in these areas provides data, then a search for the suspected person can be started. Once that person is located, arrest and interview should follow.

Proactive approaches

Once the three key activities in the reactive, or offence-based, approach have been completed, there is nothing further that can be done for that single offence if the inquiries have been unsuccessful. However, that is not the end of the matter, as a choice of three further approaches can still be considered (see Figure 9.2).

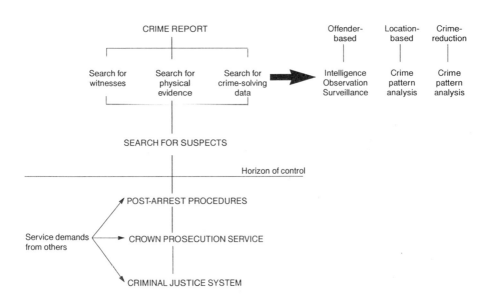

Figure 9.2   Offender-based, location-based and crime-reduction approaches

The crime-reduction approach

The crime-reduction approach is not usually considered an investigative activity but is so closely involved with the investigation that it should be included. It is an acknowledgement not only that every crime cannot be solved by investigation but that it would be better if the offence had never happened in the first place. The data from individual crime investigations can be used to fuel the construction of crime-reduction strategies ranging from crime-prevention campaigns on the general and specific to 'designing out' crime and installing sentinels alerting the community to the need for action.

The location-based approach

The location-based approach can be used where a crime pattern has been established from the data available from a number of reactive investigations. In this method, the investigator is looking for common points such as day/time, geographic venue, method or type of victim.

This approach is useful where there are few or no clues to the identity of the offender from individual or collective reactive inquiries, although a profile, primarily a description of the offender, might be constructed. However, by looking at the pattern identified, it may be possible to predict, within reasonable limits, where and when the next offence in the pattern might be committed, and thus plans could be made to be ready to catch the offender in the act.

Outlined like this, the location-based approach looks very simple. In reality, patterns tend to be swamped by the sheer volume of crime reports and the lack of distinguishable trends. It is thus only in the rarer, more serious or unusual cases that a sufficiently clear pattern emerges. The key to this method is a definable geographic area for investigators to monitor.

This approach has been used to great benefit in series-rape cases, where there may be few clues to the identity of the offender.

The offender-based approach

The offender-based approach similarly comes into play when the individual reactive investigation has failed. Like the location-based approach, the data on individual crimes are still important. This approach is useful when investigators believe that they have strong grounds to suspect an individual, that they have intelligence connecting the individual to a number of offences, but sufficient evidence is not available from any single investigation.

This approach will obviously raise concerns regarding civil liberties, and quite rightly so. The greatest danger of which to beware is the tendency to

make the evidence and intelligence fit the beliefs of the investigators. As a result, intelligence, which is the prime source of this approach, is carefully controlled, its analysis subject to check and counter-check, and any resulting operational decisions are constantly monitored and reviewed.

The theory of the approach is that intelligence is collected and analysed. When significant material is available which shows that a particular person is likely to be responsible for a group of crimes, this approach is used to collect evidence. Unlike the location-based approach, which uses passive observation in a defined geographical area to bring the inquiry to a conclusion, the offender-based approach, once triggered, is developed by further information and intelligence collected through a variety of activities, including active observation and surveillance. The investigators' objective is to arrest the offender in the commission of his or her next offence, or in circumstances where evidence is available regarding their past activities.

The last two approaches are summarised in Figure 9.3.

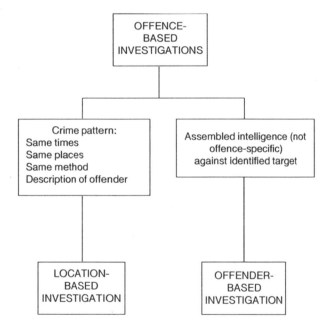

Figure 9.3　Location-based and offender-based investigations

A case study

We will now consider the relevance of these methods to investigating organised abuse.

A 10-year-old boy reveals that, prior to three months ago, he was repeatedly buggered and indecently assaulted over a period of six months by a man. He has named the man and given his address. The reactive investigation has been started and the issues of witnesses and physical evidence completed.

A video interview has been conducted with the boy, who has provided a substantial and realistic account of abuse. All offences have occurred while the boy has been alone with the man, so there are no witnesses to any of the acts. It is clear from the description provided by the boy that he has spent substantial amounts of time in the man's flat. Physical evidence has been pursued: a medical examination of the boy reveals 'injuries' which are generally consistent with his account but are not sufficient to provide corroboration that he has been assaulted. There is no forensic evidence (such as semen) available to provide material for comparison because of the period of time before the boy spoke out.

There is no need to pursue crime-solving data because the identity of the suspected person is clear from the boy's account. The next step in the reactive investigation would be to interview the suspect. However, our experience will tell us that, if he is a paedophile, he is unlikely to admit the offence even if he does not exercise his right to silence during interview. In these circumstances, the reactive investigation has been completed and leaves the Crown Prosecution Service with an unenviable choice of starting a prosecution where a 10-year-old boy's account is unsupported by any independent corroboration.

By broadening our minds to the alternative methods of investigation, we look beyond the individual pathology. In this case study, the boy has told us that a small number of other men of a similar age visit the suspect's flat and that a substantial number of other boys aged between 10 and 14 years visit the premises. Research into the suspect's background shows a classic profile of a paedophile, with substantial convictions for child sexual abuse, but also that he has been acquitted on a number of occasions.

This information provides material prompting consideration of an offender-based investigation. Observation can confirm or disprove whether there are substantial numbers of children visiting the premises and whether other adults are resorting to the premises. It should be possible, given appropriate resources, to identify the men visiting, research their backgrounds and identify the children. If the information derived from these inquiries continues to develop the picture of inappropriate relationships with the children, a tactical approach can be devised to bring the inquiry to a more fruitful conclusion than that likely from the reactive inquiry.

Management and resource issues

As with the location-based approach, described in this way, the offender-based approach appears to provide a simple and effective method of investigation. However, both of these proactive approaches require significant management time and the application of expensive resources in comparison with the individual reactive investigation which deploys one investigator on one allegation. Each of these inquiries will require an individual management structure and the reassignment of personnel and equipment from other activities. For those reasons, the application of these methods is always subject to managerial choice.

The benefits and disadvantages of the location- and offender-based approaches are summarised in Figure 9.4.

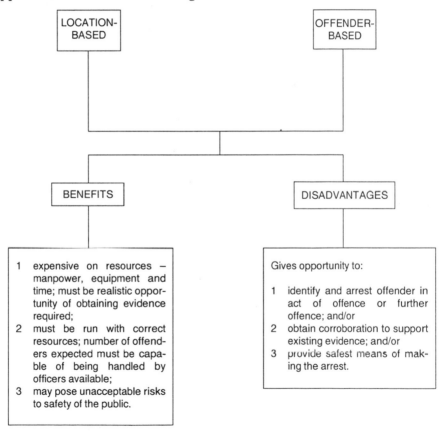

Figure 9.4　Benefits and disadvantages of the location-based and offender-based approaches

Managerial considerations

In deciding whether to go ahead, managers are jointly faced with three areas of decision-making before embarking upon a proactive response. These are based upon priorities, effectiveness and feasibility:

- *The nature and scale of the case*

  - Is the case one which has already been identified as a priority within local objectives? If not, does the seriousness merit stepping outside the defined local objectives?

- *The degree of activity of the suspect*

  - Does the activity suspected occupy a substantial amount of the subject's regular activity? If not, can a reasonable assessment be made of the times and places at which the activity takes place?
  - Is the activity observable and researchable to an extent which is likely to provide additional information?

- *The feasibility of the proposed action*

  - Do the resources available match those required?
  - What practical action can be taken?
  - What might be achieved by this action?

The conduct of a proactive investigation of organised abuse requires control at all stages by an identified manager or managers and will need support and co-ordination through various levels in both the Social Services Department and the local police area. Figure 9.5 shows the various responsibilities of each level. It is produced in this simplistic way since the police and Social Services have the statutory investigative responsibility. However, as shown in Chapter 11 in this book, there are roles to whom similar responsibilities should be given in all other agencies with a child protection responsibility. (A recommended structure is included in Chapter 11, together with an analysis of some of the problems that have to be overcome.) The most important feature in this figure lies not in the titles of the post holders, which are only indicative. The key to an effective investigation is for the strategic, tactical and action roles to be undertaken by different people, in order to give professional distance and objective reviewing of the investigation.

Those involved in strategy must first consider the needs of any children involved. In the case study above, the boy was safe and they could ensure that he did not return to the suspected man. Where the matter cannot be so easily resolved, there will be a temptation to intervene quickly. In fact, the

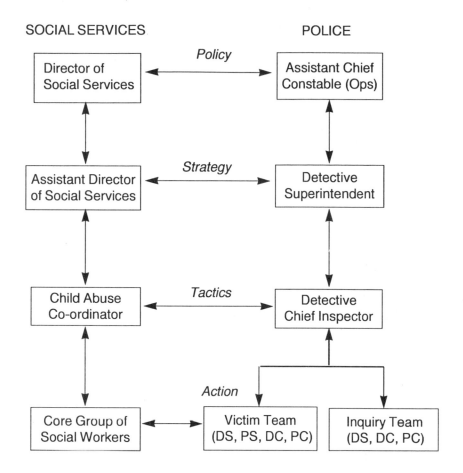

Figure 9.5   Responsibilities within a proactive investigation of organised abuse

moment of intervention is one of the most crucial points of an investigation, from which there is no turning back. It is frankly no use removing a child who in due course has to be returned because of the failure of the investigation to provide sufficient evidence upon which a court could act. The risk of premature intervention has to be balanced against a common desire in proactive investigations to always wait for that 'better moment' which one hopes is round the corner. Never should an investigation embark on a course of action which it can be foreseen would put a child at risk.

The second major difficulty facing an investigation that wishes to pursue a proactive approach is the need for secrecy. For entirely valid reasons, all guidance to date on the investigation of child sexual abuse has

recommended the involvement of all agencies, and group consultation at appropriate stages. By definition, a successful proactive investigation must be conducted covertly, with only those individuals who need to know being involved. This does not rule out a strategy meeting: rather it puts the responsibility firmly in the hands of the strategy level to decide who needs to know at each stage and what the extent of their knowledge will be. It almost goes without saying that every decision at the strategy level and the information upon which such decisions were made should be recorded at the time.

Each ACPC will need to consider the mechanisms that they require to ensure that triggers are in place so that organised abuse cases receive the early and detailed consideration they require. Once a proactive investigation is started, all data collected must be recorded and analysed. As in the case of the strategy level, all tactical decisions must be recorded.

For a response to organised abuse to be successful using a proactive approach, a full commitment is required from both police and Social Services. Experience shows that the unlocking of resources, the contingency arrangements necessary to provide cover for personnel who have been allocated to the inquiry and the persistence required to steer the investigation need commitment from all levels in both organisations.

Management during the proactive inquiry

The process of determining whether to start a proactive investigation should be fully documented at the time of each decision, recording not just the chosen course of action but the information then known. As information comes in, it gets progressively more difficult to record accurately what was known at each stage if such a record is not made contemporaneously.

Once started, the same discipline of record-keeping must be maintained. This is not simply to demonstrate retrospectively that the best decisions were taken, but to show the integrity of the investigation. If evidence is to be given of what was seen and done, either by those under investigation or the investigators, then the records must stand the most stringent tests. No short cuts are permissible or desirable.

Such an inquiry must be monitored on a daily basis. The object is to protect any children believed to be at risk, and once evidence to prove the risk and provide sufficient justification for action is available, no delay is acceptable. A structure for managing the day-to-day operation and for reviewing the evidence as it is accumulated must therefore be created. The strategy level has the responsibility for creating this and must have confidence in the ability of this structure to make the tactical decisions leading to any intervention which might occur.

Whatever the structure determined, the review of progress should con-

sider both evidential progress and the organisation and direction of what is being done. Typical issues are shown in Figure 9.6.

Of crucial importance is the flexibility of the operation. It cannot be stressed too strongly that nothing ought to be allowed which exposes children to risk. An ill-timed intervention, however, is not in the best interests of the children, and the description of the methods adopted by paedophiles

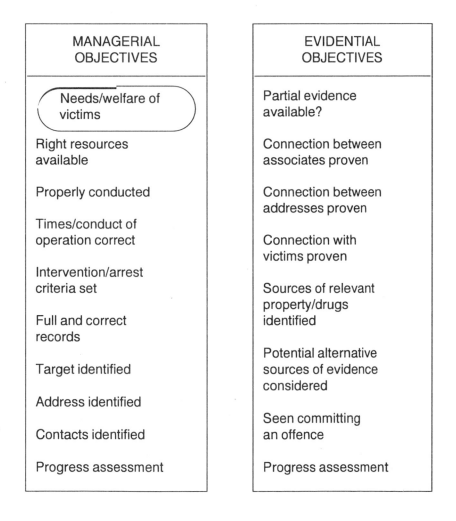

PURPOSE: To assess whether the operation is achieving its objective

MANAGERIAL OBJECTIVES	EVIDENTIAL OBJECTIVES
Needs/welfare of victims	Partial evidence available?
Right resources available	Connection between associates proven
Properly conducted	Connection between addresses proven
Times/conduct of operation correct	Connection with victims proven
Intervention/arrest criteria set	Sources of relevant property/drugs identified
Full and correct records	Potential alternative sources of evidence considered
Target identified	
Address identified	Seen committing an offence
Contacts identified	
Progress assessment	Progress assessment

Figure 9.6   Assessment of progress

outlined in Chapter 4 indicates that they may spend considerable time in the company of their victims or intended victims before abuse occurs. Adoption of a proactive investigation requires that an intervention plan be created to cope with the situation should all the worst fears or suspicions be proven correct. That intervention plan must not rely on all aspects of the inquiry going to plan and falling neatly into place in order. The alternative possibilities must be thought through and all members of the inquiry team briefed on what is expected of them should some unexpected event occur.

Consideration of the methods adopted by paedophiles described in Chapter 4 will show that any investigation will be difficult and complex. The reactive investigation is frequently hampered by an absence of corroboration. The proactive investigation provides an opportunity for securing such corroboration but requires proper resourcing, careful management and shrewd judgement. However, the proactive investigation is more likely to provide joint investigators with more substantial grounds for a successful intervention.

References

Clyde, J.J. (1992) *Report of the Inquiry into the Removal of Children from Orkney in February 1991* (The Clyde Report), Edinburgh: HMSO.

10 Help for children and their families

Anne Peake

Stories of boys: A group for boys all abused by the same paedophile

This chapter describes a group which was run for eight boys abused by the same paedophile. It has implications for all those involved in helping children and families cope with their experiences of being abused.

The abuser ('Mr B') was a 59-year-old divorced man who lived on his own in a one-bedroom council flat. Over a period of years, he actively encouraged a great number of children (approximately 69) to visit his flat by bribing them with sweets and money. The ages of the children visiting Mr B's flat ranged from 6 to 14 years.

The bribes were left around the flat, encouraging children to help themselves as and when they pleased. Numbers of children were also allowed to view pornographic literature, consume alcohol and smoke cigarettes.

The author and Maria Godfrey ran a 12-week group for the eight boys who had disclosed abuse. Each session lasted $1\frac{1}{2}$ hours. The aims of the group were to:

- help the boys to talk about their experiences of being victims of sexual abuse;
- place their abuse in a helpful context, in which the responsibility for the abuse is placed with the abuser;
- help the boys recognise and talk about the effects of the abuse on themselves;
- help the boys understand the responses of agencies such as the medical service, the police and Social Services;
- provide a programme of child sexual assault prevention work.

The group was for boys only. It excluded one girl known to have been abused by the same person. She was included in a different group run for girls who had been abused. Gender is such a major aspect of children's lives that it would not have been helpful to have placed this girl in this group of boys. Experiences of children who are abused are different according to gender. Gender issues for boys include concerns about AIDS and homosexuality (Peake, 1988).

Socialisation processes result in boys and girls dealing with pain and anger in quite different ways. The male ethic of self-reliance means that boys have fewer adult models of males as survivors of abuse. This is isolating and silencing.

There is clear societal expectation and approval that boys and young men should be sexual. Boys are often confused about sexual incidents with adults, unclear whether they are a rite of passage or abuse. The experience of being abused by a man carries both the stigma of abuse and implications for their view of their own sexuality. In our homophobic society, boys will fear being perceived as homosexual. They will link AIDS with their experiences. This can lead to boys denying their fears. Some become sexually predatory towards girls or young women in order to deny homosexual fears, or sexually intimidate younger children to deny their own sense of powerlessness and of being a victim.

Quite frequently, the police are the first agency to meet abused boys, as a result of their presenting behaviours. If boys have been involved in lawbreaking and violence as a consequence of the abuse, then their status as victim is less clear to them, and to their families and society.

The power that a paedophile can wield is all too often underestimated. He exhibits deliberate, organised, abusive behaviour that is very powerful. He is seen by the children as in an unassailable position. Mr B told the boys he knew the Chief of Police and so had nothing to fear.

These pressures and dilemmas have a major impact on boys. First, abused boys often have difficulties talking about the full range of feelings. They will often focus on trivial aspects of the therapeutic experience such as the food, games, the best chair, as a way of avoiding the core of their pain. In addition, child treatment agencies fail to put as many resources into prevention, recognition and treatment for abused boys as they do for abused girls.

The fact that the boys were related and/or close friends living near each other affected the dynamics of this particular group:

● The boys had similar backgrounds and attitudes. They immediately brought long-standing hierarchies and agendas to the sessions. This made the group more cohesive, but also excluded the workers from the special relationships. It also made it harder for boys to express views, different from the majority of the group.

- They used the common mores and group secrets to challenge the group workers' positions. Challenges to one boy were often taken as a challenge to the group.
- The cohesiveness did have its positive effects too. Once one boy was able to tell more of the abuse than had been disclosed initially to the police, the others quite clearly felt the reassurance of the group in doing likewise.
- The pre-existing links between the boys were at times silencing for some. One boy had been able to tell his aunt things he couldn't tell his mum. He worried that his mum would be told by his cousin from the group or his aunt.

The workers hoped that, as the boys were all abused by the same person, the group could focus much more on the nature of the abuse and the effects of it. However, the boys' reluctance to talk about the abuse meant the workers had to work hard to get them to discuss the abuse.

While they shared some experiences, it became clear that there were differences in their experiences which were hard to discuss. These included how the agencies dealt with the boys – differential use of statements and medicals – and the differences in sexual acts committed against them. When asked to talk about the events, they would trivialise or so sexualise the differences that it would become a group joke or a matter of hierarchy between them.

The boys viewed their abuser differently, according to their ages, temperaments and type of abuse. It was hard for the boys to express this verbally, for fear of challenging the group. They expressed much more in their writing and drawing than they did in discussions. Towards the end of the group, they wrote more and shared less. One boy sat in a corner and wrote of his dreams, which prompted others to do likewise.

The age range of the boys was from 8 to 13. This is a wide age range, but was due to the circumstances of the abuse and the need to help the boys as soon as possible.

The chronological age range of the group was less than the emotional/developmental range. The group contained an immature 8-year-old who acted out. The group also contained a quiet, bookish 13-year-old who liked to draw and was proud to do well in school. This range was hard to contain.

With hindsight, it is now apparent that the quieter boys had less space than they needed and may well have felt unsafe. At least two of the boys had such limited communication skills that they needed help to understand any written or spoken material. Other boys had quite obvious artistic or dramatic talents.

The group of eight boys was too large, and control issues surfaced. The number of boys was also a given factor – they were the boys who had disclosed, from a much bigger group visiting the paedophile's flat.

The workers

The debate about the gender of the group workers needs to take place before planning work with abused children, even when choices are limited. The vast majority of abusers are men (Finkelhor, 1984). The reasons for this may well relate to the nature of male socialisation (Frosh, 1988). It is not helpful to boys abused by a man to have two male workers. (This group was unusual because there were two female workers. This choice was largely determined by the facts of availability in a busy Social Services Department.) However, using a male worker for some groups could demonstrate to boys that there are positive male figures active in child protection work. Given that male socialisation is an issue, the inclusion of at least one female worker means that there is an alternative adult model in the group for the boys, supporting their efforts and in a position to challenge male perspectives. However, there is evidence that groups co-run by female and male workers produce less task completion (Peake, 1987a).

We need to consider the impact of two female workers dealing with this group of boys abused by a man. Only two of the boys lived in families where their natural fathers continued to be a part of the household and care for them. The others were cared for by lone parents – their mothers. They were accustomed to women caring for them. The absence of consistent, positive, male figures in the boys' lives was a feature of all their histories. It might well have been helpful to them to have such a model in one of the workers. However, it is unlikely that exposure to one person over such brief periods in a time-limited group would have had a major impact. It may be that, as there were two female workers, the boys felt more able to talk about their fears and pain. There were times when the boys used the women as carers and comforters, in ways which suggest they felt safe to do so.

Any decision concerning who will co-run a group has to rest initially on interest, availability and willingness to work together. A major factor in this case was a shared theoretical perspective on the nature of child sexual abuse, seeing it as an abuse of power and linking it with inequities in society and violence in its different forms. Finally, and perhaps most importantly, the workers had worked together before on a different project. This meant they were familiar with each other's style of work, and there were signs that the relationship was a robust one. This is an important factor in co-workers.

One of the workers had been working with the boys and their families prior to the group being set up. Arrangements were made for the other worker to visit each family in turn and spend time on a one-to-one basis, completing the pre-group questionnaire with each boy. This was useful. The worker who was less familiar with the details of the abuse, and the complexities of the case, needed to put time aside to read the documentation.

The roles of the workers in the group were interchanged in a planned way

to avoid the workers being split into 'good' and 'bad' figures. These included:

- leading the discussion in a session;
- helping the virtual non-reader in the group;
- making the drinks and refreshments;
- 'laying down the law'.

Being co-workers with a group has parallels with being married. The relationship is for better or for worse, though thankfully, it is time-limited. We discussed stresses in regular debriefings, with humour and tolerance.

Transport

All the boys were transported to the group sessions by taxi. Providing transport was one tangible way the workers could model strong, protective adult care, and it supported boys through the anxieties of coming to and leaving the group. It would make them less vulnerable to further targeting. Providing transport was a sign of our insistence on knowing the boys were safe, and of the extent to which their attendance at the group was being sought, but there was a pragmatic reason, too: it ensured they arrived together. Managing some of the group while waiting for the others was a difficult task. When there were delays for one of the taxis, we would regularly lose boys temporarily to the local Woolworths.

We tried to use only female drivers. There would always be one boy who was picked up first or last to be taken home. Safety and a sense of safety would be best achieved with female drivers, and arranging for a female driver meant it was much more likely that the drivers would be the same each week. When a female driver was not available, a mother agreed to be picked up first with her sons and act as a reassuring escort for boys.

The venue criteria included:

- The room should be private, uninterrupted and not overlooked.
- There should be access to toilets, and telephones for messages.
- It should be warm and comfortable with an appropriate amount of space for eight boys.

In the event, the only room available to the group was in the local Social Services office. Whilst the room did meet all of the above criteria, there were also some disadvantages, including:

- The building is large with lots of rooms and corridors, so the boys had space to run around.

- The other rooms could not be locked, and had expensive equipment, and other items which the boys could take, for example rubber bands, pens, etc.
- There were other professional and office staff in the building, who were a distraction to the boys and towards whom the boys were at times difficult.

The rules of the group

The group was planned with a core set of rules. These included:

Turn-taking and sharing

Each boy should contribute to the group in turn during each session. Silence or a refusal to join in would not be accepted. For one boy to be silent when others have shared upsetting information about their experiences leads to an imbalance of knowledge and power in the group which could leave boys feeling unsafe and which could be misused. Various techniques were used to encourage turn-taking and sharing.

These included a 'newsround', during which each boy told his news from the previous week to the group. Brainstorming activities were useful for topics about which any one boy would find it hard to say much. This offered a 'safe' context for turn-taking and sharing. All that was expected from each boy would be one sentence.

There was always a sense that this was a rule of the workers which needed continual prompting and work to maintain.

Respecting individual differences

We had not devised this as a rule at the beginning. Early on in the group, one boy became very distressed, so he was given individual, private time with a worker. We then realised that such a practice could reinforce a message that boys should only cry in private. We discussed this with the boys. In future, we gave one-to-one time if need be, but within the group room.

The workers would support and encourage the actions of boys who expressed different feelings to the rest of the group. This included work on their dreams.

There were times when family agendas and peer-group loyalties clashed. Then all the workers could do was keep the peace.

The prevailing culture of the group was of loud and challenging behaviour. The workers were faced with a continual task to defend and enhance space for the one quiet boy. We could only imagine that he faced this all the time.

Confidentiality

The rules with regard to confidentiality were twofold:

1   The boys were asked to agree to keep the names and the experiences shared in the group confidential to the group. The boys felt very intensely that other people could not guarantee confidentiality, given media interest in the case and local gossip. It was hard to ask them to do what so many adults and children around them couldn't do.
2   The boys were told that the bounds of confidentiality ended where there were reports of them breaking the law, including theft, or reports of them or other children being victimised in any way. (The Social Services waiting-room Christmas tree lights never did reappear.)

After one too many breakdowns in order in a session, the boys were asked to write additional rules. These were:

● Don't throw food or cans of Coke at people.
● Don't shout.
● Don't threaten or hurt people.
● Stay in the room.

Control problems

It is true to say that the workers could never confidently manage control of the group: at times boys broke up the surface of the ceiling, stole from nearby offices and shops and hit each other.

The boys chose some solutions to the incidents of lost control, but these were more honoured 'in the breach' thereafter. However, some boys recognised that the solutions had been of their choosing and helped to contain the group.

The group had a pre-planned, highly-structured curriculum for the 12 weekly sessions. Details of the curriculum are published in full in Peake (1995).

Direct work about being abused

There were examples of how experiences of abuse colour everything for victims, causing them fears and limiting their capacities to cope. During one session, the boys were able to complete a piece of work on the effects of the abuse on them. These included:

1   It changes your whole life and scars your brain.
2   It has made it hard to go to sleep at night.
3   It makes me naughty.
4   I think about it every day.
5   Sometimes I worry about AIDS when people talk about sexual abuse at school Biology.
6   Not being able to trust anybody any more.
7   We think about sex more.
8   Seeing B instead of Freddy in a horror film.
9   Hearing noises at night.
10   Running about because I don't want to hear about it.
11   I think I'm perverted.
12   I think I'm dirty.
13   I would be afraid of telling a girlfriend what happened to me in case I get chucked.
14   Anger with the police for only putting him away for six years.
15   My dad doesn't want to hear anything about it.
16   My mum cares, she asks what we have been doing in the group.
17   My brother doesn't want to sleep with me – he thinks I'm a pervert.
18   You think someone is walking upstairs behind you.
19   I get reminded of him when I see fat men.
20   I don't wear white pants because it reminds me of him.
21   I just keep drinking out of people's glasses at parties and get legless.
22   He has taken my sex life away.

Warning signs boys might show when they are being sexually assaulted

The group identified how boys show by their behaviour that something is wrong, including:

1   doing badly at school;
2   hiding things;
3   being embarrassed;
4   having a sore arse;
5   can't get foreskin back;
6   shitting yourself;
7   coming home with things and money;
8   refusing to go to school;
9   not smiling;
10   going to the library to look at rude books.

Direct work with children about abuse can quite properly form part of a comprehensive assessment. It is useful because whether a child tells the full

story about what happened to them will depend on what the child perceives to be the consequence of telling in the first place. Misconceptions a child may have – for example about who is to blame for what happened – can be aired and discussed. The child's perceptions of the consequences of telling can be explored. Plans can be made to minimise the effects of silencing. When children can see that what they have to say is believed and discussed with them, the likelihood is increased that they may feel safe to say more.

When children do disclose, many have broken months and years of silence to do so. This has been very hard for them. A structured piece of direct work allows them to continue talking to alleviate some of the negative feelings they have.

Children who have been abused need encouragement and support to make Criminal Injuries Compensation claims. Claims were made on behalf of all the boys after the group ended.

Talking to children directly about the abuse they have suffered gives them the clear message that abuse can be spoken about, and that time has been set aside to listen to the child.

The reasons why boys cannot disclose about being sexually assaulted

1   they get embarrassed to tell;
2   I would commit suicide;
3   some kids think they will get told off;
4   people get suspicious;
5   frightened he would hurt you;
6   they took sweets and money from him;
7   might have AIDS;
8   because our mums would kill us;
9   looks like you are gay;
10 we could be said to have done something wrong by going there and letting him do things;
11 if he found out we'd told, he'd come back and get us;
12 it's hard to tell when you are young and little;
13 feeling scared of actually telling everyone.

Why do direct work in a group?

Previously, some of the boys had been involved in individual direct work. The reasons for offering the eight boys a treatment programme in a group setting were:

● Group work is one way in which to enable children to know they are not alone in their experiences of being abused.

- Groups can offer children the scope to develop appropriate contact skills. The boys needed some work to be done with them.
- Groups can offer children a practical approach to confidentiality in a way which is an alternative to the secret of the abuse, and is therapeutic.
- Locally-based groups are a basis for future self-help and networks of support. The boys all knew each other before the group and were all abused by the same man. The hope is that the group will have been such a positive experience they will be more able to approach each other for help in the future. (Peake, 1987b)

Each boy made a book about his abuse. It consists of a record of each boy's story and copies of the group discussions. It can 'contain' a lot of the memories and feelings that are so hard to think about. The book can then serve to place on record and validate the child's feelings about those experiences. The books became the property of each boy to do with as he wished. He could look back to the wider discussions of the group and draw on those in the future (Peake, 1995).

The boys were initially very anxious about who would see what they had drawn and written. First, they knew their parents would disapprove of some of their sexually explicit language and drawings. Second, many boys told the group more details about their abuse than they had been able to tell during the investigation. They worried what their families would say about what really happened. Over the duration of the group, the workers persuaded the boys to show their books to their parents.

The workers also decided to run a brief, parallel group for the parents to prepare them for what the boys would show them and to help them develop a framework for understanding the pressures on the boys during the abuse and subsequently.

Evaluation

It is important that professionals who intervene in the lives of children and families are accountable for the work that they do. Accountability depends on a reliable system of evaluation, which assesses the impact of the work and whether the impact is consistent with the aims. For this group, the workers used a simple questionnaire completed with each boy individually before and after the group. There were clear changes in the boys' capacities to talk about what happened. For example, in response to the question 'How do you feel now about what happened to you?', there were many more positive responses after the group. Also all of the boys had shown their books to their mums, and most had shown them to other family members. In a very basic way, the books had enabled the boys to tell their stories. The questionnaire

would be repeated after a year to look at whether the changes and their views were durable over time.

A group for the parents

Parents of children who have been sexually assaulted have, in a sense, been assaulted too. Offering parallel programmes of help is useful.

The workers who ran the boys' group also ran a brief group for the boys' parents during the duration of the boys' group. Sexual assaults on their children raise major dilemmas for parents. Their sense of their own competence in terms of being a person and parent is completely undermined. Parents need information and the opportunity to air their feelings, if they are to be able to help their children.

When children are offered direct help to talk about what has happened to them, they begin to be able to talk more about their abuse. Their thinking and feelings change and develop. The parents' abilities must develop alongside those of their children, if they are to respond appropriately to their children at home.

It has been found that many of the mothers of sexually abused children have themselves been abused as children (Damon and Waterman, 1986). When women who were sexually abused as children recognise and respond to the signs from their children, they may well need support to work through their feelings to allow them to respond to their children.

Once it was obvious that a parents' group was needed, the workers with the boys' group felt they were in the best position to offer support. It would be more reassuring to use the two workers who were familiar with the details of the case and knew something of the boys' individual needs. One of the parents' major complaints was that professionals they had met previously were not aware of the case and the consequences for the community, and so were unable to be helpful.

The workers were beginning to get to know the boys well. The parents' group provided an opportunity to use what they knew to help the parents cope with what had happened. The work of the boys had a powerful impact on the parents who could often understand so much more when they could read it in the words of their children.

On the other hand, the boys had begun to tell the workers more about their abuse than they had been able to tell their parents during the investigation. For some time in the group, the boys were all adamant that they did not want their families to know more. The fact that the workers were planning to meet regularly with a group of their parents made the boys distrustful and anxious. The agreement was made with them that only group views would be shared with the parents. The boys became more reassured as the weeks went by and it became clear that the agreement was being kept.

It was difficult for the workers to work with both groups simultaneously. The sessions for the parents were specially designed with information and as much support for the discussions as we could manage.

With hindsight, it would have been useful to have planned the parallel parents' group from the beginning and been part of a team of four workers working in pairs. The workers were left with an impression that the fact that they were working with both groups was important for the parents.

The aims of the sessions were:

- to give the parents information;
- to provide time to discuss feelings;
- to give parents support.

The content of the sessions was planned around the parents' concerns and those of the boys. Initially, they were asked, individually and as a group, to list and discuss the consequences for them of the recognition of the abuse of their child(ren).

The parents were unanimous in saying they had needed more help sooner. They were critical of the way agencies worked to their own agendas and seemed not to understand the impact on the parents. Most of all, they were hurt and frightened.

In the second week, they tackled the key issue of why parents do not know when their child is being abused. Parents take pride in knowing their children, what is best for them and the way they behave as parents. Learning that their child has been abused for a time strikes at their sense of self-worth.

Why parents may not know about the abuse at the time it is happening

1   the abuser often undermines the parent – letting the kids have money;
2   parents trust the local postman;
3   he knew everybody;
4   he offered to help parents;
5   belief that sexual abuse only happens to unsupervised children;
6   trust people in uniform;
7   targeted single-parent mums;
8   children threatened into silence;
9   he was Father Christmas for a few years;
10 you think you have brought them up right and they won't do that;
11 believing anything rather than abuse;
12 believing we will recognise an abuser;
13 he was investigated, so that meant he was in the clear;
14 not knowing what the warning signs of abuse are.

The third session was led by Belinda Wilson, a probation officer who works with groups of sex offenders. It was helpful to get the parents to examine the public image of the abuser and to see how he had deceived the whole community.

Before the abuse was known, his image was:

1 looked like Father Christmas or Captain Birdseye;
2 thought he had a wife there;
3 looked like a homely type;
4 always looked happy;
5 would say 'Hello, my love.'

This public image compared very sharply with what the boys had to say of him:

1 hairy body;
2 fat slob;
3 dirty pervert;
4 bastard;
5 he didn't have a wife because he wanted to do it with children;
6 he made a girl drunk and had it with her;
7 white vest;
8 a lot of money;
9 chase after them and they fought him;
10 he bruised easily;
11 old;
12 veiny;
13 porno mags;
14 flab on his arms;
15 drinks;
16 he had a big float (fishing float);
17 he had a hook which he threatened us with;
18 he was always pissed;
19 he is queer;
20 watched the news in case boys grassed him up.

The fourth session was planned to raise the boys' worries about HIV and AIDS. Some boys had said that this was one reason why they couldn't disclose that they were being assaulted. The parents came away from the session knowing more, with information leaflets and details of helplines.

The final session looked at the effects of the abuse on the boys now. The parents were concerned about how best to help their sons now the abuse was known. The boys were presenting problems at home, and the parents wanted advice.

The parents' views of the effects of the abuse

1   stealing from shops;
2   saying there is someone in the cupboard;
3   nightmares;
4   soiling himself;
5   telling lies;
6   secretive;
7   trouble at school;
8   being rude – saying dirty things;
9   wanting to stay up late;
10   swearing;
11   needing to have a light on at night.

A framework to plan helpful and effective strategies was devised; this included helping the parents to:

- separate out which behaviours are negotiable and which are not;
- agree with the boys what is expected of them;
- identify what are the proportionate and consistent consequences of fulfilling or not fulfilling these expectations;
- help the boys to feel better.

The sessions were written up for the parents and the notes assembled to make a resource file which each parent could keep. This meant that when the boys finished their stories, the parents had their own stories too.

The parents of one boy did not attend any sessions. He was conscious that they hadn't attended and was disappointed. It was all the more noticeable as the boy's father was the brother of a mother who did attend. It was no surprise, months later, that these parents asked for continued support from Social Services.

There was no formal evaluation of the parents' group. Most of the parents attended, and they were very engaged and forthcoming when they did. The parents found the ending of their group hard to accept. We needed to be clear about the end of our involvement and about sources of support for them in the future.

References

Damon, L. and Waterman, J. (1986) 'Parallel group treatment of children and their mothers' in K. Macfarlane and J. Waterman (eds) *Sexual Abuse of Young Children*, Austin, Texas: Holt, Rinehart and Winston.

Finkelhor, D. (1984) *Child Sexual Abuse: New Theory and Research*, New York: Free Press.

Frosh, S. (1988) 'No man's land?: The role of men working with sexually abused children', *British Journal of Guidance and Counselling*, 16 (1), 1–10.

Furniss, T. (1989) 'Group Therapy for Boys' in H. Armstrong and A. Hollows (eds) *Working with Sexually Abused Boys: An Introduction for Practitioners*, London: National Children's Bureau.

Peake, A. (1987a) 'An evaluation of group work for sexually abused adolescent girls and boys' in J. Thacker (ed.) *Working with Groups*, Leicester: British Psychological Society, Division of Educational and Child Psychology Occasional Papers, 4 (3 and 4), 189–203.

Peake, A. (1987b) 'Tackling treatment issues with group work', paper presented to the Annual Conference, British Psychological Society, Brighton.

Peake, A. (1988) 'Issues of under-reporting: The sexual abuse of boys' in A. Peake and G. Lindsay (eds) *Child Sexual Abuse*, Leicester: British Psychological Society, Division of Educational and Child Psychology Occasional Papers, 6 (1), 42–50.

Peake, A. (1995) *Group Work: Ideas for the Content of Work with Sexually Abused Children*, Oxford: Oxford Brookes University.

Russell, D.E.H. (1986) *The Secret Trauma: Incest in the Lives of Girls and Women*, New York: Basic Books.

11 Problems of liaison

Peter Bibby

In Chapter 9, which looked at organising a response, the matrix reproduced in Figure 11.1 is described (see page 123; Figure 9.5 shows the same matrix as in Figure 11.1). The rationale for this structure is followed through further here.

Figure 11.1 is based on the legal requirements on police and Social Services as the statutory investigators of child abuse allegations. There is, however, a

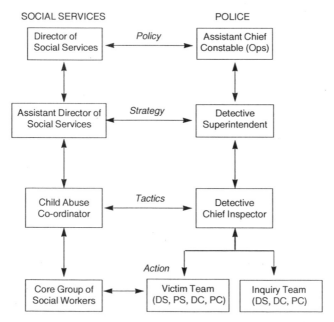

Figure 11.1   The liaison matrix

need for contact at similar levels in all agencies as the investigation, trial and treatment timetables unfold.

In reality, many agencies need to be involved at different times in the process, from initial receipt of information through to investigative interviewing; medical investigation; access to education and health records; the court case; and on to aftercare and therapy. The position is even more complicated when the children are from different local authority areas, and/or the offences took place in different police areas.

The Castle Hill investigation (Brannan, Jones and Murch, 1993) used a joint strategy group (the JSG) and a joint investigation team (the JIT), and developed links with outside agencies as shown in Figure 11.2.

In comparing this model with Figure 11.1, we see that in that investigation the ACPC was the level at which policy was decided, the JSG took the strategic role, and the JIT contained the different people with the tactical and action roles. The potential weakness of the tactics and action being conflated was overcome by very clear supervisory lines in the JIT.

For simplicity's sake, I shall comment on liaison within the matrix of Figure 11.1, then move on to liaison with other agencies, and finally, comment about other liaison issues.

Examples of good practice show that all the links within the matrix hold, both vertically *within* agencies and laterally *between* agencies. Unless there is a common approach across all links, the stresses inherent in such difficult investigations may well break the links, leading to failure to assist children. This common approach does not necessarily require complete agreement on every aspect, but it does require agreement about how to disagree and debate, and to respect and understand the position of each agency. If the disagreements are fundamental, then the senior managers need to strive to establish a working arrangement at all levels.

Two examples will help to illustrate this matter. It appears that in the Orkneys case, the police and Social Services were in agreement about the approach to be taken until the evening before the children were to be removed from home. The plan was that the police would arrest the parents at the same time as the children were removed. The police, for probably very appropriate reasons, changed their mind but did not inform the Social Services Department of this. We do not know whether such communication would have affected the plan, but it would at least have ensured that the other agency's decisions were made in the full knowledge of all the facts.

Another example appears to have occurred within the Nottingham Social Services Department around the same time. Initially, the senior managers appear to have been supportive of the investigating staff; then they appeared to change their minds on a number of occasions, dependent on changes in external circumstances. This left the fundamentals in tatters and the whole matter of joint working in chaos.

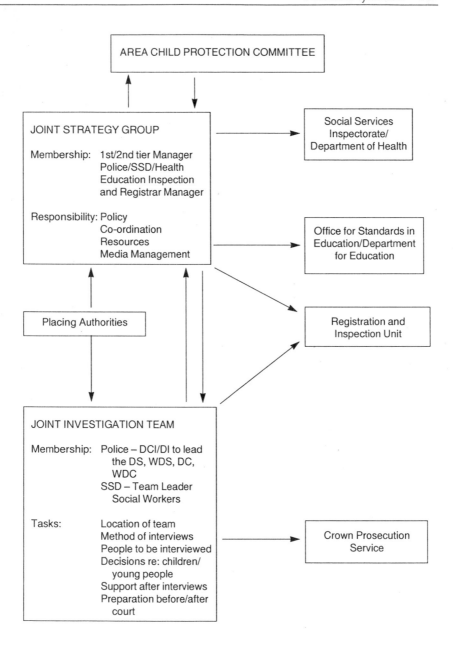

Figure 11.2 Organisational model for action on organised abuse cases

Source: Shropshire County Council

Compare this with examples where, despite difficult situations, the liaison has held up. Good examples of this include the Castle Hill investigation. In such examples, joint ownership of the investigation has been maintained, difficult issues have been discussed, common approaches agreed and workers in each agency have stuck to their respective roles.

There are four roles:

- policy-maker;
- strategic planner/manager in any particular case;
- tactical manager in the particular case;
- front-line investigator.

The roles of policy-maker and strategic planner may overlap. However, it is never good practice for the strategic managers to also be the tactical managers, or for any manager to undertake any of the tasks of the front-line worker.

This is only a re-statement of what might be considered good practice in any organisation. However, at times of great stress, unless there are predetermined structures, procedures and training, people become anxious and move into inappropriate roles. This leads to a failure in executing key tasks and reviewing progress properly.

The start to this process is the development of a common understanding of policy on organised abuse – this will lead to a policy, a definition, identification of the trigger mechanisms and agreement on a structure that will be used on initiation of an investigation. It is still of concern that there are ACPCs that have policies that state only that a senior manager should be alerted and that she or he will decide on the necessary action. This ignores the concept of the multi-agency strategy group and can induce the strategic manager to serve as the tactical manager. In these circumstances, it is not surprising that there will be panic reactions, rather than planned responses.

The wider liaison

One of the first problems arises when there is a need to widen the propagation of information to agencies other than the prime investigators. This is not a major issue where agencies are familiar with working together, but it certainly is where the history is one of vested interests or even outright antagonism. At an early stage in an investigation, there may well be a need to let schools, the Education Department and paediatricians know that something is happening. This need is in tension with the need for security of an investigation.

We must act as though there are active paedophiles and people sympa-

thetic to their cause in all organisations. Providing wider information can therefore compromise a secret investigation and put investigators and subjects at risk. This is a particular issue if there are anxieties about specific members of staff who may be in key posts. Ways of discussing these anxieties should be included in the policy. However, whatever the policy states, it is almost certainly true to say that, at some time, information will need to be given to a wider and potentially less secure group. This may result from the need to gain access to resources or to obtain information. In these circumstances, information must be given in controlled circumstances. If a leak should then occur, it may be possible to pinpoint when and how it occurred.

What issues are involved in liaison with non-investigatory agencies?

Health Services

Links with the Health Services are predominantly with paediatricians, GPs and primary healthcare workers. Any of these may be the first people to come into touch with allegations of organised abuse. They therefore need to be clear about the correct channels for informing the investigatory agencies. They may also be sources of important information that will give substance to or dispel the theories being developed during investigations. Investigations may require decisions to be made about medical examination of large numbers of children over a short period, often at fairly short notice. Once the investigation has reached the stage of diagnosing the needs of individuals, then these services will require the policies to be clear about informing, liaising and making resources and support available to individuals or groups.

At present, the split between the purchasing and provision functions is leading to significant changes in relationships with health professionals on ACPCs. The services required from paediatric trusts and/or primary healthcare providers need to be identified by health purchasers in advance and negotiated into contracts, or a clear policy needs to be established regarding how these services will be bought in when they occur.

Education Services

Likewise, liaison with the Education Services is changing. A few years ago, all schools were the responsibility of Local Education Authorities (LEAs). This resulted in a common approach on all matters of child abuse, in theory at least. Matters of disagreement might be resolved by the ACPC. The development of Local Management of Schools and the central funding of an increasing number of grant-maintained schools has resulted in each school

individually deciding how it interprets central government guidelines. The LEA cannot insist that common procedures are followed.

This is compounded by the guidance issued by the Council of Local Education Authorities (CLEA), which indicates that abuse allegations brought to the attention of head teachers do not necessarily need to be brought to the attention of the child protection agencies. The head teacher may exercise discretion.

The problems in schools are magnified if the abuse is taking place within the institution itself. If the CLEA's guidelines are followed, the alleged abuser is likely to be asked about the abuse before the investigating agencies become involved. It is vital that individual schools and their governors decide that confidentiality should be maintained until some agreed moment. If this cannot be achieved, it is likely that information will be withheld from people who can be of assistance to the children. I believe that the root of this current approach is a serious misunderstanding by the CLEA of how paedophiles work, a lack of knowledge about the nature of children's allegations, and confusion between responsibilities to children and staff.

Assuming that relationships remain good, then the Education Department can be a vital source of information, protection and support for children and staff, through the school psychological services, education social workers and the school pastoral scheme. Each of these will also be of importance in links with the local community and neighbourhood.

It is likely that a number of abused children will be attending the same school, due to the localised nature of many abusing patterns. Teachers and governors need increased awareness to be able to trigger referrals, and an understanding of the needs of the victims.

If one extends the matrix model to include the education system, then there are many more linkages that need to be sustained to effect a successful intervention.

Changes in the investigatory authorities

There are also changes in the structures of the main investigatory bodies. In the case of the police, a proposed structural trend outside London is towards larger authorities, whilst delegating more decision-making locally. The effect of this would be to create larger units for deciding policy, while increasing the number of units where case strategy will be decided.

It is in the nature of any organisation, that has to justify its existence, that it will give priority to those areas where it can demonstrate results. The resources required for a medium-size (say ten-offender) paedophile ring will be well outside the authorisation of the local inspector. This then leads to issues of obtaining resources from some regional resource committee: an extension of what happens now. However, when the resources are not

within the remit of the person who has agreed the local ACPC policy, there is a danger either of policy existing without the means to implement or support it, or no policy operating at all.

The trends in Social Service provision are pushing the other way. First, virtually all Social Services Departments are increasingly splitting their adult services between purchasing and provision sections. Often the policy-makers devise large-scale contracts, whilst care managers purchase for individual people. An increasing number of departments are replicating this in their children's sections. Purchasers may not have provided childcare. This results in the historical representatives on ACPCs being unable to influence practice. Similar issues apply to those outlined in the section on the Health Services above. The policy-makers may not serve as line-managers for the service-providers. The relationship is becoming a contractual rather than a command one. ACPCs need to take account of this change in their policies and composition and structures.

In addition, changes are to take place in local government in 1996, with counties being reduced in size and split to form unitary authorities. This will lessen the ability to provide certain specialist services in-house. It could affect labour-intensive actions such as organised abuse investigations. Change is always disruptive, and great care will be needed if current policies and inquiries are not to be disrupted. Likewise, there will be new authorities with new councillors who may have no experience of Social Service matters, and new directors who will have to make their mark amongst an existing group of chief officers. Integrated services will have to be split into a number of separate services. All of this means that current links will be subject to major turbulence.

The current situation between small Social Services Departments and large police forces – as in London, West Midlands, Yorkshire and the North-west – gives an indication of some of the problems that will have to be overcome.

In the case of a recent pan-London ring initially thought to extend to 12 boroughs, the police required one strategic Social Service manager for the whole case, rather than attempting liaison with 12 senior managers. This worked, mainly due to the co-operative way in which the London authorities were prepared to give this role to one authority's contracted employee.

The author was employed by the initiating local authority to act as the Scotland Yard Liaison Officer (SYLO). He was accountable to the lead authority's Director of Child Care. The main tasks of this post were:

- to maintain an effective liaison between New Scotland Yard (NSY) Obscene Publications Branch, and the respective local authorities (LAs) over the operation;
- to advise NSY concerning LA procedures and practice;

- to advise LAs concerning the actual and potential progress of the operation, including likely resource demands and timing of key events;
- to identify issues of concern, resolve them at an early stage, and to report unresolved issues to the lead director;
- to take a lead in Social Service links with the media, in relation to pan-London issues;
- to co-ordinate LA responses that involve more than one LA.

In this case, it seems to have worked well, but there are greater complications compared with an investigation in one local authority. It would not have been possible to have run this case as smoothly without a single linkperson with knowledge of organised abuse and strategic local authority experience.

The recent developments sponsored by the Department of Health to establish agreed pan-London definitions, trigger criteria and procedures are to be welcomed. These have the potential to lessen inter-agency skirmishes. We have seen what happens where relationships between different local authorities are antagonistic, as between Strathclyde Region and the Orkneys in 1991. The matrix fails between different local authorities. This situation will worsen as police forces become bigger and Social Service providers become smaller.

The position of politicians

Another area which has to be discussed and agreed is the matter of liaison with politicians. Here again, Social Services and other agencies are moving in opposite directions. It is possible that local authorities in London may have some involvement in police strategic management, but elsewhere, the Police Committees have no control over operational issues.

The Health Authorities have lost local authority representation, as have an increasing number of schools. More and more politicians are removed from the influence of all agencies, other than Social Services.

Politicians of any party like to feel that they are in control, and do not want anything to happen that may reflect badly on their administration at the next election. One way of coping with this is for them to seek to become involved in the handling of individual cases. Even if they achieve this, they want trouble-free services; this is always an unobtainable goal in Social Services, because its provision is strewn with risky decisions and cases. Therefore, whenever something goes wrong, officers and the party in power are likely to be blamed as part of a political football match, rather than on the merits of the case.

As part of a damage-limitation strategy, chief officers often decide to inform their chairs and/or party leaders of high-risk issues. The politicians sometimes insist on their general right to have access to all paperwork.

Now apply this scenario to the 'need-to-know' ethos of an organised abuse investigation. There is a tension between the politically sensitive (we hope) Social Services managers and other agencies who pride themselves on their political independence. The police will fear disclosures made for political ends, and all agencies will resist political direction in the strategy or tactics of any particular case. There have been cases where the chair of a local authority committee has been involved.

This being so, it is incumbent on the ACPC to develop policies and procedures that will respond to these tensions. In any particular case, the strategy group must thrash out who is to be told what and when. It is for each agency to respect the fixed position of others, whilst trying to reduce their own fixed position. As the structures are changing so rapidly, it will be necessary for systems to be set up that can be changed quickly and finely, as one or more participants in the committee have their ground-rules changed.

Best practice shows that this fluid but substantive form of liaison can be achieved. It is not best achieved at the time of an investigation, but by the ACPC taking a proactive approach to liaison between agencies. This has to be spread beyond structures and policy to continuous ACPC-driven training and a commitment to continuous improvement based upon the latest good practice and changes in knowledge and legislation.

Oxfordshire ACPC has a sub-committee which actively develops improved responses to child abuse. It analyses difficult cases, or cases that have gone wrong, and scours publications for developments on a wider front. Then, on a multi-agency basis, it revisits the internal procedures and practices in the light of what has been produced. It is fortunate in having a group of committed professionals who are determined to work together to improve services. These committed people can be found in most of the agencies and have been given a considerable degree of delegated authority within the agreed policy framework. This shows that it is possible for people with goodwill and commitment to make progress and for those with the appropriate knowledge to be encouraged to develop policies and practices on the wider scale, as well as at the individual case level.

References

Brannan, C., Jones, J.R. and Murch, J.D. (1993) *Castle Hill Report – Practice Guide*, Shrewsbury: Shropshire County Council.

12 Institutional abuse

Catherine Doran and Chris Brannan

Context

Newell (1991) suggests:

> our law and culture . . . still condone deliberately hurting and humiliating children and young people as punishment, [education] or treatment as part of child-rearing and care. Until we have successfully challenged and changed that culture we all share responsibility for 'pin-down' and other similar exercises in our institutions and in children's own homes.

In this chapter, we attempt to examine the context of children within society, the characteristics of institutions and abusers, the detection, investigation and finally, the prevention of abuse. The lack of research and the piecemeal implementation of recommendations following a number of inquiries leaves one feeling that professionals have not addressed their 'responsibility' for the abuse and protection of children. We all have an active part to play and should not displace the problem solely onto the abuser – we have a collective responsibility for every child in our care and under our protection.

Defining the institutional abuse of children requires professionals and society to assume ownership of the context of children's place in communities, in families and in all institutions. When reviewing the literature and research on institutional abuse, we were struck by the limited definition of 'institutions'. There was a definite bias towards institutions for working-class and vulnerable children. Perpetrators came from all social classes.

This bias is one of the strongest and least acknowledged. The result is that institutions are viewed through a lens of social class, filtering out certain establishments. Although much of the literature recognises the nuclear family as a key site of abuse, the middle-class nuclear family is, nevertheless, the

155

most revered construct in our culture: not just from a moral standpoint, but from legal, economic and social perspectives as well. So even non-nuclear family institutions that mimic or replicate aspects of the middle-class nuclear family are rarely considered as potential sites of abuse.

There was, or possibly still is, an underlying acceptance that modern institutions (children's homes and psychiatric hospitals) emulate eighteenth- and nineteenth-century workhouses, asylums, borstals and poorhouses, with the undercurrent of abuse and abuse of power. Somehow we expect the abuses that were a daily feature of eighteenth- and nineteenth-century institutions to be replicated to a lesser degree in institutions today. Is this because we expect or accept that the poor, disadvantaged, disabled or mentally ill have fewer rights or cause problems to us as professionals?

The irony is that, historically, all children, regardless of class, experienced physical abuse, which was seen as a necessary part of their eduction and learning. The purpose of the abuse was to instil a sense of discipline, a fear of authority and a sense of order. For working-class children, this meant 'knowing their place'. For middle- and upper-class children, especially boys, this was seen as a means of character-forming for leadership.

Although the incidence of corporal punishment may have been universally reduced, abusive power and denial of the rights of children are still fundamental to all institutions that are responsible for the care of children. And whilst the sexual abuse of children is now accepted as taboo, the recent outrage that has been expressed over high-profile cases masks a more sinister acceptance that there has always been (will always be?) sexual abuse of children, throughout all classes.

Abuse in institutions comprises any system which violates the rights of a child to healthy physical and psychological development. Newell further states:

> instead of trying to compensate . . . [for] out-dated concepts of professional discretion and parent [and state] ownership of children, we must follow the United Nations Conventions' principles . . . set out in primary legislation that children shall not be subject to humiliating or degrading treatment or punishment.

Positive legislation and guidance over the last ten years still have fundamental flaws which need to be addressed to ensure that the protection of children is guaranteed. *Working Together* (DoH, 1991) seeks to establish better community/institutional procedures and relations as a means of reducing abuse to children. However, educational legislation, and gaps in the existing Children Act legislation, still leave children in private schools and private children's homes facing degrees of vulnerability and stymie professionals' ability to intervene in a proactive way.

There has been no systematic survey of the incidence or prevalence of

institutional abuse in the UK, or for that matter, in the USA. Yet certain researchers suggest that abuse is widespread and may occur at *higher* rates than those reported for intra-familial abuse. Because there is no central mechanism in this country for reporting or recording investigations and findings regarding institutional abuse, we remain ignorant of its true scope. Until there is compulsory recording and reporting of all investigations and findings, and such data is centrally compiled, it will be impossible to gauge the extent of institutional abuse. What we do know is that, since there has been heightened public awareness, professionals are reporting much higher levels of abusive activity coming to their attention.

Continuing ignorance of the scale of abuse, combined with an inability to negotiate the difficulty and complexity of this area, means that it is impossible to plan for it organisationally, emotionally and professionally. This means that we will continue to be both reactive and uncoordinated. This is exacerbated by the skill and cunning employed by child abusers to perpetrate their crimes.

Characteristics

The dynamics of institutions are characterised by their isolation and their hierarchical and unequal power relationships. There is more potential for denial of abuse than in the wider community, the abuse is perpetrated by adults unrelated to the child, and all this is contained in a bureaucratic environment.

Within this context, there are other key factors which further disempower children and allow abusers more control. Residential institutions that educate and care for children inevitably place them in a vulnerable situation. Those which cater for children with special needs – children in care, disabled children and those with learning difficulties – compound this power imbalance even more. Having control over the physical and emotional care of children creates a fertile environment for abuse to take place. If abusers have access to the intimate and personal details of children, this increases their power. Research indicates that the double re-victimisation rate of sexually abused children may be as high as 30 per cent. We also know from research (Moss, 1990; Singles, 1989) that abusers can exert control over the child's subsequent placements or future care.

Targeting children with disabilities and learning difficulties may be on the increase. Certainly, intelligence suggests that organised paedophile rings are shifting their activities to prey on such children, possibly due to the greater alertness of professionals to abuse generally. Children with disabilities and learning difficulties are also less likely to be believed by social work and legal professionals. Their vulnerability is compounded by their potential

communication problems and the abusers' awareness that the criminal justice system tends to discount the testimony of these children. As Sloan (1988) states: 'Severe powerlessness appears to be a key factor in inhibiting children from reporting their abuse.'

Another factor which seems to increase the likelihood of abuse is the isolation of the institution from the larger network of care. This isolation can be exacerbated by geographical considerations. Physical isolation ensures that outside professionals and families visit less frequently. Local authority, educational and childcare establishments which are situated long distances from the placing authorities or the children's families and are not networked into the larger organisation feature in a significant number of investigations. Abusers can thrive in these isolated environments. Failure to create regular professional and organisational management monitoring procedures and guidelines that ensure the protection of children, and to provide for the training for staff in such isolated environments, has led to chaos and to a vacuum which allows abuse to flourish.

These very hierarchical, well-networked and over-bureaucratic institutions are so highly controlled that no one can permeate their structures. The abuser in this type of organisation is more commonly an authority figure in the institution. Such abusers are in a position to create an exclusive power base and a system of abuse. Economic control of the institution compounds the impregnability of such establishments. This is particularly relevant to privately-run schools or homes. Regulatory authorities should be particularly cautious when dealing with owners or large investors who either spend unsupervised time in an institution or who actually run it.

The 'pindown' case highlighted the use of 'expert knowledge' as another form of control. It is an effective way to isolate management and fellow professionals, as well as to disempower staff caring for the children.

The above factors of isolation, chaos or over-control lead to a dysfunctional and distorted process which makes it practically impossible for children or for other carers to disclose abuse.

There are two principal archetypes of institutional abusers. The first is the charismatic, articulate, well-networked 'caring professional' who is usually part of the leadership of the institution. The second is not well integrated into the social network of the institution and could be characterised as just an isolated, but dutiful, staff member who is perhaps over-helpful to colleagues and children, and frequently does things outside normal duties. This simultaneously enhances relationships with staff, children and, sometimes, the children's families. This is the 'grooming' stage. Although this term is usually only used in connection with the relationship between the abuser and the child, we believe that it should be extended to recognise the techniques abusers successfully use to cultivate other adults – most notably family members and professionals.

The commonality of language, education, training and social class between these abuser archetypes and most members of the regulatory authorities often makes it easier for institutional abuse to escape detection. The very consistent, conventional, credible and respectable façade that such abusers are able to project enables professionals to deny and collude with institutional abusers. Past examples where many of these abusers have been allowed to slip away or to continue to practise are indicative of how difficult it is for professionals to confront this issue.

The damning reality is that it has taken media exposure of these large institutions not only to reveal that widespread abuse is incubated inside, but also to force the hierarchies of such organisations to admit to it and to deal with the abusers they have been ignoring and sometimes hiding. The very power that these institutions wield – such as the Catholic Church in Ireland – militates against families, social workers and criminal justice professionals being able to expose or prosecute these abusers.

Investigation

The effective prevention and investigation of abuse within institutions is dependent on an ability to understand and address the complex and multi-faceted nature of their internal and external hierarchical and power systems. An awareness of the relationship between these aspects is critical to the establishment of appropriate and objective preventative or investigative techniques.

In addition to the structural complexities, the nature of abuse within institutions is also complicated and cannot be defined in a narrow manner. Stein (1993) suggests that there are at least four different and distinctive forms of abuse:

> Sanctioned, institutional, systematic and individual – themselves enveloped by wider structures of inequality and therefore at the outset a crude homogeneity and an implicit standard or single response in addressing abuse in residential care must be discarded.

In an effort to conceptualise these factors, a broader definition, including organised and multiple abuse, must be developed. Figure 12.1 depicts the potential relationship between various abusive practices, in addition to possible vehicles chosen by perpetrators to achieve their goal, which in many cases will ultimately be the sexual abuse in isolation to the other forms of abuse utilised. It is also necessary to be aware of the relationship between the abuse and the structural aspects of the vehicle used.

A complicating factor when considering abuse within institutions is the lack of any systematic research data and the consequent difficulty in trying

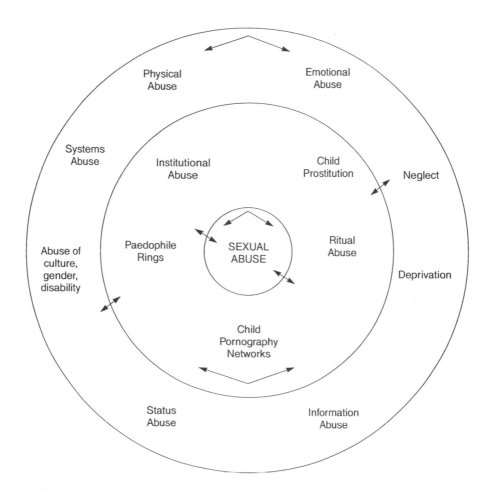

Figure 12.1   Conceptualising organised/multiple abuse

to formulate effective preventative and investigative procedures – a factor further compounded by a level of professional disbelief and denial due to the absence of such 'hard' research.

On reviewing the available literature, a significant number of high-profile cases are available, all of which have had far-reaching and devastating effects on the victims, institutions and the placing and monitoring agencies. Some of the more prominent cases are worth mentioning, as they are relevant to the context of this chapter:

- Kincora Home in East Belfast (Hughes, 1985)
- Beeches Children Home, Leicestershire (Kirkwood, 1993)

- Leeways Children Home, Lewisham (Lawson, Ambrose and Clough, 1986)
- Castle Hill School, Ludlow (Brannan, Jones and Murch, 1993)

These cases are only a small sample of the information available and are significant in that the failures that allowed these regimes to develop and exist have, in one form or another, been formally reported. Many lessons were identified, but how many have been learnt and acted upon is a matter for considerable debate. Before moving on to address preventative and investigative strategies, it is necessary to explore the reluctance of the caring professions to acknowledge the dangers inherent in institutional care.

In cases such as Castle Hill and the Beeches, the main perpetrators, Ralph Morris and Frank Beck respectively, were seen as powerful, charismatic and knowledgeable 'experts'.

The exposure of their long-standing regimes brought with it a level of corporate guilt for all professionals and agencies involved in the placing, monitoring and care of children in those institutions. In an effort to minimise and deal with this guilt, Morris and Beck were elevated to the status of being cunning deviants, which had enabled them to operate despite the good offices of all the agencies involved. The reality is that in both cases (and many others), basic but thorough checks and monitoring systems would have either prevented the regimes developing at all or, at worst, stopped them at a far earlier stage. The fact is that Beck and Morris, like others, were able to operate with impunity *because* of our fragmented and disjointed care system, rather than *despite* it. The tendency to view such cases as sensational, extreme, one-off occurrences inhibits professional development, and the number of one-off cases shows that this view is wrong. Having drawn a pessimistic picture, it is only right to attempt to balance this by highlighting the changes that have taken place.

Prior to 1991, there was no formal recognition of the difficulties faced by social workers in investigating such complex cases. The Department of Health (1991) offers some acknowledgement of the problems by referring to cases of organised abuse. Whilst the guidance offers no detailed information on how to deal with these matters, it at least recognised that there were difficulties and problems that needed to be addressed.

Legislation prior to the Children Act 1989 did nothing to identify the responsibilities of statutory agencies in inspecting or overseeing institutions and residential establishments. During the passage of the Children's Bill through parliament, an amendment was introduced requiring registration and/or inspection by Social Services Departments of some independent establishments. This followed issues raised by the Castle Hill and Crookham Court inquiries, where abuse in these residential boarding schools had been proven.

At the time of the Castle Hill inquiry, the investigating officers found very little formal guidance to assist them in identifying the extent of the problem or in formulating an investigative plan. As a result of this, the team were requested by the Department of Health and the Department for Education to document their experiences and to provide a practice guide for those professionals involved in future inquiries.

The *Castle Hill Report* (Brannan, Jones and Murch, 1993) offers practical guidance for those involved in large-scale abuse investigations. Whilst acknowledging the need to address each individual case on its own merits, it seeks to provide a framework and focuses on areas relevant to any major inquiry of this nature. The report identifies six main areas and confronts the issues from both a strategic and operational perspective. These six main areas are:

1   pre investigation;
2   investigation plan;
3   aftermath;
4   preparation for court;
5   court;
6   aftercare.

Preventative strategies

It is of great importance that investigation strategies and practices are in place to address any concerns that may come to light. It is unlikely that we will ever be able to exclude the possibility of an abuser infiltrating our care system and gaining access to vulnerable young people. However, the main commitment must surely be to re-structure and re-organise our recruitment, monitoring and evaluation systems in order to prevent the development of abusive regimes as far as is possible.

Major reports such as Warner (DoH, 1992), Hughes (1985) and Lawson, Ambrose and Clough (1986) have made recommendations for key preventative strategies. A summary of these recommendations includes:

1   progress and performance monitoring for staff;
2   clear job descriptions;
3   better staff training and development;
4   improved recruitment systems;
5   provision of statements of aims and objectives;
6   unannounced visits; independent visits;
7   complaints procedures and access to enable residents to disclose;
8   local registration and inspection.

These recommendations, along with many others, have been wholeheartedly welcomed by professionals and have been refined and reinforced by subsequent inquiries and reports. The fact that, since these were made, other major cases such as Castle Hill have emerged causes one to question the effectiveness of such measures.

However, it is not the quality of the recommendations that needs to be addressed, but the commitment of the responsible agencies to implement them fully in a concerted and co-ordinated fashion. It is relevant to list some of the more prominent subsequent reports:

- Utting (1991);
- Kirkwood (1993);
- Williams and McCreadie (1992);
- Levy and Kahan (1991).

These identify specific needs in the provision of residential care that echo those in the reports mentioned earlier. They address matters of recruitment, policy and practice, monitoring and inspection. Whilst they are of great value, they can only be effective if implemented in a consistent and standardised manner. The fact that they provide only recommendations has meant, in times of resource shortages, they have been utilised in an *ad hoc* fashion, depending on local circumstances. Furthermore, whilst they successfully analyse the dynamics of residential provision, they generally fail to analyse the dynamics of the committed abuser and, therefore, commence at a point somewhere along the continuum, rather than at the point of origin.

Most of the reports recommend training and staff development. Enthusiastic staff members can enrol themselves on a variety of in-service courses. The elevation of the NVQ as a recognised qualification is impotent and unsatisfactory, providing a low level of training with an elevated status, so staff can increase their credibility and value by seeking these qualifications, without scrutiny and evaluation as to their suitability for the work. This is an issue not only at this basic level, but in all social work accreditation.

There were high expectations that the establishment and broadening of the Social Services Registration and Inspection Units would lead to greater protection of children within residential facilities. However, it is clear that whilst they have made some impact in closing some unsatisfactory establishments, many of these units have never been fully staffed, and some have come under tremendous pressure from the public-school lobby. Recently, amendments to the Children Act have watered down some of the original duties placed on the inspection units. For example, it is proposed that whilst previously there were annual inspections for schools with over 50 residents, these inspections will now only take place every four years, and the schools

can ask other agencies or organisations to undertake these inspections. Many of the reports failed to acknowledge the issue of power in the abuse of children within institutions. The Kirkwood Report, however, did draw attention to the disproportionate power Frank Beck wielded, even with senior managers. Utting (1991) refers to the head of the children's home as the single biggest influence upon the home, in some cases a determining influence upon the home's culture, ethos and practice.

Heads of homes should be responsible for managing all the resources of the home and should be equipped to do so by appropriate training, experience and supervision. The difficulty in failing to deal with people who wield this power inappropriately is that the hierarchical nature of institutions remains unchallenged, and this situation is likely to be reinforced when the head of the home is the owner and responsible for the staff's livelihood. There is still no legislation or policy to prevent a person both owning and running a residential home.

All the inquiries and reports previously referred to recommend steps to be taken to empower children in residential care in relation to access to telephones, independent visitors and complaints procedures. They are best summarised in recommendations 51–3 of *Choosing with Care* (DoH, 1992).

There is evidence in some of the above cases that many of these recommendations had been formally accepted but were latterly controlled and monitored by the staff who were carrying out the abuse. At Castle Hill, Ralph Morris had set up a scheme covering many of these earlier recommendations, but he was still abusing young people. The Warner Report team conducted a survey on the level of unannounced inspections in children's homes. They found that private-sector homes in particular were not receiving adequate inspections from local authorities. The report quotes local authorities' claims that independent inspections of homes would be made no less frequently than once every six months. However, less than a quarter of authorities reported that they had mechanisms to ensure that their policy requirements regarding inspections were being carried out.

In the light of recent public sector cut-backs, increasing local authority responsibilities and the growth of private-sector provision, the likelihood is that many establishments are not subject to even minimal scrutiny.

The question of educational placements must not be overlooked when considering placing young people away from home when they are the subject of a Statement of Special Educational Need (Education Act 1981). These educational needs will be the only consideration governing placement at a specific school. If this is deemed to be a residential special school, the only obligation is to inform the Social Services Department in the child's home area.

Children in these situations have no allocated worker outside of the school and will be visited once or twice a year by an education officer or an educa-

tional psychologist. Their brief is to assess educational progress only. No enquiries are required or made in relation to the child's welfare. If we consider the vulnerability of children with severe learning, physical or sensory impairments, then the consequences for them in abusive regimes are appalling.

When we consider the development of operational child protection procedures, there have again been major policy changes. Section 47 of the Children Act 1989 requires local authorities to investigate concerns about the welfare of any child in their area. Therefore it is the responsibility of the authority where the home is located to investigate allegations of abuse. In order for those investigations to be effective, there needs to be good co-ordination and co-operation from authority to authority and police force to police force. The Act is diluted by different local procedures and practice.

An unfortunate omission from all the reports is the need to assess vulnerability in young people prior to placement. They comment, retrospectively, on how vulnerable young people were, but do not enter the field of assessment.

The current shrinking local authority provision and climate of public opinion favouring punishment of young people, particularly adolescent boys, militate against good practice in relation to vulnerability issues. The social work profession is again in a dilemma between care on the one hand and a demand for control by society on the other. Therefore, what has developed is a growth of alternative private provision offering specialist, skilled services outside local authority areas in remote, isolated locations. Placements are again being made for convenience. The lack of alternatives highlights many of the issues raised in some of the inquiry reports, including distant placements, poor planning, infrequent visits and the status and expertise of caregivers.

Policy and good practice demand that young people be placed in their own locality, but eking out scarce resources and the need to find *any* sort of provision are again the priorities. Whilst many residential resources are genuine facilities, the whole culture of institutions operates against the interests of vulnerable young people. There is little doubt that career paedophiles are operating within residential provision in this country.

It is difficult to make sense of the experiences of children and young people without recognising the construction of childhood as a period of dependency and powerlessness, and perceiving children and young people as an indefinable social group with their own sets of interests (Frost and Stein, 1989).

A young victim from the Castle Hill School case was interviewed by Yorkshire Television and stated:

> Morris had [total] hold over our lives at the school, at home, the lot. He had us right where he wanted us, under his thumb. He was a very convincing man.

It is important for us to listen to the victims and understand the power and influence that perpetrators of institutional abuse have over them, and also the power and status that we invest in the abusers.

References

Brannan, C., Jones, J.R. and Murch, J.D. (1993) *Castle Hill Report – Practice Guide*, Shrewsbury: Shropshire County Council.

Department of Health (DoH) (1991) *Working Together Under the Children Act: A Guide to Arrangements for Inter-Agency Co-operation for the Protection of Children from Abuse*, London: HMSO.

Department of Health (DoH) (1992) *Choosing with Care: The Report of the Committee of Inquiry into the Selection, Development and Management of Staff in Children's Homes* (Warner Report), London: HMSO.

Frost, N. and Stein, M. (1989) *The Politics of Child Welfare*, Hemel Hempstead: Harvester Wheatsheaf.

Hughes, W. (1985) *Report of the Committee of Enquiry into Children's Homes and Children's Hostels* (The Hughes Report), Belfast: HMSO.

Kirkwood, A. (1993) *The Leicestershire Enquiry 1992*, Leicester: Leicestershire County Council.

Lawson, E., Ambrose, K. and Clough, R. (1986) *Leeways Report*, Lewisham: Lewisham Social Services Committee.

Levy, A. and Kahan, B. (1991) *The Pindown Experience and the Protection of Children: The Report of the Staffordshire Child Care Inquiry 1990* (The Pindown Report), Stafford: Staffordshire County Council.

Moss, M. (1990) *Abuse in the Care System: A Pilot Study by the National Association of Young People in Care*, London: NAYPIC.

Newell, P. (1991) 'A new age of respect', *Community Care*, 25 July, 12–14.

Singles, T. (1989) 'Child sexual assault in which the alleged offender is a child care professional', *Australian Social Work*, 42, 21–8.

Sloan, J. (1988) 'Professional abuse', *Child Abuse Review*, 2, 7–8.

Stein, M. (1993) *The Abuses and Uses of Residential Childcare: Surviving Childhood Adversity*, Dublin: Social Services Press.

Utting, W. (1991) *Children in Public Care: A Review of Residential Child Care*, London: HMSO.

Williams, G. and McCreadie, J. (1992) *Ty Mawr Community Homes Inquiry*, Cwmbran: Gwent County Council.

13 Pornography and the organisation of child sexual abuse

Catherine Itzin

This chapter reviews the literature on the nature and extent of pornography and organised abuse, drawing on existing data on the incidence and prevalence of child sexual abuse, child pornography, prostitution and the international traffic in women and children. It uses a case history to explore the phenomenology of being used in and abused by pornography as a child. From this perspective it is possible to see the processes by which child sexual abuse is organised inside and outside of the family and the role of pornography in it. This approach highlights some of the limitations of current definitions and categories of child sexual abuse based on sex offender classifications. It also provides the basis for a model, based on the experience of the child, which conceptualises the organisation of child sexual abuse as a continuum in which pornography is a part of all forms of intra-familial and extra-familial abuse and is itself a form of organised abuse. The chapter includes a discussion of some characteristics of pornography and child sexual abuse extrapolated from the case study, including: gender, generation, coercion and compliance, 'cycles of abuse', prostitution and the function of incest as a form of 'pimping' for the perpetrator(s) within the family and as grooming for extra-familial abuse.

The nature and extent of pornography and organised abuse

Current knowledge about pornography and child sexual abuse

A review of the research and the clinical literature indicates a general lack of consistency in the terminology used to define and to categorise 'child sexual

abuse', and specifically in definitions of 'organised child sexual abuse'. The term 'child sexual abuse', for example, has been used interchangeably and synonymously with 'sexual victimisation', 'sexual exploitation', 'sexual assault', 'sexual misuse', 'child molestation', 'sexual mistreatment' and 'child rape' (Russell, 1983, p.133).

Another definitional category is 'paedophilia'. Some research has used the clinical diagnostic criteria of the American Psychiatric Association (1980) to define paedophilia as: 'the act or fantasy of engaging in sexual activity with prepubertal children as a repeatedly preferred or exclusive method of achieving sexual excitement' (Langevin and Lang, 1985, p.404). Finkelhor (1986) has defined paedophilia as: 'adult sexual contact with a child or adult masturbation to sexual fantasies involving children' (p.90). Kelly's review of the research (1987) identified the three most common distinctions as being made between paedophiles (men whose sexual interest is restricted to children), child molesters (men whose sexual interest includes both children and adult women) and incest offenders (p.54). Kelly categorises incest as a sub-category of child sexual abuse. Waterhouse, Dobash and Carnie (1994) classify their sample of convicted child sexual offenders as 'random abusers, paedophiles, incest offenders and deniers' and then sub-classify paedophiles as 'professional, committed and latent' (p.vii). Russell (1983) categorises child sexual abuse as either extra-familial: defined as one or more unwanted sexual experiences with persons unrelated by blood or marriage, ranging from petting (touching of breasts or genitals or attempts at such touching) to rape, before the victim turned 14 years, and completed or attempted forcible rape experienced from the ages of 14 to 17 years; or intra-familial: defined as 'any kind of exploitative sexual contact that occurred between relatives no matter how distant the relationship before the victim turned 18 years old' (pp.135–6).

Seng (1986) categorises child sexual abuse as a sub-category of child abuse which includes 'intrafamilial child sexual abuse or incest'; child molestation, defined as sexual abuse involving 'an adult and child who are not related by blood or marriage' (p.51); and paedophilia, defined as 'psychosexual perversion in which children are the preferred sexual object' (p.52). Seng's typology makes a distinction between incestuous fathers (most of whom are not paedophiles) and child molesters (most of whom are paedophiles) and considers 'multiple victim behaviour' as characteristic of child molestation but not incest. Seng categorises 'sex ring activity' as child molestation which occurs in groups with multiple victims and/or multiple offenders. 'Sexual exploitation' is another category of child sexual abuse, involving 'a subtle shift from use of children for personal gratification to the use of children as objects' (p.56). One form of sexual exploitation in Seng's typology is prostitution, in which he includes the 'exchange of children among syndicated sex rings' (p.59). The most common form of sexual exploitation, however, according to

Seng, is 'the use of children in the production of pornographic photography' (p.56).

Generally, however, pornography has not been conceptualised and categorised as a form of child sexual abuse; nor has the role of adult and child pornography been seen as instrumental to other forms of child sexual abuse. Information on the nature and extent of pornography and 'organised abuse' currently comes, therefore, often incidentally, from a range of sources: from child pornography, from prostitution, from the international traffic in women and children, from some of the research on child sexual abuse generally, and specifically the child sexual abuse that has been defined as 'organised'.

Quite a lot is known about the incidence and prevalence of child sexual abuse. Kelly (1987) quotes abuse prevalence findings in different studies ranging from 12 per cent to 38 per cent with variations explained by differences in methodology, age and definition of abuse. A survey of over 4,000 readers of *Cosmopolitan* magazine in the UK found that 13 per cent of women reported having been sexually abused as children (Itzin and Sweet, 1990). In the USA, Russell (1983) found, in a probability sample of 930 women in San Francisco, a prevalence of 16 per cent for intra-familial abuse before the age of 18, and 31 per cent for extra-familial abuse.

Only a minority of studies have produced data on the ways in which pornography is implicated in child sexual abuse. Respondents in the *Cosmopolitan* survey described a range of circumstances in which they had been abused with pornography as children by different family members: by fathers, grandfathers, uncles, brothers, and by their friends (Itzin and Sweet, 1990). In another study, women have reported being used to pose for child pornography and then living into adulthood in dread of finding the photographs published; pornography being used to initiate and legitimise their sexual abuse ('if she can, you can'); and the devastating effects of 'simply' finding their father's pornography ('shock, confusion, disgust, guilt, fear and utter hopelessness about sex'). 'I feel', said one woman, 'as if my whole life has been poisoned by it' (Itzin, 1996, in press).

The most obvious source of information on child sexual abuse and pornography is child pornography itself, which is now generally regarded as the evidence – recorded on film or video tape – of serious sexual assaults on children (Tate, 1992; Kelly, 1992; Hames, 1993). This kind of material ranges from 'posed photographs of naked and semi-naked children, through more explicit shots of their genitalia thumbed apart to still, film and video recording of oral, vaginal and anal sex' (Tate, 1992, p.203). Amongst the material seized by Scotland Yard's Obscene Publications Branch have been items showing:

a boy of about eleven being forced to sit on top of an erect penis, in visible discomfort and pain as he is positioned to show as much of the genitals as possible to the

camera and penetrated anally; a woman placing a female child (aged about eight) on top of a man's erect penis; Portuguese boys masturbating and performing oral sex; a female child (aged about four or five) being forced to perform fellatio on an adult male; several children of both sexes lying together being urinated on by an adult male. (Itzin, 1992a, p.51)

Ennew (1986) records the contents of a booklet of child pornography obtained by mail order from an address in Denmark, described as 'photographs imported from the USA', including children as young as 2 with genitals exposed to the camera, penetrated vaginally and orally, presented precociously, posed provocatively and 'inviting' sexual abuse (pp.121–3).

Police in the USA and in the UK have identified as a characteristic of paedophile behaviour the recording of their abuse of children and its collection as a record of the abuse for purposes of masturbation and to share and exchange with other paedophiles (Tate, 1992). Records of child sexual abuse in photographs and films are also used to blackmail abused children to prevent them disclosing the abuse, and to seduce other children (Burgess and Hartman, 1987). In some cases of paedophilia, the abuse is organised to meet the immediate sexual needs of the perpetrator, but is also recorded for explicitly commercial purposes 'as an item of trade' (Hames, 1993). John Bulloch, for example, convicted in 1985 on 13 counts of the abuse of two 12-year-old girls, described 'the child pornography business he built up as a by-product of his paedophilia' (Tate, 1992). The trade in child pornography is part of the multi-million pound international pornography industry (Baxter, 1990).

Further evidence of the relationship between child sexual abuse and pornography is available from research and clinical work with sex offenders. In Canada, Marshall (1988) found, in a study of non-incarcerated sex offenders, that over a third reported being incited by pornography to commit an offence, and over half of those who committed child sexual abuse said they deliberately used pornography in preparing to commit the offence. In the UK, clinical work with sex offenders has shown that for a substantial proportion of offenders, pornography is implicated at every stage: in fantasy arousal to abuse, in predisposing men to commit abuse, in legitimising and normalising abuse, in creating and reinforcing false belief-systems about victims of abuse, in reducing and overcoming internal and external inhibitions to abuse, in targeting victims and overcoming victim resistance, in initiating and carrying out abuse and in reinterpreting victim behaviour to support further abuse (Wyre, 1992). In the USA, Carter et al. (1987) found amongst sex offenders at a treatment centre, that child molesters were likely to use pornography prior to and during their offence.

Another source of information on pornography and child sexual abuse is prostitution. Research has shown that the median age for entry into prostitution is 14 (Weisberg, 1985, cited in Baldwin, 1992, p.101). Silbert and Pines

found that 70 per cent of the 200 street prostitutes they surveyed in San Francisco were under 21 years of age. Of these, 60 per cent were under 16, and many of those who were over 16 had started to work as prostitutes under the age of 16. Some were only 10, 11 or 12 years old (Silbert and Pines, 1984, p.862, cited in Russell, 1993, p.114). Allen (1981) found that the average age at which the child prostitutes in his study had first experienced sexual intercourse was 12 years old, the youngest being 9. Eighty-two per cent of a sample of prostitutes in New York had had sexual intercourse before the age of 13 (Janus and Heid Bracey, 1980, cited in Ennew, 1986).

In evidence to public hearings held by Minneapolis City Council in 1983, Barry described how:

> pornography is used by pimps as part of the illegal action of procuring and attempting to induce young girls and women into prostitution by presenting young women and girls with pornography which fraudulently represents actually painful sexual practices and acts as pleasing and gratifying to the female represented in pornography . . . Many pimps 'season' or break down their victims through sessions of rape and other forms of sexual abuse. Sometimes these sessions are photographed or filmed and used in a variety of ways which include the personal pleasure of the pimp and his friends, blackmailing the victim by threatening to send them to her family, and selling them to the pornographers for mass production.

In Barry's view, 'pornography is a form of prostitution and consequently pornographers are pimps' (1988, pp.29–30).

Prostitutes giving evidence to the hearings said:

> One of the very first commonalities we discovered as a group, we were all introduced to prostitution through pornography, there were no exceptions in our group, and we were all under 18. Pornography was our textbook, we learned the tricks of the trade by men exposing us to pornography and us trying to mimic what we saw. I cannot stress enough what a huge influence we feel this was. (p.71).

Silbert and Pines (1984) found that 38 per cent of their sample of prostitutes described having been 'involved in the taking of sexually explicit photographs of themselves when they were children for commercial purposes, and/or the personal gratification of the photographer' (p.866). 10 per cent of their respondents had been used as children in pornographic films and magazines, all of them under the age of 13 when they were victimised. 22 per cent of the 178 cases of juvenile sexual exploitation mentioned the use of pornographic materials by the adult prior to the sexual act: this included both adult and child subjects for purposes of their own and the child's sexual arousal, to legitimise their action, and to persuade the child to participate.

This corroborates, from the experience of the victims, what is known about the use of pornography from the perpetrators of child abuse. (The information on pornography in this study was unsolicited and was volunteered incidentally: it almost certainly, therefore, represents an under-reporting of the incidence of pornography-related abuse.)

Another source of information on pornography and child sexual abuse is the international traffic in women and children for prostitution and pornography (Ennew, 1986; Sariola, 1986). This trade has seen a major development in the form of 'sex tourism' (Ireland, 1993), a business which 'involves the use and abuse of Third World women [and children] as part of the sexual recreation of Western men, including paedophiles' as a 'planned item of state national income' involving 'the interlocking interests of air carriers, tour operators and hotel companies' (Barry, 1992). There was evidence in 1991 that 'several hundreds of thousands of young children between the ages of six years and fifteen years had been forced or sold into prostitution' (EFCW, 1993). It has been estimated that 60 per cent of all tourism in Thailand and 50 per cent of tourism in Kenya, the Philippines and South Korea is sex tourism (Groner, 1992). Many of these prostitutes will be children who are poor and black, who, like women who are poor and black, are 'disproportionately targeted for prostitution' (Baldwin, 1993, p.77). The United Nations recognises 'child prostitution and pornography . . . as a vast national and transnational problem'; that 'child pornography is often interrelated with child prostitution; that 'there are major child pornography markets in North America and Europe'; that 'Eastern Europe has emerged as a new market'; and that Asia is a key area of concern in regard to 'transnational trafficking of children for sexual purposes' (Muntarbhorn, 1995, pp.60–61).

Current knowledge about pornography and 'organised' child sexual abuse

There is very little empirical data on the incidence and prevalence of organised abuse or the role of pornography in it, and, like child sexual abuse, 'organised abuse' has been defined differently in various studies. Research in the USA has shown that child pornography is a core activity in most organised abuse where an individual or group of adults abuse large numbers of children (Burgess, 1984). In one study, Burgess and Hartman (1987) distinguished between three kinds of 'sex rings':

   i.   a solo ring consisting of one adult who is sexually involved with small groups of children [which] has no transfer of children or photographs to other adults;
   ii. a syndicated ring including several adults who form a well-structured organisation for the recruitment of children, the production of pornography and the establishment of an extensive network of customers and;

iii.   a transitional ring [where] there may be more than one adult involved with several children [and] pornographic photographs may be sold. (p.248)

All of these forms of organised abuse involved pornography.

In another American study, the multi-disciplinary team of clinicians in the Sexual Information and Trauma Team in a Family Development Centre identified a sub-group from their population of sexual abuse victims, of children who had been sexually abused by a ring (defined as 'a group of adults, male and/or female, who gather for the express purpose of sexual exploitation of children') all of which had involved child pornography (Hunt and Baird, 1990, p.196).

In the UK, a survey of 71 NSPCC child protection teams identified child pornography as a form of organised abuse, in addition to 'network' and 'ritual' abuse, and found child pornography to be involved in 16 per cent of cases (Creighton, 1993). A study of the prevalence of sex rings in Leeds (Wild, 1989) found 31 sex rings identified by police over a two-year period within a geographically-defined population of 710,000. A total of 47 male perpetrators aged 16–82 and 334 children aged 4–15 were involved. In this study, adult pornography was found to have been shown to a third of the children. Child pornography was produced in two rings, and in one ring, 'socially deprived boys . . . were sometimes blackmailed into participating after videotapes of them engaged in sexual activities had been made' (p.556).

A survey of police forces, Social Services Departments, and the NSPCC in England and Wales covering the four-year period from January 1988 to December 1991 produced an estimated national incidence rate for organised abuse of 967 cases over four years, or an average of 242 cases per year, but no data on pornography (Gallagher, Hughes and Parker, 1994; see Chapter 16 in this volume). La Fontaine (1993) defined organised abuse as 'abuse by multiple perpetrators, some of whom are outside the immediate household and who act together to abuse the child/ren' (p.230). La Fontaine's (1994) report on the extent and nature of organised and ritual abuse in the UK defined organised abuse as 'multiple abuse, involving more than one adult and, usually, more than one child' (p.3). It considered four categories of organised abuse: ritual abuse, paedophile networks, family-based abuse and institutional abuse. Child prostitution was considered to be possibly another 'distinct type of organised abuse', but it was not discussed and the study did not consider the links between pornography and organised abuse.

In the absence of a body of research on pornography and child sexual abuse or common definitions of what constitutes 'organised abuse', it is possible in this way to draw on a range of knowledge and research from different perspectives to build up a picture of the relationship between pornography and child sexual abuse. It is also possible to see, through this process, that much of this abuse is 'organised' in significant ways. In child

pornography, for example, some of the child sexual abuse recorded will have been perpetrated by individual adults on individual children, but much of it will have involved more than one child and more than one adult. All of it will have been organised for purposes of publication and for sale or exchange in the form of child pornography. Prostitution is itself frequently a form of organised abuse of women and children: most prostitution is organised and controlled by pimps, and it is a major business and source of income for organised crime internationally (Baxter, 1990; Baldwin, 1992).

At the same time, the process of looking at a wide range of child sexual abuse and how it is organised suggests that our understanding of organised abuse is limited, both in scope and in how it is conceptualised and defined. There is a need to establish a better understanding of the nature of child sexual abuse: how it is organised and the role of pornography in it. There is also a need to recognise the limits of knowledge based on incidence and prevalence data, and the potential for developing knowledge, understanding and theory by exploring the phenomenology of being used in and abused with pornography as a child, focusing on (in the words of one of those victims) 'what is done to the person or persons involved' (Kroon, 1980).

Pornography and the organisation of child sexual abuse: A case study

Methodology

There are, from various sources, personal accounts from survivors of their experience of pornography and organised child sexual abuse (Kroon, 1980; Danica, 1988; Minneapolis Hearings, 1988; DeCamp, 1992; Davies, 1994). These accounts have often been published with a view to providing evidence and 'proving' that organised abuse exists and the role of pornography in it, and to overcoming the disbelief and denial which is a common response to accounts of both intra- and extra-familial abuse and to research showing a high level of incidence and prevalence. The study in this chapter uses 'auto/biography' for a different purpose: to develop a more complex and sophisticated conceptual understanding of organised abuse that captures the way in which abuse is organised in and across different contexts, and the different ways in which pornography can be – and often is – implicated.

The case history in this study was selected from a sample of 132 women who, in response to a Channel 4 *Dispatches* programme on pornography in 1992, contacted a helpline for people who felt they had been harmed by pornography, a number of whom agreed to participate in a pilot study researching their experience of pornography-related harm (Itzin, 1996, in

press). The data in this study were obtained, retrospectively, by the author, from 'Alice', one of the respondents in the *Dispatches* research, using a semi-structured, life-history interview schedule. Aged 53 at the time of the interview, Alice described her experience as a child and adolescent: of incest, of organised abuse within her family, of organised abuse outside her family, of being prostituted and of being used in and abused with pornography. The interview is presented in the next section of this chapter in the form of a narrative which illustrates the nature of the abuse and the role of pornography in it at different stages in Alice's childhood. It is followed by a final section which extrapolates some of the characteristics of pornography and organised abuse from this study and discusses these in relation to other 'auto/biographical' accounts.

Incest as grooming for organised abuse

My first conscious memories are from when my sister was born when I was 2½, I was sent to my grandparents and stayed with them. My abuse started there. I have a memory then of my grandfather holding me, putting his fingers into me, touching me and watching me naked, especially wanting to see me naked. I also remember sleeping in a bed with an aunt, who also wanted me in the bed naked. They all lived in the same house.

I've always had these memories. I've never forgotten them. I remember it – and the time – because it was the first time that I was sent away from my mother. It was at the birth of my sister, and she was born on Boxing Day. I don't know how long I was there, but it felt a long time. I did go back to visit my mother with the baby, but I didn't stay back at home. My brother, who was in hospital with pneumonia, was a year younger than me. There were three of us in two-and-a-half years.

I was born illegitimately, early: a premature, illegitimate baby. My mother was sent away by her family to another town, as it was a disgrace. She knew of a man she'd met at a cinema who offered to marry her, and she accepted that in order to not go back to her own family. They were married and lived in this very damp rented house. My mother used to go out to the local pub to play cards and to drink, and her brothers and her sisters used to come and baby-sit whilst my stepfather was working. My stepfather always used to work until about 9 or 10 o'clock at night, in order to fund my mother's drinking and spending. We were very poor, and my stepfather often went to the soup kitchen to feed us because it was wartime.

My mum was one of 11 children: six girls and five boys. She was the third-eldest child. My mother would never profess to be an alcoholic, but she drank daily, quite a lot daily. I remember her often drunk. She smoked continually. She was very unemotional, very cold, very distant. And she was obsessively linked to her mother: she could never be apart from her mother. But she didn't return home

after she had me. I think she wanted to be away from that environment. I think she thought I'd be at risk from my grandfather.

One of my aunts, who is now dead, told me that my grandfather was my father. My mother would never tell me who my father was, she told me it would 'never do me any good to know'. Those were her words. But I believe that I was probably the child of incest between my mother and her father. My mother's eldest sister told me this when I was in my twenties, after I'd had an illegitimate child of my own when I was 19, and my mother was furious with me. My aunt was reassuring me that my mother had no need to be cross because, in her words: 'history was repeating itself except that the fathers were different'.

I think my mother's leaving home was quite an act of love. It took me a long time in my adult life to realise that she had actually tried to protect me from them, because then she went on to abuse me, so it became very contradictory.

My mum's abuse of me was physical and emotional and it had long-lasting effects. I've since been reliably told that my mother also sexually abused me, but I don't remember it. I was told by a man my mother had an affair with that my mother had sexually abused me too. She told him she'd been abusing me from infancy and it had turned her on, that she'd been sexually aroused. I think this is likely to be true, but I don't remember it.

My grandfather had his own business. He used to have a workshop near to where we lived, and we (my sister and brother and I) used to have to go down and see him at the workshop. We were abused at his workshop. Separately, not together. We would be told to go down and see grandad, take him something down or give him a message. We were actually sent – by my grandmother, by my mother. Once I took a school friend down, and she wouldn't come with me again after that. He abused both of us. He sexually assaulted us. He made us take our knickers off and touched us and orally abused us.

My stepfather did not abuse me. He was never there. He used to be up first in the morning, and he'd come in last at night. If we were still awake, once the baby-sitters had gone, he'd read us a story. He was fabulous, he still is. He didn't know that all of this was happening.

Abuse organised within the family

My mother didn't acknowledge that she knew what was going on, but I know that she knew, because she saw it and turned and walked away. On one occasion when I was 8 and my grandfather was abusing me, I heard footsteps coming up the stairs. I was in a position to see my mother standing in the doorway. She stood for a while, and then turned and went away. That memory was very destructive for a long time. It was probably worse than the abuse itself, watching while my mother turned away.

I told my stepfather once, because one time when he came home from work, I was crying because I'd been hurt. My uncle had abused me and hurt me. My step-

father wanted to know why I was crying, and I told him what had happened. He told my mother. She came and got me out of bed. I told her, and she took me to my grandparents. I was 8, I think, 8 or 9. She took me in to confront my grandparents and my uncle because he lived with them, with his parents. I was told I was fabricating, it was a lie. I stood and said to my grandfather 'you know it's true, you know this is happening'. He told me I'd got an overactive imagination. My mother hit me, and put me in the back room for telling lies, and making her look stupid. But she knew it was true, because she had seen us. So the whole thing was totally confusing. I got punished for talking, so I never did it again.

I was abused by my mother's younger brothers – my uncles – when they were baby-sitting, and also by the older aunt. They told me that they'd been taught by their father, my grandfather. I also know that my mother and her brothers were abused by their father, and from what my aunt told me about my parentage, that I was probably the product of father–daughter incest.

The sexual abuse I experienced from my uncles when they were baby-sitting would be intercourse, oral sex, anal sex, and at times both. The physical abuse included needles put under my toenails and fingernails, being tied up, being frightened. The psychological abuse was always threats, the unknown, never knowing whether they would actually do what they threatened they would do. The emotional abuse was one moment to do things that indicated they cared about me, and then the next moment to hurt me. They'd tell me I was really nice and they cared about me, and they'd offer to give me a sweet and then take it away. They'd say they wouldn't hurt me, and then they would. They threatened to make up stories to my mother to get me into trouble. They said they'd tell my teachers things about me that weren't true.

They terrorised me until I did what they wanted me to do. It wasn't just what they did to me that terrified me, but the things I was told they would do at different times if I didn't obey them. Like they said they would catch me coming home from school and would take me away and hang me unless I did what they told me to do, which could be the sexual abuse, or it could be the photography.

Pornography and intra-familial abuse

My uncle would make me look at pornographic literature and then take photographs of me doing it naked when he was baby-sitting. This is age 4 to 11 that I remember. He'd show me photographs of adults, men and women with whips and leather and children and animals. It would be photographs of oral sex, penetrative sex, both vaginally and anally. Somebody must have given him these, because he was only a teenager. Then he would make me act out some of them. If we were alone, this would be putting things inside myself, or he would put them in and then take the photographs. Sitting in provocative positions, masturbating; in sexually provocative poses and smiling. That was always the big criterion of photographs: smiling.

I don't know where his camera came from, so it's quite possible that someone had given him the money and a camera to take the pictures with. He knew ways of making money, and later he used to sell me to his friends anyway. He used to charge them to have sex with me, so it is quite possible that someone had paid him to take photographs.

One of the friends' fathers was a contact of my grandfather's. He was a photographer, and his shop was only yards away from the school. If we were at his friend's house – the photographer's house – then often, his father would be involved and he would take photographs of the boys, the teenagers, with me and with their dog. This was just filming at home by individuals, it would just be photographs at home. Pornography was the filming later in the groups. At home it was just still photographs.

Pornography and extra-familial abuse

This was from the age of 4 to 11 or 12, when we moved. We left that house when I was 12, and went to live next door to my grandmother and grandfather, and aunts and uncles. I think it was my twelfth birthday we left. I can only remember up to 11, and then I have a complete blank from 11 to 13. I still have a complete blank of two years, I can't remember any of it. But we did move, and I know at 13 my memory returns and I'm at the other house. By 13 we had moved, and then the sexual abuse accelerated with other uncles, with uncles' friends and my grandfather's friends. Prior to that, it had just been family and family connections, then it just seemed like it was everybody.

And pornography started. One of the forms of organised abuse would be to make pornography. Me on my own, and in groups and with other children I didn't know. At 13, my younger uncles were older than me, ranging from five years upwards. They were in the senior level of the same school. By this time, they were making money by selling me to their friends. So when I was supposed to be at school playing netball, I was being sold for sex to my uncles' friends and to their friends' fathers, including the photographer.

I didn't know who this man was when I first met him. But when my uncle wanted me to go back with him and his friend to the friend's house, I realised I'd been there before, that I'd met this photographer before when I was younger. This man had a studio at the back of his house, it was like a town house, terraced, but at the back they had a long garden with a big studio. He had cameras, and white umbrellas set up in there with lots of big lights, chairs and some tables. He took children's portraits. That was his job, taking photographs of children. He would have a cine camera in there as well as a stills camera. I'd be taken there in order to be photographed. And there'd be other children and other adults there, and my uncle and his friend, the photographer's son. At this point, I knew that he was a friend of my grandfather's, but I didn't know in what context. But later, I knew my grandfather was involved in the pornography, because I saw him paying him for the pictures.

There were groups there, and group sex. It would all be organised before I got there. When I'd be taken there, the people were already there, the extra children were already there. I would then be made to be a perpetrator, and I would have to be involved in sexual abuse with younger children. Oral sex or penetrating their vagina or rectum. And that included abusing my brother. I would also be abused by other older children and by male and female adults. There were babies involved too. They would be naked. They would have their penises sucked, or they'd be involved in creating the picture. A baby could be breastfeeding while her mother was being penetrated by an adult and orally stimulating an older child. So she'd be having intercourse with an adult whilst feeding the baby. Any scenario you could think of happened, virtually. The babies weren't being penetrated, so you couldn't prove sexual abuse. But fingers would be in vaginas, rectums. I don't know about new babies, or tiny babies, but certainly toddlers would be penetrated. Sometimes we would be involved in going in big bathrooms, and photographs would be taken of children playing in the bath and then the adults joining in, and that could involve all of the things that I've said before. Afterwards, we'd be given sweets.

For me, my greatest fear was I'd suffocate. As a small child I was terrified I would die by suffocation, and ever since being a small child, whenever I vomit I swallow it, and I still do it. After coming round from theatre when I've been for surgery, I wake up vomiting and swallowing. Because we had to swallow semen. The penis in our mouths would make us gag and retch, and we had to swallow before anything came up. If we didn't swallow it and made a mess, we had to lick it up.

In the pornography, there was also violence – tying up, restraint. There was pushing things inside us: instruments, bottles, rods, in our vaginas and rectums. Fruit, bananas, cucumbers, things like that, ice cubes. Being hung upside down, being tethered with a dog collar round our necks and on all fours. Animals mounting us in that position. There was also recording: recording pain, recording sexual excitement. Not just photographs, there were recorders going, and then they were reel-to-reel tapes, not the little things like today.

Child prostitution

Another form of organised abuse was to be prostituted. In my early childhood, in addition to what was going on at home – the incest as I later learned it was – I'd be taken to places for group sex, group pornography and group prostitution. It had already been mapped out before I actually got there. We were taken out to places where it was already planned out. This is what I mean by 'organised abuse', and the organised abuse included pornography. We were taken out where we met strangers and other children. Me and my brother and sister were taken there. I have memories of going, my sister has some memories, but my brother doesn't want to talk about it. I was taken by an aunt, by uncles, by my grandfather.

It was after one of these sessions – where we'd be in group sex, but without the cameras – that I saw my grandfather buy the pictures, and I knew that he must have been involved in the pornography too. In the making of pornography, prostitution is taking place. They go together, and I was prostituted to make the pornography. But also I was just prostituted, sold for sex. Sometimes, there was a combination of prostitution and filming. Whereas the pornography was set up for pornography, prostitution was set up so you could be sold for sex, but sometimes filmed. This film wasn't necessarily sold, it was for the individuals that were there, as distinct from the pornography which was to make pornography for sale.

The prostitution could be with just one person, or two or three, or a group, but on those occasions, there wasn't just an emphasis, like there is in pornography, on the image – the emphasis was on sexual satisfaction, and on sexual gratification, and everybody there got it. In the prostitution, I had to sexually meet everyone's needs. That wasn't always so with the pornography, where the main point was to take photographs or make film.

Perpetrator networks

Where there was prostitution with photographs, money was flying around, you know, not only for the photographs, but also for the sex that was happening at the same time. I became aware of this when I saw money being exchanged between my grandfather and the father of my uncle's friend. I couldn't separate what the money was for: whether it was for the photographs, when they were handed over, or whether it was for the sex. But I knew there was some kind of networking between my grandfather and other people. He was involved in it in one way or another.

There was a network of people whose paths crossed for these purposes. It could be to do with their work or socially, their paths crossed: not just related to the abuse, their paths crossed in other ways. One of our local policemen was part of the group that was into the pornography, and also one of the local doctors was a part of it. And two of the local teachers were part of this abuse network. My grandfather was a freemason, and a lot of the abusing people were in high places. We knew that by the cars they used to come in, and in those days there were very few cars, it's not like now, and by the kind of clothes they wore.

No one ever told me not to say anything, not ever, but I knew I shouldn't. That came from my mother saying to me once, when I was telling her what somebody else did in their house, that it was none of my business to know what other people did in their house, and it was none of their business to know what we did in ours.

Coercion: The obedient smile

My fear has always been that the photographs of me will turn up. An ongoing concern all my life is that the pornography that was taken is going to turn up

somewhere, and if it doesn't, I'd like to know who has it, where has it gone to? When I was in my twenties, I saw some of it: my uncle showed me some that he still had. It was me at age 9. It was photographs taken in the shed, this sort of shed place at the back of the pornographer's house, with younger children and men and women. He had about six of these photographs. And then, when my mother died, this was 11 years ago when I was in my forties, he came to the funeral and he said to me 'are you still as good as you always were?' He put his arms round me, and then he said he'd still got the photographs, did I want to see them again, would I like more sessions?

My response when I saw the photographs was total horror. And the thing that struck me more than anything else, was how small I was. I'd always felt I'd been a big girl, but I just looked so small. And the other thing that struck me was that my eyes were dead, but I was smiling. I couldn't believe that I was hurting so much and smiling. But they asked me, they told me to smile. I'd learnt from a very early age obedience was the name of the game. This was about total obedience, it wasn't about questioning anything. From babyhood, I'd been taught to be obedient, not just in the smiling but in everything. Don't vomit, be quiet, do this, do that, and I did it. I was like a human robot, that when someone clicked, I jumped. And when they let me go and finished with me, I used to say thank you. The reward was being a good girl.

Consent: The sexualised child

The biggest thing for me was being told that I was a good girl, patted on the head. That was the only affection I ever got, and I'd do anything for that. I'd go out to the park and not actually look for people to abuse me, but I'd be very friendly with someone, and if they abused me, I'd do anything if they'd tell me I was a good girl. They'd smile at me, they'd put their arm around me, they'd stroke my head, they'd just tell me 'good girl' and it didn't matter how much they hurt me in between any of those things. That happened in the local bakery and in the park numerous times. So I was a willing accomplice to sexual abuse, having learned I could be told 'good girl'. It was the only positive feedback I had growing up.

At the bakery, for example, we were playing hide and seek one day. My brother and sister were hiding, and I was supposed to be finding them, and the man on the bread-cutting machine said they may go down in the basement, have a look down there. So I went into the basement, and he followed. He started to sexually touch me, and then he had intercourse with me. He told me I was a good girl, gave me a cake and told me to come back the next day without my knickers. I went back the next day without my knickers, and he did it again.

In the park, I was talking to this man who was really nice to me. My sister and I were on the see-saw, and I went down. After he'd finished with his hand in my knickers and his fingers in my vagina, I went back to play with her. She told me she'd seen me, and I told her she hadn't, she was lying. He was a complete

stranger, I hadn't a clue who he was. What he did felt nice, and he was nice, and he told me I was a good girl, and he gave me a sweet.

I used to go swimming to get clean, because we hadn't got a bath in our house. On the way home from the swimming baths, almost daily for a long, long time, seven years or so, there was a man in the local rec, where I had to go through to get home, and he was one of the men that was nice and made me feel nice who I ended up having intercourse with. I'd be 10 or 11 then. At about this time, sexual activities had become the norm. I didn't even know it was wrong.

It just felt like this is what you do to please people, and if you don't get hurt, you're lucky, and if you feel nice, it's great, and sometimes you get a sweet, sometimes you don't, sometimes you get a pat on the head. Both were good: in fact, a pat on the head was better than the sweet. And I knew how to be nice, I knew how to smile, and by this time I was an expert in knowing what to do to sexually arouse. I'd been taught a whole lot by the time I was 11. My grandad used to say: 'Alice, when you've been taught all that I need to teach you, the world will be your oyster.'

I knew what I had to do, I never questioned it. I'd learned what was expected of me. The feedback was that I was doing well, that I was pleasing, and as long as I did what I was told, I'd continue to be pleasing. I didn't think it was wrong. It was a place that I fit into, I used to say it's the place I belong to best, it's the thing I'm best at. It's what I knew best, and I always felt confident in being able to do well by the time I got to 11. The rewards were affection and praise. I was desperately seeking approval, and this gave it.

Normalising child sexual abuse

I didn't know I was doing anything wrong until I went nursing at 17. I went to a lecture on sexually transmitted diseases, and it was there that I first heard all about incest, not only that it was wrong, but that it was illegal. It was like being absolutely hit over the head, and I was more terrified of being put in prison for doing something illegal all of my childhood than what had actually happened to me. Although I could easily have died from what was done to me as a child, the thought of being incarcerated in prison for what I'd done frightened me so much that I took an overdose.

From the moment that I heard about incest being illegal, then I had to look at what the rest of it meant, the sex with strangers, what did that mean, and the pornography. The whole lot of it just felt devastating. Everything that I'd done and felt I'd had to do I discovered at the age of 17 that I didn't have to do, that most people don't have to do it, but I had. I was then to discover the enormity of the damage that had been done to me. But that's another story.

Some characteristics of pornography and the organisation of child sexual abuse

Gender and generation

Incest, although most commonly perpetrated by fathers on daughters, may (as Alice's story illustrates) also be perpetrated by grandfathers (although Alice's grandfather may also have been her father) and by uncles and aunts. Mothers, too, may be perpetrators of sexual abuse. La Fontaine (1994) found women more commonly implicated in family-based abuse, and that 'nearly two thirds of the cases of paedophile networks involved no women at all' (p.12). She found that the majority of alleged perpetrators were men, but women were also significantly represented amongst alleged perpetrators as 'implicated jointly with a partner, as knowing of the abuse, not protecting the child or assisting a male abuser' (p.12).

Danica (1988), for example, describes how her father sexually abused her at and from the age of 4, and how, on the first occasion, her mother had 'listened' from the bottom of the stairs, much as Alice recalls her mother doing. She describes how her father began his 'training' of her from the age of 11, with her mother as an accomplice, instructing her in what to wear, waking her in the night to send or to take her to her father, sometimes watching while the abuse was perpetrated. A woman interviewed by Davies (1994) said her mother allowed, even encouraged, her father to abuse her and her two young brothers and sometimes joined in the abuse. Alice's mother was actively a perpetrator of physical, emotional and psychological abuse. With respect to the sexual abuse, her role was more passive – in failing to protect her child, in permitting and enabling the abuse to take place and in failing to prevent it or to stop it happening.

Incest as grooming for organised abuse

The incest in Alice's family was more than the abuse of a child for the sexual purposes of the abuser: it was also part of a process of grooming and seasoning for organised abuse within the family and outside the family. It is an example of what Baldwin (1992) describes 'as a form of seasoning, a practice of a father pimping his daughter to himself' (p.113), or in this case, grandfather/granddaughter. It is also an example of (grand)father pimping a (grand)daughter for prostitution. This is not uncommon, and has also been reported in other 'auto/biographical' accounts. Davies (1994) interviewed a woman who described 'being conditioned' from the age of 4 or before, so much so that she thought it was 'the normal condition of all children to receive almost daily sexual attention from an adult' (p.14).

Danica (1988) describes how, at the age of 9, her father had taken her to the stock car races, and how he and his brother (her uncle) had sold her through the afternoon to a steady stream of customers in the back of the car in the field where the cars were parked. Alice's grandfather and uncles sold her to their friends. This form of family-based abuse is child prostitution, and in these cases, the extra-familial abuse is organised by the family for people outside the family and may then involve both family members and non-family members.

Pornography and prostitution

Like Alice, one of the women interviewed by Davies (1994) was filmed: 'more than 15 years of it, hundreds of scenes, thousands of feet of film'. Like Alice, she said that although she didn't understand it at the time, she now thinks 'they used to plan it all in advance, map it out'. A typical event would involve adults (which sometimes included her mother and father), and children as young as 2 or 3 through to teen age. The abuse would include anal, oral and vaginal penetration of the children by the adults and by each other, with objects as well as fingers, hands and penises, tying up, gagging, blindfolding and whipping. The men who filmed were also perpetrators, and she was beaten if she was not compliant, or if, like Alice, she gagged and choked on semen. This woman's experience is similar to Alice's and also Danica's.

The case material used by Davies (1994) illustrates the symbiotic relationship between pornography and prostitution, and how even the women and girls who claim to consent to their participation can be seen to have been induced by poverty and drug addiction and 'predisposed' to participate by their own previous experiences of child sexual abuse. Davies, for example, quotes a woman who described herself as 'happy to make pornography', including 'sadistic stuff if the money was right'. She was a drug addict and a prostitute who 'could make £20 opening her mouth for some stranger's penis on the streets of Kings Cross or £250 for doing the same thing in the tatty temporary studio in the front room of someone's flat'. Davies also cites the example of the man who 'persuaded a 13 year old girl to make pornographic videos for him simply by offering her an escape from her thoroughly deprived background' (p.17).

Networks of perpetrators

One of the women interviewed by Davies (1994) said friends of her parents took part, and she described 'a network of adults who shared a secret and obsessive interest and who used each other's children, sometimes separately and sometimes in grotesque gatherings devoted to abuse without limit, endless rape and whippings and [how] always there were cameras' (p.14).

Danica (1988) describes her father building 'what he called a studio' in their basement, and parties which her parents organised which ended up in the basement. She describes on one occasion being raped by three 'very important men', a judge, a lawyer, a doctor, and then by her own father. The filmed record of this 'gang rape' was subsequently sold by her father (pimp and pornographer) to the participants. Alice also describes the involvement of eminent men in the community in her abuse, and a network likely connected with her grandfather's freemasonry.

Coercion and 'consent'

The compliance of children in child sexual abuse, prostitution and pornography is sometimes achieved through the use of violence and threats of violence. This was the experience of Danica, who was beaten into submission. Alice's submission was achieved through systematic emotional and physical abuse and neglect, such that the sexual abuse itself was perceived less as abuse than an opportunity to win favour and approval.

The 'smile' of the victim (child or woman) in pornography is often cited as the evidence of her consent. Davies (1994) describes a video of a 'girl with her wrists and ankles chained to an iron bar in the ceiling and a grotesque dildo hanging out of her'. The pornographer who was showing the video pointed to the girl's smile as evidence of her consent. Davies acknowledges the 'tired kind of smile' on the girl's face, but also describes 'the mark in her make up where a tear had rolled down to her jaw' (p.17).

Danica (1988) recalls how, at the age of 11, her father called her to the basement and showed her some photographs of her mother: 'naked. Smiling that smile I know. The smile I have learned to make for the camera too. The smile I make when he says, wet your lips, lift your head, smile. The clenched teeth. The eyes of the hunted facing the camera. Caught. Powerless . . . ' (p.41). She didn't believe her mother would do this, but her father had said: 'She does whatever I tell her to do. Just as you'll learn to do what I tell you to do.' Alice always smiled, however much she was being hurt. She was happy to smile. This pleased people. They told her she was a good girl. They gave her sweets. These were her only pleasures and happiness in an otherwise miserable, emotionally deprived and abusive childhood.

Denial and the silencing of victims

One of the most extreme examples of child sexual abuse organised for the purposes of making pornography is quoted by DeCamp in his book on the cover-up of a paedophile network in Lincoln, Nebraska in the USA. DeCamp was a state senator and the attorney representing one of the victims of a paedophile network, who testified under oath to his part in the making of

pornography in which one of the victims was sexually murdered (called 'snuff pornography'). In response to their testimony, the boy and a young woman victim of the same organised abuse network were convicted of perjury and given prison sentences. But, wrote DeCamp (1992, p.225): 'I have not a shadow of a doubt that her story [like his] is true.'

It is another characteristic of organised abuse that the victims, when they do tell their stories, are not believed, particularly when the alleged perpetrators are men of power and influence in the community, or in government. But the evidence of the truth of the accounts – and the evidence of the organised child sexual abuse – is to be found in the pornography itself. The corroboration, as Davies (1994) described it, is the 'widely distributed, easily available, for sale to anyone who would like to look – images of pornography in Britain in 1994' (p.14).

Pornography and 'cycles of abuse'

Perpetrators

Abuse within the family may be intra- as well as inter-generational. The abused in one generation may become the abusers of and within the next generation. In Alice's family, her uncles (her mother's brothers) as well as her mother had been victims of incest perpetrated by their father. The extent to which abuse is learned through the experience of abuse and then perpetrated or repeated in the same or similar forms of either victimising or victimisation is documented by different sources.

The view that 'today's child molester may well be yesterday's incest victim' (Seng, 1986, p.49) is supported by empirical data. Briere and Runtz (1989) found amongst the most 'significant predictors of self-reported sexual response to children amongst university males' to be 'negative early sexual experiences and self-reported likelihood of raping a woman' (p.71), and that 'the "bad experiences" item was one of the most powerful predictors of sexual interest in children' (p.73). Fagan and Wexler (1988) found that 'sex offenders more often came from families with spousal violence, child abuse and child sexual molestation according to both official and self reports' (p.363). Seghorn, Prentky and Boucher (1987) found that the 'incidence of sexual assault in childhood among child molesters was higher than the incidence of such abuse reported in the literature' (p.262). Carter et al. (1987) found that 57 per cent of the child molesters in their study were themselves molested as children, and 'of the sizeable proportion of child molesters who were molested, 77 per cent were assaulted by strangers or casual acquaintances' (p.200).

Briere and Runtz (1989) also found that masturbating to pornography as well as sexual abuse during childhood was a significant predictor of adult

sexual interest in children. Carter et al. (1987) found that the childhood sexual assaults on the men who later became child molesters 'often involved pornographic materials' (p.206) and that their subsequent sexual assaults on children frequently involved the use of pornography 'prior to and during their offences' (p.205). Burgess (1985) reported on the 'increasing frequency of a history of childhood sexual victimisation in sex offenders'. She explains this as a process of 'identification with the exploiter', whereby 'the child has already introjected some characteristics of the adult and has transformed himself from the person threatened into the person who made the threat' (p.123), or alternatively where the child 'maintains a victim rather than a survivor position, and is at risk for future victimisation' (p.119).

Victims

The 'causal effects' of childhood sexual abuse and pornography on the subsequent behaviour of victims is also reflected in research on prostitution and pornography. Allen (1981, cited in Ennew, 1986) found that 90 per cent of girls and boys who were exploited as prostitutes reported having been physically abused by parents and 50 per cent claimed to have been sexually abused. Weisberg (1985, cited in Baldwin, 1992) reported 66 per cent of prostituted girls and women having been sexually abused by fathers or stepfathers. The Silbert and Pines study (1984, cited earlier) found that 60 per cent of the 200 prostitutes they interviewed reported having been sexually abused as children, and 73 per cent reported having been raped; 10 per cent of the sample had been used, as children, in pornographic films and magazines, and 38 per cent had had sexual photographs taken of them as children.

Alice was 'sexualised' by her sexual abuse as a child to the extent that she subsequently prostituted herself in the playground, on the streets to and from school and in the local shops: anywhere, anytime. To her, this was 'normal' behaviour, and it was not until she was 17, attending a lecture on sexually transmitted diseases, that she realised that her sexual abuse was not 'normal'. Burgess, Groth and McCausland (1981) found that child victims of organised abuse often went on to become prostitutes and pimps and to repeat sexual acts on younger children. Wild and Wynne (1986) illustrated 'how abnormal and sexualised the behaviour of children involved in a sex ring may become' with the example of girls who had been victimised subsequently deliberately seeking out a replacement perpetrator when 'their' perpetrator had been apprehended, including trying to recruit men in their homes with sexually provocative behaviour (p.184).

The rest of Alice's story tells of living with the trauma, and trying to recover from the effects, of having been sexually abused as a child: of the 'traumatic sexualisation, betrayal, powerlessness and stigmatisation' described by Finkelhor and Browne (1985), and in the words of the woman

herself, the 'torture and its legacy of self-injury, self-abuse, attempted suicide and life-long depression'. Her belief that being abused in and through pornography aggravated the trauma of the child sexual abuse she experienced is supported by the clinical observations of Hunt and Baird (1990) that 'being photographed while being sexually abused exacerbates the shame, humiliation, and powerlessness that sexual abuse victims typically experience', and that 'denial of the abuse becomes even more important . . . and is achieved at greater cost' (p.202). Hunt and Baird (1990) found the effects on children of being photographed in the act of being abused as 'devastating'. The record of their sexual abuse is 'then used to reinforce the children's sense of responsibility for the abuse and to ensure their silence' and the children 'become the instrument of their own torture' (p.201). Burgess, Groth and McCausland (1981) found that having been used in pornography was a poor prognosis factor for victims of child sex rings.

Conclusion

Defining child sexual abuse to include pornography

Alice's account of her abuse, and other survivor accounts, suggest that the existing definitions of child sexual abuse which ignore pornography and isolate paedophilia from incest, incest from extra-familial abuse and all of these from something called 'organised abuse', are misleading. In a recent Scottish study, Waterhouse, Dobash and Carnie (1994) categorised 48 per cent of their sample of 500 convicted sex offenders as 'familial' (where the perpetrator was related to and/or responsible for the victim) and 52 per cent as 'non-familial' (where the perpetrator was not related to or responsible for the victim). In the USA, Finkelhor (1979) found that fathers and stepfathers were implicated in up to half of the cases. But Waterhouse, Dobash and Carnie (1994) also found that only 10 per cent were strangers (i.e. not known) to the child victims; that 61 per cent of the offences were committed in the home of the child victim; and that 'the majority of the perpetrators were not strangers to the child and indeed usually lived in the home of the victim at the time that abuse occurred' (p.iii). An earlier UK study had found that child sexual abusers were unknown to the child victim or to the child's family in only about 25 per cent of cases (Mrazek, Lynch and Bentovim, 1983).

From a clinical perspective, a typology which categorises child molesters by predictable patterns of beliefs, sexual preferences and behaviours may be useful in assisting the understanding and treatment of individuals who sexually abuse children. But typologies based on offender classifications, or on whether the abuse occurred inside or outside the family and judgements about its seriousness, usually defined in terms of penetration and/or use of

force, have 'real limitations' and provide 'little insight into the nature of the trauma experienced by the child' (Finkelhor and Browne, 1985, p.537). On the assumption that 'intrafamilial abuse was expected to be generally more upsetting and traumatic than extrafamilial abuse', Russell (1983, p.135) used a broader definition of what constitutes intra-familial abuse, but then found that 'children who are sexually abused outside the family are abused in a significantly more serious manner' (p.142). This suggests that there may not be significant, qualitative differences in the degree of damage experienced by children abused within or outside the family. Conceptualising paedophilia as separate from incest and organised abuse, and pornography and child prostitution as further separate conceptual categories, also obscures the fact that one and the same perpetrator can appear in any or all categories. Seng (1986) acknowledges that the distinctions between sexual exploitation (including child pornography), incest and child molestation can become blurred by the fact that the offenders may very well be the same: 'that is, an incestuous father may involve his daughter as a participant in child pornography and child molesters are indeed very apt to involve their victims in pornography' (p.56).

These kinds of typology of abuse do not reflect the complex and cross-cutting factors that characterise child sexual abuse, such as: the relationship between the abuser and the victim; the length of time over which the abuse takes place; the number of different abusers in time and over time; the nature of the abuse, the level of violence and/or intimidation; the role of pornography in the abuse, and the short- and long-term effects of the abuse on the victims. Even the diagnostic definition of paedophilia as 'the act or fantasy of engaging in sexual activity with prepubertal children as a repeatedly preferred or exclusive method of achieving sexual excitement' is not supported by research. Langevin and Lang (1985) found that 66 per cent of heterosexual paedophiles were married at some time, 91 per cent had vaginal intercourse with an adult female and even 50 per cent of homosexual paedophiles had done so. They found that 'empirical controlled studies' did not support the view that paedophiles were 'shy, unassertive, sexually ignorant' and have 'an aversion to adult females' (p.405). From the child's point of view, it probably does not matter if the perpetrator's sexual interests are only children or also adults.

From his clinical work with sex offenders, Wyre (1993) has categorised all child molesters within a paedophile typology as 'parapaedophiles', 'fixated paedophiles', 'inadequate paedophiles', 'inadequate fixated paedophiles' and 'regressed paedophiles'. Wyre's category of 'parapaedophile' includes incestuous fathers and other men who may also have sex with adults as well as, or even more than, with children. All of Wyre's categories include the use of adult and/or child pornography. This particular conceptualisation of child sexual abuse from the perpetrators' per-

spective has the advantage of being consistent with the child's perspective, for whom the experience of the abuse is paramount, and not the particular profile of offender behaviour.

Conceptualising pornography and the organisation of child sexual abuse as a continuum

Kelly (1987) conceptualises 'sexual violence as a continuum' in order to reflect the extent and the range of sexual violence reported in a study of 60 women. Kelly's concept of continuum was developed to capture the 'basic common character underlying the many different forms of violence' reported (of the 'abuse, intimidation, coercion, intrusion, threat and force men use to control women'), and the fact that sexual violence is 'a continuous series of elements or events that pass into one another and which cannot be readily distinguished' (p.76). Similarly, the study in this chapter illustrates a continuum of child sexual abuse ranging from incest to sharing children for sex within the family, to sharing children for sex outside the family (with other families/with other adults), to selling children for sex (child prostitution), to the making of pornography. All of the abuse in Alice's childhood was organised, and pornography was one of the forms of organised abuse. Pornography was also part of the organisation of all the other forms of abuse. The transactions included both personal sexual gratification and profit, in the exchange of money for child sex and for child and adult pornography. Figure 13.1 illustrates this diagrammatically.

Figure 13.1 also includes a category of national and international traffic in children as another form of organised abuse, where children are treated as commodities for the purposes of prostitution and pornography. Although this was not Alice's experience, when it does occur, it may involve abduction or kidnap, or it may involve families, or the collusion of families, or networks of 'paedophiles'. The distinction between this and the selling of children for prostitution and pornography in Alice's case, may largely be the size of the business – part of an international industry rather than a 'cottage industry' (Tate, 1992).

The organisation of the sexual abuse of Alice involved incest (grandfather, uncles, aunt), abuse organised within the family (more than one adult/more than one child), abuse organised between families (more than one adult/more than one child) and abuse organised for the benefit of adults outside the family (more than one adult/more than one child), and may also have involved 'fixated paedophiles'. It seems to be conceptually useful, therefore, to define all adult sex with children as 'paedophilia' (as in the Wyre typology), within which there are categories of activity defined by characteristics common to different kinds of paedophiles in different circumstances. Alternatively, it might be useful to abandon the use of the word

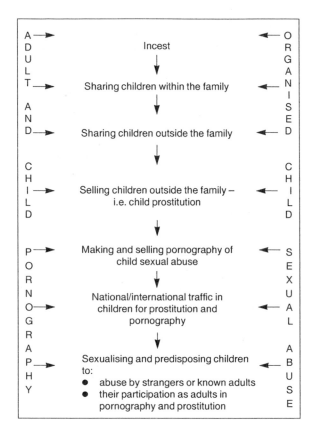

Figure 13.1 The organisation of child sexual abuse (1)

'paedophile' altogether and use, the generic category 'child sexual abusers', within which there are a range of different characteristics.

Where classifications are used, there would appear to be a need for common definitions shared within the international research community, by clinicians and child protection agencies, and for purposes of national and international policing. Whatever classifications are used, they need to take account of the range of characteristics of child sexual abuse identified in this and other studies, for example:

- All child sexual abuse is carried out by people who think it is acceptable to have sex with children.
- Sometimes it is carried out by fathers (biological or step) or cohabiting males in a parental role who are heterosexual in their adult relationships and have sex with their female partners, but who may have sex with either male or female children.

- Sometimes it is carried out by unrelated or non-custodial males who may either be strangers or known to the child (as 'trusted' adults), who may be either heterosexual or homosexual and who may or may not also have adult sexual relationships.
- Sometimes it is carried out by men who are primarily interested in having sex with children and not with other adults (the so-called 'paedophiles'), who may be homosexual or heterosexual in terms of sexual preference, but who may have sex with women in order to get access to children, and who may have sex with either male or female children, but who may be 'fixated' on certain age or gender or physical characteristics.
- Sometimes, when carried out by any of the above, it may involve more than one adult and/or more than one child (what is usually called 'organised abuse').
- Whatever the relationship of the perpetrator to the victim, and whatever the sexual preference of the abuser, the majority of abuse occurs in the home of the child and only a small proportion (10 per cent to 25 per cent in different studies) is perpetrated by strangers.
- Coercion and/or violence occur in all of these circumstances.
- All of this abuse is 'organised' in the sense of being 'planned' and/or 'engineered'.
- However the abuse is organised, it really just represents different ways of initiating and carrying out the sexual abuse of children. This is also true when the abuse is organised around or to include elements of ritual. There may be differences which are important for purposes of police investigations or perpetrator treatment, but they are not significant phenomenologically: they are just different ways of being a child sexual abuser.
- Pornography, in the form of adult and/or child pornography used to season/groom/initiate/coerce children into agreeing to be abused, or the production of child pornography (the records of children being sexually abused), is implicated in every form of child abuse, however it is organised.

Figure 13.2 conceptualises the organisation of child sexual abuse as a continuum in the form of concentric circles. The outer circle is the boundary of child sexual exploitation and includes all those who believe it is OK to have sex with children for their own personal gratification or for profit. Within this boundary, there are the variety of different ways in which the abuse may be organised (in the form of incest, sharing and selling children within and between families, with adults outside the family, between groups of unrelated adults and in the making of pornography). These are overlapping rather than discrete categories which may involve the same perpetrators and the same or similar activities. In addition to the form of abuse which is organ-

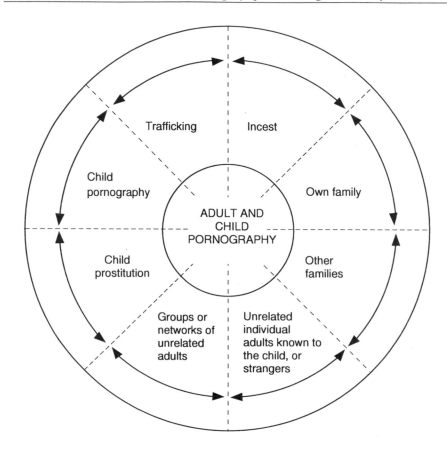

Figure 13.2   The organisation of child sexual abuse (2)

ised for the purpose of making child pornography, Figure 13.2 shows, in its inner circle, how all the other forms of abuse can and do involve the use of adult and child pornography and the recording of the sexual abuse of the child.

Summary

From case studies and the range of sources cited in this chapter, a picture begins to emerge of the nature and extent and the characteristics of pornography and child sexual abuse, which suggests that both adult and child pornography can be instrumental to the abuse of individual children by individual adults, and that the use of and the making of pornography may very well be a characteristic of most or all of the abuse of more than one child by one or more adults. It would also appear to be the case that there is consider-

able overlap in the experience of the victims between incest, organised family-based abuse and extra-familial abuse. The value of a phenomenological approach is its ability to generate theory and conceptual models. Further research could usefully explore the extent to which these characteristics of pornography and the organisation of child sexual abuse are true across larger samples. The value of incidence and prevalence data is their power to validate individual accounts and to override the 'denial' which is typically the response of perpetrators and commonly the response of 'ordinary' people to disclosures of pornography and organised abuse.

References

Allen, E.E. (1981) 'Testimony before the Committee on the Judiciary United States Senate 1981' by the Chairman of Jefferson County Task Force on Child Prostitution and Pornography, quoted in Ennew (1986).

Baldwin, M. (1992) 'Split at the Root: Prostitution and Feminist Discourses of Law Reform', *Yale Journal of Law and Feminism*, 5, 47–120.

Baldwin, M.A. (1993) 'Strategies of Connection: Prostitution and Feminist Politics', *Michigan Journal of Gender and Law*, 1, 650–79.

Barry, K. (1979) *Female Sexual Slavery*, New York: Avon Books.

Barry, K. (1988) 'Evidence to Minneapolis Public Hearings 1983' in *Pornography and Sexual Violence: Evidence of the Links*, London: Everywoman, 29–30.

Barry, K. (1992) 'The Penn State Report – International Meeting of Experts on Sexual Exploitation, Violence and Prostitution' in *The Penn State Report*, State College, Penn: UNESCO and Coalition Against Trafficking in Women.

Baxter, M. (1990) 'Flesh and Blood: Does Pornography Lead to Sexual Violence?', *New Scientist*, 5 May, 37–41.

Briere, J. and Runtz, M. (1989) 'University Males' Sexual Interest in Children: Predicting Potential Indices of "Paedophilia" in a Nonforensic Sample', *Child Abuse and Neglect*, 13 (1), 65–75.

Burgess, A.W. (1984) *Child Pornography and Sex Rings*, Lexington: Lexington Books.

Burgess, A.W. (1985) 'Dangerous Sexual Offenders: Commentary', *Medical Aspects of Human Sexuality*, 19 (2), 119–23.

Burgess, A.W. and Hartman, C.R. (1987) 'Child Abuse Aspects of Child Pornography', *Psychiatric Annals*, 7 (4), 248–53.

Burgess, A.W., Groth, A.N. and McCausland, M.P. (1981) 'Child Sex Initiation Rings', *American Journal of Orthopsychiatry*, 51, 110–19.

Carter, D.L., Prentky, R.A., Knight, R., Vanderveer, P.L. and Boucher, R.J. (1987) 'Pornography in the Criminal and Developmental Histories of Sexual Offenders', *Journal of Interpersonal Violence*, 2 (2), 196–211.

Creighton, S.J. (1993) 'Organized Abuse: NSPCC Experience', *Child Abuse Review*, 2 (4), December.

Danica, E. (1988) *Don't: A Woman's Word*, Dublin: Attic Press.

Davies, N. (1994) 'Dirty Business', *Guardian*, 26 November, 12–17.

DeCamp, J.W. (1992) *The Franklin Cover-Up: Child Abuse, Satanism and Murder in Nebraska*, Lincoln, Nebraska: AWT.

Dworkin, A. (1981) *Pornography: Men Possessing Women*, London: Women's Press.

Ennew, J. (1986) *The Sexual Exploitation of Children*, Cambridge: Polity Press.

European Forum on Child Welfare (EFCW) (1993) *Child Pornography and Sexual Exploitation*, EFCW Position Statement, London: Barnados.

Fagan, J. and Wexler, S. (1988) 'Explanations of Sexual Assault Among Violent Delinquents', *Journal of Adolescent Research*, 3 (3–4), 363–85.

Finkelhor, D. (1979) *Sexually Victimised Children*, New York: Free Press.

Finkelhor, D. (1986) *A Sourcebook on Child Sexual Abuse*, Newbury Park, Calif: Sage.

Finkelhor, D. and Browne, A. (1985) 'The Traumatic Impact of Child Sexual Abuse: A Conceptualization', *American Journal of Orthopsychiatry*, 55 (4).

Gallagher, B., Hughes, B. and Parker, H. (1994) *Organised and Ritual Child Sexual Abuse, Research Report to the Department of Health*, Manchester: Department of Social Policy and Social Work, quoted in La Fontaine (1994), 7.

Gagnon, J. (1965) 'Female Child Victims of Sexual Offences', *Social Problems*, 13, 176–92.

Groner, L. (1992) *The Opinion of the Committee on Culture, Youth, Education and the Media*, Committee on Civil Liberties and Internal Affairs on Pornography, B3-0420/92, quoted in EFCW (1993).

Hall, R. (1985) *Ask Any Woman*, Bristol: Falling Wall Press.

Hames, M. (1993) 'Child Pornography: A Secret Web of Exploitation', *Child Abuse Review*, 2 (4), December, 276–81.

Hunt, P. and Baird, M. (1990) 'Children of Sex Rings', *Child Welfare*, LXIX (3), May–June.

Ireland, K. (1993) 'Sexual Exploitation of Children and International Travel and Tourism', *Child Abuse Review*, 2 (4), December.

Itzin, C. (1992a) ' "Entertainment for Men": What It Is and What It Means' in Itzin (1992b), 27–55.

Itzin, C. (ed.) (1992b) *Pornography: Women, Violence and Civil Liberties*, Oxford: Oxford University Press.

Itzin, C. (1996, in press) *Women's Experience of Pornography-related Harm*, Bradford: Violence, Abuse and Gender Relations Research Report No. 12.

Itzin, C. and Sweet, C. (1990) 'What You Feel About Pornography', *Cosmopolitan*, March, 8–12. Also in Itzin (1992b), 222–36.

Janus, S.S. and Heid Bracey, D.H. (1980) *Runaways – Pornography and Prostitution*, quoted in Ennew (1986).

Kelly, L. (1987) *Surviving Sexual Violence*, Cambridge: Polity Press.

Kelly, L. (1992) 'Pornography and Child Sexual Abuse' in Itzin (1992b), 113–24.

Kroon, L. (1980) 'Personal Experiences in the Pornography Industry', Women Against Violence in Pornography and Media: *Newspage*, IV (8).

La Fontaine, J.S. (1993) 'Defining Organised Sexual Abuse', *Child Abuse Review*, 2 (4), 223–31.

La Fontaine, J.S. (1994) *The Extent and Nature of Organised and Ritual Abuse: Research Findings*, London: HMSO.

Langevin, R. and Lang, R.A. (1985) 'Psychological Treatment of Paedophiles', *Behavioural Sciences and the Law*, 3 (4), 403–19.

Leidholt, D.A. (1993) 'Pimping and Pornography as Sexual Harassment: Amicae Brief in Support of Plaintiff-Respondent' in *Thoreson v. Penthouse International Ltd*, *Michigan Journal of Gender and Law*, V, 107.

Marshall, W.L. (1988) 'The Use of Sexually Explicit Stimuli by Rapists, Child Molesters, and Non Offenders', *The Journal of Sex Research*, 26 (2), 267–88.

Minneapolis Hearings (1988) 'The Complete Transcripts of Public Hearings on Ordinances to Add Pornography as Discrimination Against Women: Minneapolis City Council, Government Operations Committee, December 12 and 13, 1983'

in *Pornography and Sexual Violence: Evidence of the Links* (1988) London: Every-woman.

Mrazek, P., Lynch, M.A. and Bentovim, A. (1983) 'Sexual Abuse of Children in the United Kingdom', *Child Abuse and Neglect*, 7, 147–54.

Muntarbhorn, V. (1995) 'Violence Against Children: The Sale of Children, Child Prostitution, and Child Pornography' in *Children in Trouble*, Proceedings of the United Nations Expert Group Meeting on Children and Juveniles in Detention: Application of Human Rights Standards, Vienna: Austrian Federal Ministry for Youth and Family.

Russell, D. (1984) *Sexual Exploitation*, Beverly Hills: Sage.

Russell, D.E.H. (1983) 'The Incidence and Prevalence of Intrafamilial and Extrafamilial Sexual Abuse of Female Children', *Child Abuse and Neglect*, 7 (2), 133–46.

Russell, D.E.H. (1993) *Making Violence Sexy: Feminist Views on Pornography*, Milton Keynes: Open University Press.

Sariola, H. (1986) *Child Prostitution, Trafficking and Pornography*, Finland: Report for Defence for Children International and Central Union for Child Welfare.

Seghorn, T.K., Prentky, R.A. and Boucher, R.J. (1987) 'Childhood Sexual Abuse in the Lives of Sexually Aggressive Offenders', *Journal of the American Academy of Child and Adolescent Psychiatry*, 26, 262–7.

Seng, M.J. (1986) 'Sexual Behaviour Between Adults and Children: Some Issues of Definition', *Journal of Offender Counselling, Services and Rehabilitation*, 11 (1), 47–61.

Silbert, M. and Pines, A. (1984) 'Pornography and Sexual Abuse of Women', *Sex Roles*, 11/12, 857–68. Also in Russell (1993).

Tate, T. (1990) *Child Pornography*, London: Methuen.

Tate, T. (1992) 'The Child Pornography Industry: International Trade in Child Sexual Abuse' in Itzin (1992b), 203–17.

Waterhouse, L., Dobash, R. and Carnie, J. (1994) *Child Sexual Abusers*, Edinburgh: Scottish Office Central Research Unit.

Weisberg, D.K. (1985) *Children of the Night: A Study of Adolescent Prostitution*, quoted in Baldwin (1992), 101.

Wild, N.J. (1989) 'Prevalence of Child Sex Rings', *Paediatrics*, 83 (4), 553–8.

Wild, N.J. and Wynne, J.M. (1986) 'Child Sex Rings', *British Medical Journal*, 293, 19 July, 183–5.

Wyre, R. (1992) 'Pornography and Sexual Violence: Working with Sex Offenders' in Itzin (1992b), 236–48.

Wyre, R. (1993) *Working with Sex Abuse: Understanding Sex Offending*, Birmingham: Gracewell Clinic.

14 A police view of pornographic links

Mike Hames

The body of knowledge that has been and is being constructed about the phenomenon of organised abuse is, as has already been pointed out, of very recent origin. The links with pornography which often form an essential element of this type of abuse are also part of the picture of a subject that is both complex and, from a law-enforcement point of view, extremely problematic.

Child abuse recorded on film and photograph (commonly referred to as 'child pornography') has five main purposes for paedophiles:

- It serves as a permanent record of the child, frozen in time at the preferred age; it is mainly used for masturbatory purposes.
- It can be used as part of the seduction process, to sexualise the victim and to normalise the activity.
- It can be used to validate and to confirm their belief-systems. The production and exchange of material services their inherent need for acceptance by their own kind. It is often so crucial to their activity that they will keep it despite the knowledge that they may be in imminent danger of discovery; it has often been observed that the loss of a 'collection' is far more devastating to a paedophile than any prosecution.
- It can be used to blackmail the victims. The knowledge that pictorial evidence of abuse exists often strikes terror in the hearts of the victims, and the most casual threat of exposure is sufficient to silence almost any child or, indeed, an older victim.
- It can serve as an item of trade. The material has great value, in terms of the first three purposes listed above, to other paedophiles, and their fantasies are fuelled by the exchange of films, photographs and stories recounting abuse, whether they are fantasy or not.

The term 'child pornography' is widely regarded as inappropriate when

197

describing the material under discussion. It has a tendency to minimise the true nature of it, and the term 'kiddy porn' is even more unacceptable, carrying with it overtones of acceptability which are misleading in the extreme.

The way in which so-called 'adult pornography' is used in abuse cases is self-evident. It is used to sexualise children and to normalise the behaviour which the perpetrators intend to participate in with the victims. The notion that 'if it is seen on a television screen then it is acceptable' is often used.

The relative difficulty that paedophiles have in obtaining child pornography has been catered for by the 'adult' industry by using subjects who are over 16 years old but are underdeveloped and dressed in children's clothes, or images which are computer-enhanced to superimpose a child's body onto an indecent pose.

Knowledge about the way in which paedophiles use indecent and obscene images of both adults and children has been gained by the police over the last ten years as increasing amounts of evidence of child abuse on film and photograph has been seized by the Obscene Publications Branch at New Scotland Yard.

During the late 1970s and early 1980s, the branch, whilst dealing mainly with the distributors of adult hard-core pornography, noticed that an increasing amount of material that they seized portrayed the abuse of children.

At the same time that this was becoming apparent, the self-styled Paedophile Information Exchange organisation took a conscious decision to attach itself to the Campaign for Homosexual Equality and to lobby for acceptance as a minority group with particular sexual predilections. This gross miscalculation exposed, for almost the first time, the existence of an organised body of (mainly) men which had as its *raison d'être* the sexual abuse of children. The distorted thought-processes which lie at the heart of a paedophile's belief-system were therefore directly responsible for the initial exposure and subsequent investigation of their secret networks. The response of the police and media to the outrageous assertions of the lobbyists led to universal condemnation, several prosecutions and an attempt by the lobbyists to retreat from the public spotlight. Whilst these developments were widely regarded by the public – and indeed elements of the police – as having effectively dealt with the problem, the Obscene Publications Branch, alerted to the reality of the situation, began to commit more resources to the investigation of those who sought to obtain and use the material.

The inexorable advances in technology which have enabled paedophiles to create and copy images in quantity and in secret have produced an increasing amount of material. The Polaroid camera and, subsequently, the camcorder have enabled them to film without the need to have the resultant products developed, and the video recorder is used to reproduce them in high quality as well as quantity.

The most recent misuse of technology in this area involves computers. It is now possible to transmit indecent and obscene images of children all over the world via computer links at high speed with relatively little risk of discovery. It is also generated and copied onto floppy discs at almost no cost, and the distribution of this material is growing apace with the increasing popularity of the medium. Law-enforcement agencies across the world are alert to the problem and are working with the computer industry and responsible user groups to tackle the situation. Several successful prosecutions have been concluded in the UK. The Criminal Justice Act 1994 closed any potential loopholes in legislation by extending the Obscene Publications Act 1959 and the Protection of Children Act 1978 to include computer-generated images. The rapid growth of the medium, and in particular the use of the Internet, does, however, pose a significant problem in terms of the resources available to detect such misuse.

Prior to the enactment of Section 160 of the Criminal Justice Act 1988, which amended the Protection of Children Act 1978, it was an offence to *distribute* indecent photographs of children, but it was not illegal to *possess* them. The 1988 Act, which made it possible to seize such material and prosecute those who possessed it, was crucial to the fight against paedophiles and to the investigation of the network of abusers who use it.

The increase in knowledge of the identities and the behaviour patterns of paedophiles in the United Kingdom has been enhanced by extensive contacts with law-enforcement officials throughout the world via Interpol. In particular, the links with the authorities in the United States (FBI, US Customs Service and US Postal Service) were, and are, crucial in the fight to combat the problem. The US National Center for Missing and Exploited Children has also been at the forefront of the build-up of knowledge. An international approach to the detection of paedophile rings has also been driven by the discovery in many different countries of child pornography which features the same children.

In one particular case, copies of a video film of a young boy who was depicted being abused by several men were seized in England, Holland, France and Germany. He had been filmed as he was tied up, gagged, beaten and buggered. The seizures occurred over a period of about six months. In every case, the authorities made the identification of the victim a priority. Contact between the police agencies was extremely efficient, and the boy was soon identified. It transpired that he was English and had been taken to Switzerland by a Swiss national and abused there by an organised ring. The film was extremely marketable in the paedophile world and had therefore been much in demand.

Whilst the nature and application of the material can be analysed, it is difficult to establish the extent of its use and availability. The analogy with the misuse of drugs is a useful one. In the case of drugs, measures such as

seizures and the registration of addicts, together with surveys of target populations, give rough estimates. Self-reporting by paedophiles in prison or community treatment programmes, the testimony of victims and the volume of seizures help to gauge the level of criminal activity in the area of child pornography. However, this is a very inexact science.

The continuum of paedophile behaviour ranges from a sole person masturbating to innocent images of children – perhaps gathered from newspapers, magazines or trade catalogues – to predatory paedophile murderers who may act alone or in concert. Within this vast area of activity, fuelled and driven by fantasy, the images of children, either in abusive situations or not, play an important and essential part. Whether this involves tangible material or not, it is vital that this aspect of their psychological make-up is understood and accepted. Unless this is so, any attempt to investigate and combat the behaviour will be weakened.

Another crucial aspect is that indecent and obscene material must be seen for what it is, high-grade forensic evidence of crime. For an investigator, it is the next best evidence to actually witnessing the abuse as it takes place. It offers the opportunity to identify the victims as well as the perpetrator(s). If such evidence is available, it often leads to a plea of guilty and obviates the need for the victims, be they children or adults, to give evidence, with all of the trauma that this inevitably entails.

Therefore, it should be made almost a matter of routine to search any and every premises to which a suspect has access for tangible evidence of the offending behaviour. After all, if police officers deal with burglars, they look for stolen property and fingerprint evidence of their presence in the premises that have been broken into. If they deal with an allegation that a victim has been assaulted, they search for the weapon, which may be items of clothing such as boots. Why not, then, search for items that may have been used in an assault on a child, such as indecent films and photographs, written descriptions or tape-recorded conversations? Having searched and taken possession of video recordings and other evidence, they should *never* be returned until they have been viewed in their entirety. The entreaties of suspects and their representatives for the immediate return of the material must be resisted at all costs.

The discovery of pornographic material may also be a crucial means by which to break into and identify rings of offenders. The Obscene Publications Branch has many examples of success in this regard.

One case in particular serves to illustrate the geographical spread of rings, the way in which obscene material is used and the opportunity that such use offers the authorities to identify and prosecute the offenders.

It has to be said at the outset that, in this particular case, the original identification occurred by accident. A school nurse, Leonard Jeans, returned to London from Amsterdam by air and landed at Gatwick. However, his lug-

gage went to Heathrow and was opened by HM Customs. Child pornography was found, and Customs officers together with police from the Obscene Publications Branch searched his flat at Notting Hill. They discovered a large amount of videos, photographs of children and correspondence. Jeans was charged with indecent assault, taking indecent photographs of a child at the school where he worked and importation and possession of obscene material involving children.

Examination of the material led to the arrest of a former schoolmaster, John Shannon from Warwickshire, who, at the time, was in Portugal, touring in a camper van, making indecent videos of children. He was charged with aiding and abetting the buggery of a boy with special needs in England by another man, which activity he had recorded on video.

Alan Bowler, the man who assaulted the boy, lived in Birmingham and was arrested, charged with the offences, and received eight years' imprisonment. Bowler had introduced the boy and his brother to another man, Thomas Brooks, who lived in Walsall. Brooks was convicted of indecent acts and received three years' imprisonment.

Both Jeans and Shannon had contacts in Holland, and a photographer, Fred Vivjer, had visited Jeans and photographed Jeans indecently assaulting a boy. The trail in Holland led to the arrest of Vivjer and two other men there. One of them was an ex-schoolteacher and the other a youth worker.

Bowler was also involved with a network of six other men in Stoke-on-Trent who were dealt with for offences of indecency against young boys aged between 6 and 14. A Belgian youth leader was also prosecuted in his own country.

The crucial and central element in this investigation was the careful and systematic analysis of the forensic evidence – photographic, filmed and written accounts of abuse, together with correspondence and diaries which served to link the perpetrators.

The way in which the Shannon ring was identified is typical of the process by which organised abuse comes to light. It is rare that the whole picture is apparent from the outset; indeed, it may well be that the true extent of the abusive network is never established. It is good practice to employ the services of a crime analyst at an early stage in any inquiry in which multiple abusers or victims are discovered, so that working models are constructed which can be easily adapted as the case progresses. This is a very valuable tool which may point up connections that are not otherwise apparent. It also illustrates ways in which the case itself may be structured in terms of inquiry and preparation for court. Figure 14.1 shows the work of one such crime analyst in the Shannon ring case.

An obvious and major difficulty which has arisen with the seizure of increasing amounts of film and photographic material is the identification of victims. Sometimes the tracing of the children is fairly straightforward and

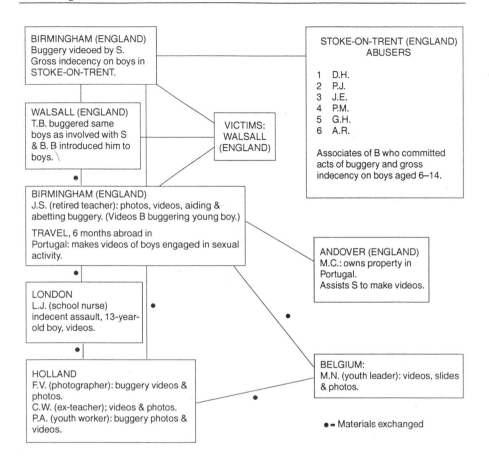

BIRMINGHAM (ENGLAND)
Buggery videoed by S.
Gross indecency on boys in
STOKE-ON-TRENT.

STOKE-ON-TRENT (ENGLAND)
ABUSERS

1   D.H.
2   P.J.
3   J.E.
4   P.M.
5   G.H.
6   A.R.

Associates of B who committed
acts of buggery and gross
indecency on boys aged 6–14.

WALSALL (ENGLAND)
T.B. buggered same
boys as involved with S.
& B. B introduced him to
boys.

VICTIMS:
WALSALL
(ENGLAND)

BIRMINGHAM (ENGLAND)
J.S. (retired teacher): photos, videos, aiding &
abetting buggery. (Videos B buggering young boy.)

TRAVEL, 6 months abroad in
Portugal: makes videos of boys engaged in sexual
activity.

ANDOVER (ENGLAND)
M.C.: owns property in
Portugal.
Assists S to make videos.

LONDON
L.J. (school nurse)
indecent assault, 13-year-
old boy, videos.

BELGIUM:
M.N. (youth leader): videos, slides
& photos.

HOLLAND
F.V. (photographer): buggery videos &
photos.
C.W. (ex-teacher); videos & photos.
P.A. (youth worker): buggery photos &
videos.

● = Materials exchanged

Figure 14.1   The abuse trail

takes place quickly. In many other cases, it is not so easy. In these circumstances, the authorities know – indeed, can see – that the children are being
abused. Sometimes the activities – when they involve the apparent use of
drugs, restraint and severe abuse – appear almost life-threatening. Decisions
have to be made about whether and how to circulate photographs of the victims. If children disappear from home, their pictures are published widely,
for obvious reasons. However, the decision to publish pictures of children
who have been abused is not straightforward. The identification of child victims is, quite rightly, prohibited when prosecutions take place. One of the
fears that victims often have is that the material in which they are portrayed
will be shown to others, and that they will be portrayed as willing partners in
the abuse. If the vast army of victims were to be given the impression that
they were indeed to be exposed to public gaze, even though it was to be car-

ried out with the best of intentions, one can imagine the agony that would be caused. The moral dilemma is obvious. Against this background, it is extremely rare for authority to be given to publicise the photographs. Thus there are literally thousands of images of children in abusive situations stored away in police files, and no further action is possible until and unless there is a policy change to allow publicity. The frustration of investigating officers is immense.

There is a need to store the photographs of the victims on computer, both nationally and internationally, so that they can be compared. This enables agencies to check whether the victims had been identified and prevents duplication of effort. The centralisation of the information may also make it possible to identify more links and break into the networks in which many of the victims have been trapped and abused.

There is much work to be done by the police in the area of detection of child pornography and the proactive targeting of paedophiles. If it comes to the notice of the authorities that a gang of men are planning to rob a bank, they are put under surveillance and arrested at some point in their criminal enterprise. Paedophiles, who by their offending behaviour patterns are classified as serial offenders, are very rarely targeted. Studies have consistently shown that individual paedophiles offend against many children and commit, literally, thousands of serious sex offences in lifetime careers of abusive behaviour. A national strategy is long overdue to address this issue.

15 Ritual abuse: Research findings

Jean La Fontaine

The problem

In the early 1980s, the first allegations that children were being abused by cults – variously described as 'witchcraft', 'black magic' or 'devil-worship' – were made in the United States. The abuse was said to be part of rituals that also included perverted sexual activity, human sacrifice, forced abortion and cannibalism. Those who were accused mostly owned or worked in nursery schools, and parents were to the fore in pressing charges against them. Later in the decade, similar allegations began to be made in Britain, and by 1990 there were enough of them to lend substance to the allegation that a new and dreadful threat to children was appearing. It was argued by some campaigners (Core and Harrison, 1991; Davies, 1991, p.8) that a national or international organisation was behind the cults. However, in Britain it was parents who were accused, and until 1993 there was no case of ritual abuse involving a nursery school. Neither in the United States nor in Britain was there material corroboration of these allegations, which provoked a bitter public controversy between those who believed that the evil rituals were taking place and those who were sceptical about the stories.

Definitions

These cases were usually called cases of 'satanic abuse', given that they involved allegations of devil-worship, or if not devil-worship, the most extreme evil. They might also be called 'ritual abuse', and there was some confusion with the psychological notion of rituals as compulsive, repetitive behaviour accompanying sexual activity. A lack of clarity about what terms meant allowed a wide range of people to accept the allegations as accurate, and in so doing give tacit support to the most extreme versions. In this chap-

205

ter, the term 'satanic abuse' is used to refer to allegations of sexual abuse that took place in rites directed to a religious objective and including human sacrifice, cannibalism, sadism and other extremes of sexual and other behaviour. 'Ritual abuse' refers to the sexual abuse of children in rituals without the other acts, where the ritual was secondary to the sexual abuse which was the main objective of the perpetrator(s). My usage follows the meaning attributed to the word by the majority of people involved in my research and excludes the less commonly-used psychological one.

The scale of the problem

Eighty-four cases were identified for the research funded by the Department of Health. Those reported to a postal survey[1] all occurred between 1988 and 1991; others added by other methods mostly fell between those dates, but there were a few cases reported earlier, predominantly in 1987 (La Fontaine, 1994, p.7). The earliest case discovered was reported in 1982, but this was a case of ritual (according to the definition above) rather than satanic abuse. The cases were fairly evenly distributed, with a peak in 1989 and 1990, but with such small numbers, any generalisation must be tentative. However, the distribution of cases over time does not suggest that their numbers were increasing. In any of these years, moreover, the proportion of such cases in the total number of cases of child protection was minuscule.

The location of allegations

The allegations were most numerous in the Midlands. There was a large concentration of cases around Nottingham, where there had been a case in 1988 that attracted great attention from the media. Further clusters could be seen in the Northwest and the Southeast. Isolated cases occurred in other areas during the period. It is not possible to offer a cast-iron explanation for the clustering, but there is some evidence that it relates to the enthusiasm of child protection workers for seeking out such cases. In one area, most of the cases reported to the police came from teams that were committed to finding evidence of satanic abuse.

Material evidence and corroboration

There is no material evidence (for example satanic paraphernalia or human remains) to corroborate the allegation that organised cults have abused children in their rituals, or that they practised human sacrifice or cannibalism. A large survey in the United States, carried out for the National Center on Child Abuse and Neglect, examined 12,264 'accusations of group cult sexual abuse based on satanic ritual' and found no evidence for it (Goleman, 1994).

There has been no corroboration of similar allegations in Holland, Sweden, Australia and New Zealand either.

There has been ample material evidence corroborating allegations of children's sexual abuse conducted in the context of rituals invented to justify the abuse to the victims and ensure both their compliance and their silence. Robes, altars and other paraphernalia mentioned in the victims' disclosures were found in three cases of ritual abuse. The accounts of the victims in these cases corroborated each other and were confirmed by the admissions of adult participants. In none of the three were the other elements of satanic abuse present, and the cases differed from the others in a variety of ways.

Characteristics of ritual abuse

The three substantiated cases each involved a central figure, a man whose sexual predilection for children appeared to be the motivation for constructing the ritual. However, two of the men appeared to have come to believe they had some supernatural or mystical powers. Even so, all of the three had abused children without ritual, when the opportunity had presented itself, so that it is possible to conclude that they were motivated by their sexual desires rather than any ritualistic aims. One of the perpetrators had earlier convictions for sexual assault. In all three cases, the stories of mystical powers were a means of involving children in activities that led to the abuse.

None of the perpetrators of ritual abuse belonged to an organised cult, although in two cases, other adults were involved: two women in one case and a man in another. In one case, the perpetrator acted alone, except on one occasion when he invited another paedophile to participate. The abusers had constructed the ritual they used themselves, and it was completely different in each case. One involved a belief in a mission given him by a Catholic saint to seek out evil and included ideas of reincarnation from the distant past; another concerned persuading young children that, if they followed his instructions, they would be witches and would achieve anything they wanted, including being able to fly. The third ended by calling himself Lucifer, one of the names attributed to the devil by some people, but his rituals were not those of any known satanist group, and they varied over time. A man whom he attempted to involve said his knowledge of the occult seemed superficial. Some of the children, mainly his young nieces, were abused with no formal ritual, merely to 'receive the power' he claimed to have in his body.

It is significant that in these three cases, the information regarding the ritual was disclosed by the children at once, in spite of the fact that in one case the children were very frightened that what they had been threatened with if they told would indeed happen. One child complained to an educational

social worker about being involved in the rituals without admitting that the rituals included her having sexual intercourse with the 'priest'. It was not until she was made pregnant by him, about a year later, that the sexual abuse was discovered. By contrast, campaigners who have spread beliefs about satanic abuse have stressed that it takes time for the children to feel 'safe' enough to tell of the rituals. It is characteristic of the cases involving allegations of satanic abuse that the children have either been interviewed a very large number of times or have been in care for some months before the allegations were made. There is thus an association between a delay in making the allegations and the nature of the allegations.

Almost all the children in the three ritual abuse cases were girls, but it seems likely, with such a small number of cases, that it is coincidence and not significant. The brother of one victim was also abused, but outside the rituals and without the knowledge of the other adult participant. Most of the children were not related to the perpetrator, although one abused his nieces as well as other children,[2] and one man had become like a stepfather to the girl he first abused, whom he used to recruit the others. In this last case, although the perpetrator of the abuse was very close to the mother of the original children and referred to them in his police interview as his children, he did not live with them. There are too few cases to conclude that the ritual stratagem is only used where the abuse goes on outside a household. However, it seems likely that parental or quasi-parental authority is strong enough not to need the additional power ritual affords.

On the available evidence, ritual abuse is not associated with victims of any particular age, although they were old enough to understand the ideas being offered them. In one case, the ideas associated with the abuse were built up over time to satisfy the children's questions. The children in the three cases varied in age from 6 to 17; in one of them, it was clear that the perpetrator liked little girls, and he began to lose interest in the eldest child as she approached puberty. In another, by contrast, the sexual abuse started when the girl was 9, full intercourse began at 11 and continued until she was 17 and pregnant. In the third case, the victims were of a variety of ages, from 8 to 16. A 1-year-old had been involved by his father in a ritual, although he had not been sexually abused at the time of the arrest.

Satanic abuse

Details of the cases involving allegations of satanic abuse are available elsewhere (La Fontaine, 1994), so it is sufficient to summarise their characteristics. These are rather different from the ritual abuse cases. The cases involve more people than the ritual abuse cases, but in nearly half of them there are perpetrators who are related to the victims. In nearly two-thirds of cases,

neighbours and friends of the children's parents are also among the perpe-trators. Unlike the extra-domestic paedophile networks, these cases involve no perpetrators described as unknown to the parents. In only ten survey cases of satanic abuse were perpetrators described as 'strangers'.

The numbers of adults involved were smaller than would be suggested by the allegations that a cult organisation was involved; in 12 cases, only one per-son was accused of the abuse. Over half the cases involved between two and nine perpetrators, often including couples, both of whom were accused. Only one in five of the cases involved more than ten perpetrators. Where large num-bers of adults were alleged to have participated in satanic rituals in which the children were abused, many of them were shadowy figures, unidentified by name or gender. This is not characteristic of other types of organised abuse such as paedophile networks, where very large numbers of both abusers and abused were precisely identified in the survey questionnaires.

A high proportion of women were accused in cases where satanic abuse was alleged; in over two-thirds of the survey cases (69 per cent), women were said to be involved as perpetrators. Both boys and girls were victims, and half the cases involved men and women accused of sexually abusing boys and girls. In this, as in other characteristics, the cases of alleged satanic abuse resemble the other large cases of family-based abuse where no satanic allegations have been made (La Fontaine, 1994, p.11).

The social context of allegations of satanic abuse

It is known that reports of child sexual abuse are not evenly distributed across the socio-economic classes (La Fontaine, 1990). The cases where alle-gations of satanic abuse are made show even more class bias. The largest sin-gle category of persons in the cases studied in detail involved the very poor; many were unemployed, often for long periods, with those who did have work earning little in unskilled jobs and few women contributing to the fam-ily income. Run-down urban estates were the homes of most of them, and the poverty of the children's families was often referred to. Social Services concerns stretching back many years were recorded in the files. Yet there was considerable resistance among some child protection workers to explaining the families' behaviour as the result of deprivation; several inter-views emphasised that other families who were just as deprived managed to care for their children normally. Often there was hostility to the families in the neighbourhood, and in some cases it would not be too strong to call these families 'outcasts'.

Few of the households involved in these cases showed a comfortable or middle-class lifestyle. Those that did involved four cases in which an allega-tion of satanic abuse had been made by a woman against her husband. By contrast, the foster-parents of children taken into care were mostly quite

comfortably off and led a conventional life. Some of them could afford holidays abroad, in one case to America, and they celebrated festivals with all the trimmings. The frequent references in the files to having to teach the children the necessity for cleanliness and showing them how to eat properly sitting at table are indications of the very different kinds of domestic life led previously by the children compared with that led with their foster-parents.

When they were taken into care, the children were often found to be developmentally delayed or even handicapped. In half the cases, there was good evidence that the children, or some of them, had been sexually abused, and there were strong suspicions of sexual abuse even where evidence was lacking. Their appearance, dirty and unwashed, often led to their being shunned by other children or bullied at school. The children showed many symptoms of their ill-treatment in their behaviour, and foster-mothers were often at their wits' end to know how to deal with them. They not only wet the bed but smeared faeces on the walls, they broke things and attacked the family pet or other foster-children. Their behaviour was often extremely sexualised and their speech not easily understood. They slept badly and displayed a variety of terrors, not merely in nightmares but on unexpected occasions in daily life. Given that some of the foster-parents were not experienced and most found the children's behaviour extremely distressing, it is not surprising that they found it difficult to explain the origin of the state the children were in. Their mistake, and that of others who found the idea of satanic abuse the answer to their questions about the children, was to look for a single cause rather than to recognise the cumulative effect of multiple forms of deprivation and abuse.

The source of the allegations

The first accounts of satanic abuse, as distinct from ritual abuse, came from adult women who claimed to have been sexually abused in rituals as children. Some of them said they were forced into abusing children themselves or confessed their continuing membership of satanic cults. The first such account to be published came out in 1980; *Michelle Remembers* was written by the Canadian Michelle Smith and her therapist Lawrence Pazder (Smith and Pazder, 1980), whom she later married. The most influential in Britain has been Audrey Harper's *Dance with the Devil*, written with Harry Pugh (Harper and Pugh, 1990). These accounts are more detailed and complete descriptions than any of those attributed to young children, but they have not resulted in the discovery or conviction of any satanic abusers. However, they have been very influential in persuading therapists, police officers and social workers to accept the reality of satanic cults and their rituals. This conviction has affected how adults have listened to the children in these cases.

The children's evidence

The lack of corroborative evidence in the cases involving children raises the question of what was the basis for the original allegations. In several of the more highly-publicised cases, it has been claimed that it was the children who had disclosed the satanic abuse.

Much attention in child protection work has been focused on interviewing children. However, in these cases, the children's evidence was actually collected in a variety of ways, of which formal interviews formed only a part. Informal conversations with foster-parents, residential care workers, social workers and others might provide the bulk of what is learned from the children. In nearly half of the 84 cases in my study, the first allegation of ritual abuse was said to have been made by the victim to a foster-parent, parent or other relative, or a teacher. Foster-parents form the largest single category of people who were reported as the first to have heard an allegation of ritual abuse. This is not unusual, but it does indicate that the evidence must be carefully assessed.

Evidence is not only collected informally, but much of what is labelled 'children's evidence' actually represents the concepts, views, ideas and possibly fantasies of the adults, who while encouraging children to speak, actually alter what they say. This is not necessarily an intent to deceive, although in a few cases this may have happened; it is merely that adults bring their own perceptions and motivations to their contacts with abused children. These determine how the children's words are heard, recorded and communicated to others. What are alleged to be 'the children's stories' are, in the majority of cases, adult constructions.

What 'the children' say depends on their ages. The cases studied involve children of a wide range of ages from toddlers to teenagers. In a few cases, an earlier conviction testified to older children having been sexually abused, but as with the younger ones, medical or other evidence for prior sexual abuse may not have been available. The teenagers in these cases were mostly sexually active, so that medical evidence of any contemporary sexual abuse was very unlikely. In two survey cases, however, a medical examination indicated the girls were virgins, despite their descriptions of abuse and, in one case, of gang rape. Teenagers, like adult 'survivors' of satanic abuse, gave full accounts of what they say they have suffered. Where younger children are concerned, it was difficult to interpret an odd phrase or some strange behaviour that was reported as evidence of satanic abuse. In some of the cases, more than one child, either siblings or friends, made allegations. Despite allegations that children all over England were saying the same thing, their stories, even in the same case, varied. Comparison of the accounts given by two sisters of what was said to be the same ritual occasion showed big discrepancies in the 'facts'. In another case, involving two ado-

lescent girls who were friends, one described the other's abortion as taking place in a ritual, a detail that seemed to surprise the girl to whom it was alleged to have happened. Supporting testimony for the pair from other teenagers agreed only on the fact that they had been smoking marijuana in the accused's house, and two others from the same peer group denied that anything else had occurred.

All in all, the teenagers' allegations of satanic abuse in these cases were not credible as descriptions of actual events (see also Weir, forthcoming). Significantly, none of them referred to beliefs associated with the rituals or described the organisation of the satanic cult. While many of these older children were clearly very emotionally disturbed, others appeared to be merely responding to the interests of the adults they were talking to. When asked why she had told her invented story of satanic abuse, Beatrice, a 14-year-old girl, made it clear that she thought she had said what was expected: 'You lot are into those things and the police and social workers wanted to hear them so I thought I had to say something and I went from there.' Others seemed to have had other motives, but the emotional damage that they showed could also have been the effect of earlier sexual abuse.

The evidence provided by disturbed small children may consist of odd words and sentences, fragments which mean little or nothing at face value. If these remarks are to be taken as evidence, rather than as indications of a child's disturbed state, they must be interpreted. In many cases, the interpretation seems to reflect adult preconceptions. The journalist Tim Tate claimed that a senior social worker described a 4-year-old chanting 'word perfect – the opening words of an historic satanic chant – in Latin' (Tate, 1992, p.28). In fact, this referred to sounds written by his foster-mother as 'Dom-i-die', and the context suggested another quite harmless interpretation of it as an attempt to describe singing scales. In another case, a consultant cited the fact that children had described going to the woods at night as a reason for considering that they had suffered satanic abuse. Traced to its source, this 'evidence' referred to a child's talking of being abused 'in the shadow'. Asked about that, she said that they were 'in the trees', explaining that she meant Christmas trees. In a final example, a child was asked to recount her dream, which the interviewer then took as an account of what had happened to her; when prodded to continue, she said: 'Then I woke up.' This ending was ignored.

It has been pointed out (Vizard, 1987) that children do not always say anything coherent, even when interviewed very skilfully, and most professionals accept that they may not always be able to discover what happened to a child. But in these cases, foster-parents or social workers were unable to accept that and continued to try and get information from them. Leading questions reflected the questioners' anxieties about the possibility of satanic abuse but also provided the children with clues as to what was wanted from

them. Play and drawings were used to provide additional clues for the adults, but both of these methods have inherent dangers of misinterpretation when used by untrained people (Cox, 1992). Research has also shown that repeated interviews or repeating questions can induce children to give quite erroneous information (Ceci and Bruck, 1993; Moston, 1987). It compounded the problems in these cases. Although much of the questioning was of an informal sort, it persisted for weeks and even months, thus increasing the likelihood that what the children said would be of little value as information.

Processing the information

As well as the inherent likelihood that what the children said might simply reflect what adults wanted to hear, or that their odd remarks might be interpreted to support adult concerns, the procedures of child protection may result in faulty recording and transmission of children's stories. Inaccurate transcription of video-taped interviews, omissions and inaccurate summaries can all destroy the sense of what children originally said. When, in addition, the children are disturbed and anxious, or difficult to understand because they are developmentally delayed or intellectually disadvantaged, then what adults present as 'what the children say' may be a purely adult concoction.

Conclusions

Adults who intend to satisfy their sexual wishes by abusing children but do not simply use their superior physical strength as a means of doing so must devise ways to induce the children to comply and then preserve silence about what happened. Men who live with their intended victims may use their paternal or quasi-paternal authority and powers to coerce them, but outsiders must use ingenuity to recruit their victims and then keep control over them so that they do not disclose. Children may be attracted by a claim to have magical powers, which may also be used to threaten and intimidate.

Sexual abuse may take many forms and involve several adults; references to dressing up, oral and anal sex and the perverse use of faeces or urine are not indications of a satanic ritual but known accompaniments of sex among some adults, that may also be used in the sexual abuse of children. Children's allegations should continue to be taken seriously, however bizarre the acts they refer to, or the allegations of magical powers they include, but care should be taken to ensure that what they are deemed to have said is what they actually *did* say. It is most important of all that we recognise how adult concerns may overwhelm children's voices, even when the general aim is child protection.

Notes

1   A postal survey of police forces, Social Service Departments and NSPCC teams in England and Wales was carried out by myself jointly with a team in the Social Policy and Social Work Department, Manchester University (see Chapter 16 in this volume). The survey covered England and Wales.
2   These unfortunate children had already been subjected to incest by their father, but (contrary to Tate 1994, p.191) he did not participate in the ritual abuse organised by his brother-in-law.

References

Ceci, S. and Bruck, M. (1993) 'Child witnesses; translating research into policy', *Society for Research in Child Development, Social Policy Report*, 20 (10).

Core, D. and Harrison, F. (1991) *Chasing Satan*, London: Quartet Books.

Cox, M. (1992) *Children's Drawings*, London: Penguin.

Davies, M. (1991) *The Rehabilitation of Satanic Cult Members*, Rhyl: Beacon Foundation.

Goleman, D. (1994) 'Proof Lacking for Ritual Abuse by Satanists', *New York Times*, 31 October.

Harper, A. and Pugh, H. (1990) *Dance with the Devil*, Eastbourne: Kingsway Publications.

La Fontaine, J.S. (1990) *Child Sexual Abuse*, Oxford and Cambridge: Polity Press.

La Fontaine, J.S. (1994) *The Extent and Nature of Organised and Ritual Abuse: Research Findings*, London: HMSO.

Moston, S. (1987) 'The suggestibility of children in eyewitness studies', *First Language*, 7, 67–78.

Smith, M. and Pazder, L. (1980) *Michelle Remembers*, New York: Simon & Schuster.

Spencer, J.R. and Flin, R. (1990) (2nd edn 1993) *The Evidence of Children*, London: Blackstone.

Tate, T. (1992) *Children for the Devil*, London: Methuen.

Tate, T. (1994) 'Press, politics and paedophilia: A practitioner's guide to the media' in V. Sinason (ed.) *Treating Survivors of Satanist Abuse*, London: Routledge.

Vizard, E. (1987) 'Interviewing young sexually abused children', *Family Law*, 28–33.

Weir, K. (forthcoming) 'Allegations of children's involvement in ritual sexual abuse: Clinical experience of 20 cases', *Child Abuse and Neglect*.

16 The nature and extent of known cases of organised child sexual abuse in England and Wales*

Bernard Gallagher, Beverley Hughes and Howard Parker

Introduction

Most of the existing knowledge regarding organised abuse has been obtained from reports in the public and professional media, rather than through more systematic studies of child sexual abuse. Even the small number of research surveys completed have had rather limited scope. As a result, there is little reliable or systematic data on either the nature or the extent of this problem (Kelly and Scott, 1993). Media reports of investigations into organised abuse in locations as diverse as Canterbury (Warren and Fowler, 1990), Manchester (Myers, 1990), Ayrshire (Clayton, 1992), Southwark (Cohen, 1993) and Dyfed (Murray, 1993) suggested that these cases could occur in any region and any type of area, in families (Waterhouse, Kingman and Cuffe, 1990), in residential homes (Millbrooke Grange – *Community Care*, 1993; Leicestershire – Katz, 1991) and daycare. Until now, much of the more empirically-based data on the nature of organised abuse has been obtained from studies on other types of child sexual abuse cases (Burgess and Clark, 1984; Wild, 1989; Finkelhor, Williams and Burns, 1988).

Specific studies of organised abuse have been primarily concerned with establishing the extent of known cases. In 1990, the BBC social affairs programme *Public Eye* conducted a survey amongst all 52 police forces in the United Kingdom, asking them to report on the number of 'network abuse' cases they had investigated in the previous three years (Bashir, 1990). A later survey by the NSPCC found that 19 cases of organised abuse (10 network, 6 ritual and 3 child pornography) had been referred to the agency's 71 projects

* This research was funded by the Economic and Social Research Council, under grant number R 000233372, and the Department of Health. The authors would like to thank all those who have contributed to this work.

in England, Wales and Northern Ireland between December 1989 and April 1991 (Creighton, 1993). Whilst these surveys were ground-breaking, their findings were of limited value. For example, each survey targeted only one of the three agencies with statutory child protection powers, rendering it likely that some known cases would have been missed. In the *Public Eye* survey, 13 police forces (25 per cent) did not reply. Furthermore, the survey used a rather narrow definition of 'network abuse': 'where abuse involves organised paedophiles'.

Given the challenge posed by organised abuse, there was clearly a need to develop a knowledge of these cases that would enhance understanding and enable agencies to respond to them more effectively. The research reported here aimed to assess the nature and extent of organised abuse, and its implications for practice. As well as studying a broad range of organised abuse cases, the research has investigated cases of child sexual abuse where there had been allegations of ritual abuse, and cases which might be said to involve 'organised abusers': *lone* perpetrators who abused in an institution for children (institutional abuse), in a number of different situations, often several families (serial abuse) or amongst a group of children who were known to one another (peer group abuse). The first stage of the research consisted of a national postal questionnaire survey conducted jointly with another research project directed by Professor Jean La Fontaine of the London School of Economics (La Fontaine, 1994). In the second stage of their work, the authors searched child protection records and interviewed police officers and social workers in eight local authority areas. This chapter discusses organised abuse on the basis of findings from the national survey and the record searches. It seeks to establish some of the basic elements of organised abuse, particularly its extent, the characteristics and diversity of cases, and the ways in which these cases are marked out from other cases of child sexual abuse.

National postal questionnaire survey

Questionnaires were sent to every police force (N=43), Social Services Department (N=116) and NSPCC team (N=66) in England and Wales in the first half of 1992. Respondents were asked to complete one questionnaire for each case of organised, ritual or institutional abuse that was reported between January 1988 and December 1991. The postal survey incorporated the following working terms and definitions:

- *Organised abuse* – a case in which there has been more than a single abuser and the adults concerned appear to have acted in concert to abuse the children sexually;

- *Ritual abuse* – a case in which there have been allegations of ritual associated with the abuse, whether or not this was a case of organised abuse and regardless of whether the suspicions were taken any further or mentioned in legal proceedings;
- *Institutional abuse* – a case in which an adult has used the institutional framework of an organisation for children to recruit children for sexual abuse;
- *Case* – the cluster of adults and children connected in an incident, or series of incidents, of the sexual abuse of children.

The questionnaire covered three main areas: *agency intervention, victim and perpetrator characteristics*, and *nature of the abuse*. Sexual abuse was not defined, but cases not involving physical contact, such as child pornography, were excluded for the purposes of the survey. Respondents were asked to assign the case to one of the five following descriptive categories: abuse by a large family (several generations), paedophile ring, commercial prostitution, a cult, or abuse in a residential institution. Alternatively, they could provide their own description of the case. Forty-four per cent of respondents replied either that none of the categories were appropriate or that they did not know how to classify the case.

Once the questionnaire data had been analysed, a new scheme for categorising cases was developed. This was based upon a combination of any classification and features given by respondents, other descriptive information that they might have provided and the researcher's own interpretation of the case. The resultant classification is shown in Table 16.1.

For the purposes of this analysis, 'ritual' was taken to refer to situations in which the abuse was accompanied by ceremonies or trappings of the occult, witchcraft or Satanism. The ritual was either part of a belief-system or behaviour designed to facilitate the abuse. Some respondents had used the term 'ritual' in a psychological sense to denote repetitive behaviour on the part of perpetrators. Other respondents equated 'ritual' with sadistic practices. These cases were not classified as ritual abuse. The term 'paedophile ring' is used to refer to groups of adults, either predominantly or exclusively male, who were at least loosely associated with one another. The remaining categories comprised a much smaller proportion of cases but showed that organised abuse could occur in many different settings and guises.

The distribution of the 211 cases over the four years covered by the survey showed no specific trend over time. Given the number of children dealt with under child protection procedures, it would appear that organised abuse accounts for only a very small proportion of work in this area: in the year ending 31 March 1991, the names of 3,900 children in England were placed on Child Protection Registers (CPRs) under the category of 'sexual abuse' (DoH, 1992); the total number of children registered that year was 28,300.

Table 16.1   Revised classification of cases reported to the national survey

Classification	N	%
Ritual[1]	62	29
Paedophile ring	43	20
Non-residential institution[1]	29	14
Family-based	28	13
Residential institution[1]	16	8
Other	28	13
More than one category/category not clear	5	2
Total	211	99[2]

Notes:

1   Some of these cases involved only one perpetrator
2   Not equal to 100 because of rounding

Having said this, it was believed that many agencies had reported to the survey only a small proportion of cases that were known to them, and had tended to report high-profile cases, such as those involving allegations of ritual abuse or large numbers of perpetrators and children. Evidence for this came from three sources: a comparison of agency reporting and agency involvement in cases of organised abuse; a search of child protection records in one Social Services Department, and reports to the research team from respondents on how the questionnaire had been completed (Gallagher, Hughes and Parker, 1994). A similar phenomenon was noted by Finkelhor, Williams and Burns (1988) in their survey of abuse in daycare centres.

The national survey revealed that organised abuse occurred throughout Britain. It described the nature of a relatively large number of the cases and suggested ways in which these cases were distinct from other cases of child sexual abuse, such as the higher representation of women amongst perpetrators and boys amongst victims (La Fontaine, 1994). However, there are doubts over the reliability of the findings from the national survey, particularly concerning the overall extent and the distribution of different categories of organised abuse.

Search of police and Social Services records

The second stage of the research – a search of police and Social Services records – was intended to provide more comprehensive and detailed information on cases of organised abuse and the response of agencies to them. This work also allowed the researchers to validate the findings of the national survey, and if need be, provide more reliable data on the nature and extent of known cases.

The records held by police child protection teams and Social Services child protection co-ordinators were searched in eight local authority areas. As the NSPCC has a policy of informing police or Social Services of all referrals it receives, it was not deemed appropriate, given the resources of the study, to search their records. The eight areas were selected to be broadly representative of England and Wales in terms of regions, types of local authority (metropolitan, shire county, London and Welsh) and numbers of cases reported to the survey. The results of this exercise are shown in Table 16.2.

Although child protection records held by the two key agencies were not as detailed or comprehensive as police crime files or Social Services case files, they were considered to be an efficient and effective means of gathering information on known cases of organised abuse. Furthermore, if clarification or additional information was required on individual cases, then these files, or indeed the relevant agency worker, were consulted. The fieldwork was

Table 16.2   Demographic and socio-economic variables: eight local authority areas (combined) compared to England and Wales

Variable	8 areas (%)	England & Wales (%)
Under-18-year-olds in population	22.6	22.6
Male unemployment	9.8	9.7
Local authority housing	22.8	19.8
Ethnically white population	94.2	94.1
Single-parent households	4.0	3.7

Source: OPCS (1992)

carried out between April 1992 and October 1993. Approximately 20,000 files were read on 32 sites in the eight local authority areas spread throughout England and Wales. Needless to say the work was extremely demanding, both physically and emotionally.

Initially, a file was searched to establish whether or not it referred to an incident of child sexual abuse that was reported in the period covered by the national survey, namely 1988–91. If it did, then it was read in more detail to determine whether there was any evidence that the abuse occurred in an organised (as defined by the survey) context. For a case to be accepted as 'organised', there had to be at least one piece of unambiguous evidence for both child sexual abuse and an organised context. Such evidence included disclosures by victims, admissions by perpetrators, medical/physical symptoms, photographic or audio recordings of the abuse and witness statements.

Seventy-four cases of organised abuse were identified during the course of the fieldwork. As a result of supplementary information provided to us by agencies after the end of the fieldwork, it was possible to classify a further four cases as organised abuse. The distribution of these 78 cases between the eight areas is shown in Table 16.3. In every one of the eight areas, the searches identified more cases than the national survey. In Area 3, for example, there was an eightfold disparity between survey and search figures. In Area 6, there was a fivefold difference. Similar comparisons could not be made in five of the areas, as they did not record any cases on the survey. However, if figures for the eight areas are combined, the national survey is shown to have underestimated the extent of organised (including ritual) abuse by a factor of more than nine.

The eight areas accounted for approximately 7 per cent of the population of England and Wales (OPCS, 1992). Therefore, if the per capita rate of known cases of organised abuse in the eight areas combined was the same as that in the whole of England and Wales, then there would have been 1,111 cases of organised abuse in England and Wales between 1988 and 1991, or a mean incidence of 278 cases per annum.

Cases of organised abuse can be classified according to a number of dimensions, such as the number, gender and sexual orientation of the perpetrators, their *modus operandi* and the number of children involved. In terms of understanding this phenomenon, the dimension with which it is perhaps most useful to begin any process of classification is that of perpetrator/victim relationship. In addition to indicating the setting in which a case occurs, this dimension gives some idea as to how cases are created and maintained, and their implications for agency intervention. Table 16.4 gives a breakdown of the 78 cases according to perpetrator/victim relationship.

The majority of cases involved only one perpetrator/victim relationship. Where cases involved more than one, they were classified on the basis of whichever type the researchers judged to be most significant in bringing

Table 16.3   Comparison of the number of known cases[1] identified in the national survey and the record searches for the eight local authority areas

Area	National survey (N)	Record searches (N)
1	4	13
2	0	19
3	2	16
4	0	8
5	0	2
6	2	11
7	0	5
8	0	4
Total	8	78

Note:

1   Organised and ritual abuse cases only

about the organised abuse. The only exceptions to this were cases involving a perpetrator who was a member of the child's family or a relative. All such cases were placed in the 'family/relative' category. The purpose of this was to highlight the significance of such perpetrators in organised abuse.

Family members and relatives were involved in almost two-thirds of all organised abuse cases. In the national survey, only 13 per cent of cases were classified under this heading. The searches uncovered six cases where, in addition to there being clear evidence of organised abuse, agencies had expressed concerns regarding ritual abuse. In all of these cases, at least one of the perpetrators was a family member. Therefore, only 8 per cent of the organised abuse cases involved suspicions of ritual abuse, compared to the national survey, in which almost one-third of all cases were classified as alleged ritual abuse.

Table 16.4   Perpetrator/victim relationships in known cases of organised abuse

Relationship	N	%
Family/relative	51	65
Neighbour/friend	12	15
Paedophile ring	8	11
Stranger	3	4
Foster-carers	2	3
Institution workers	1	1
Adoptive carers	1	1
Total	78	100

Many of the family/relative cases involved only two perpetrators. Very often, they were the children's birth mother and birth father, stepfather or co-habitee. However, a considerable range of other relatives were found to be involved in these cases, including grandparents, aunts/uncles, adult siblings and in-laws. In terms of the preponderance of family members and relatives as perpetrators, organised abuse is similar to other child sexual abuse cases (Kelly, Regan and Burton, 1991). This similarity is underlined by the fact that the second-largest category of cases (neighbours/friends) was also made up of perpetrators who were relatively well known to the child.

Previously, organised abuse has generally been thought of in terms of sexual abuse by two or more perpetrators. Definitions of organised abuse have now been refined to specify that at least one of the perpetrators should live outside the immediate household of the victim (La Fontaine, 1993). On this basis, 31 of the 51 family cases would be defined as organised abuse. Again, some of these cases involved only a small number of perpetrators and/or children, but all of these family/relative cases involved at least one perpetrator who did not live with the child.

The only other category that was of any appreciable size was that of 'paedophile ring', accounting for 11 per cent of cases. These consisted of groups of adults, predominantly if not exclusively male, who were usually only

casually acquainted with their victims. Often, these men would be associated with groups of boys involved in prostitution, so-called 'rent boys', with the abuse taking place on a quasi-commercial basis. Men and boys would frequent particular areas of a town, such as amusement arcades, clubs and public toilets, in the knowledge, sometimes acquired through an underground network, that sex could be bought or sold for money, sweets or other material goods. Although the remaining categories accounted for only a small proportion of cases, it is clear that the settings in which organised abuse occurs are quite diverse.

Table 16.5 shows that, in terms of the number of perpetrators, the majority of cases were small-scale: 55 per cent of cases involved only two perpetrators, and a further 17 per cent involved only three perpetrators. Just over a quarter of all cases (27 per cent) involved four or more perpetrators. A total of 279 perpetrators were involved in the 78 cases, or a mean of 3.6 perpetrators per case. Having said this, it must be recognised that these figures relate only to perpetrators that were *known* to be involved in a case. An individual was not counted as a perpetrator if an agency only suspected their involvement, or if a child made ambiguous remarks to this effect. Therefore, these figures must be seen as minimum estimates of the number of perpetrators involved in cases of organised abuse. The three largest cases were a family-based case with 16 perpetrators, and two paedophile rings, one involving 15 and the other involving 20 perpetrators.

In addition to the number of perpetrators, organised abuse cases were also marked out from other sexual abuse cases by the proportion of perpetrators who were female. The gender of all perpetrators was known in 77 cases. In these cases, 50 perpetrators (19 per cent) were female and 218 (81 per cent) were male. This is a far higher proportion of female perpetrators than is reported in the general child sexual abuse literature (Faller, 1987). Women were counted as perpetrators only where it was clear that they were willing participants in the abuse. In many cases, it appeared as if women did not initiate the abuse but rather were following the lead of male perpetrators. However, in a small number of cases, they did appear to be prime movers in the abuse.

The majority of organised abuse cases were also small-scale in terms of the number of children involved. As Table 16.6 shows, almost half (47 per cent) of all cases involved just one child. A further one-fifth of cases involved only two children. The remaining approximately one-third of cases involved three or more children. The largest two cases involved 19 and 20 children each. As with perpetrators, these figures refer to children who were *known* to have been involved in a case, and as such they constitute a minimum estimate of the number of children involved in organised abuse. The total number of children known to be involved in the 78 cases was 228, giving a mean of 2.9 children per case.

Table 16.5   Number of perpetrators known to be involved in cases of organised abuse identified through record searches

No. of perpetrators	Cases N	%
2	43	55
3	13	17
4	9	11
5	3	5
6	1	1
7	4	5
8	1	1
9	–	–
10+	4	5
Total	**78**	**100**

It is perhaps worth emphasising that a 'case' was defined by the process in which an incident was referred and investigated, and as such, it is an artificial construct in terms of describing the boundaries of a perpetrator's activities. Therefore the figures cited here, for example the number of perpetrators and children involved in cases, reflect the limits of particular referrals and investigations rather than the full extent of organised abuse.

A further contrast between organised and other cases of child sexual abuse was found in relation to the gender of victims. In the 75 cases where the gender of all victims was known, 119 of the victims were boys (55 per cent) and 99 (45 per cent) were girls. In respect of child sexual abuse generally, the literature is consistent in showing that the large majority of victims are female (Kelly, Regan and Burton, 1991). This finding reaffirms the existence of possible important differences between organised abuse and other child sexual abuse cases.

Table 16.6   Numbers of children known to be involved in cases of organised abuse identified through record searches

No. of children per case	Cases N	%
1	37	47
2	16	21
3	7	9
4	3	4
5	3	4
6	4	5
7	2	3
8	2	3
9	2	3
10+	2	3
Total	78	102[1]

Note:

1   Not equal to 100 because of rounding

Table 16.7 compares the gender of the perpetrators to that of the victims in the 76 cases where this information was available. Four categories of case were prominent. The largest of these was the 25 per cent of cases where men and women abused only girls. A large proportion of these cases were family/relative-based. The second-largest category (22 per cent) was composed of cases where only men abused only boys. These were typically cases involving paedophile rings, strangers and workers in children's institutions. The two other major categories were those where men and women abused boys and girls (20 per cent), and cases where only men had abused only girls

(17 per cent). The proportion of recorded abuse by men on boys is a feature of organised abuse which marks these cases out from cases of familial child sexual abuse.

Table 16.7   Comparison of the gender of perpetrators and victims in known cases of organised abuse

| | Victims | | |
Perpetrators	Only boys	Only girls	Boys and girls
Only men	17 (22%)	13 (17%)	3 (4%)
Only women	–	2 (3%)	–
Men and women	7 (9%)	19 (25%)	15 (20%)

Many of the victims were known to protection agencies before the detection of organised abuse. The abuse these children were subject to tended to be associated with the more serious and sadistic or bizarre acts. All too often, they were not receiving sustained intensive input from any agency.

Conclusion

There was considerable diversity in the nature of individual cases of organised child sexual abuse. The settings in which cases occurred included families, paedophile rings, groups of neighbours or strangers, children's institutions, a foster-home and an adoptive home. The numbers of perpetrators involved in these cases ranged from 2 to 20 and the number of children from 1 to 20. Even amongst large-scale cases, where some of the perpetrators did not live with the child, a number of different settings were evident. This diversity between cases was witnessed with regard to other factors also, such as the perpetrator's *modus operandi*. In short, there was no typical organised abuse case, but rather a set of factors that tended to cluster.

The defining characteristic of organised abuse is the minimum number of perpetrators. However, these cases were distinctive in a number of other respects, particularly the proportion of perpetrators who were female and the proportion of victims who were boys. Combined with the involvement of multiple perpetrators, these factors suggest that the 'dynamics' of organised

abuse may be quite different from those found in other cases of child sexual abuse. These differences may have important implications for both theory and practice.

It was also apparent that medium- and large-scale cases were marked out in respect of a number of other victim characteristics. Many of the children had had contact with Social Services prior to the detection of the organised abuse. Often, this was because either they or their siblings had been abused or neglected. The sexual abuse these children suffered tended to be extreme. On occasions, they would be exposed to bizarre or sadistic practices, such as being forced to eat excrement, and bestiality. Given these factors, it was not surprising that many children were very disturbed emotionally and behaviourally. This presented agencies with a major challenge, both in finding an appropriate placement for them and in offering them adequate therapy.

In terms of its extent, as measured by the number of cases, organised abuse constitutes only a small part of statutory child protection work. The 78 cases identified by the searches accounted for only 1 per cent of *all* child protection cases dealt with by the police in the eight areas and only 2 per cent of child sexual abuse cases in the period 1988–91. The equivalent figures for Social Services were 1 per cent and 3 per cent respectively (Gallagher, Hughes and Parker, 1994). However, whilst these figures are useful in placing organised abuse in some broader perspective, they tend to mask the impact which individual cases of organised abuse may have upon multi-agency work.

Several police forces and Social Services Departments have now had experience of dealing with large-scale cases of organised abuse. 'Operation Orchid' included three boys who were known to have been murdered by a paedophile ring based in London, but it is believed that as many as nine boys may have been killed. The Metropolitan, Thames Valley and Essex Police Forces were all involved in huge inquiries that ran through the late 1980s and early 1990s. The Dyfed police/Social Services investigation of family-based organised abuse which resulted in the imprisonment of five adults in 1994 was reported to be one of the biggest police inquiries ever carried out in Wales. There are numerous current large-scale investigations of which we are aware. All have presented agencies with major challenges, not only in terms of resources but also in developing their services to meet the unique difficulties presented by these cases.

Whilst agencies may have to focus more of their efforts upon large-scale cases, this should not lead to more moderately-sized cases of organised abuse being ignored. Many of the cases involving four, five or six perpetrators, and a similar number of children, also created formidable problems for agencies. Obtaining evidence as to the full extent of the 'organisation' and its abusive activities, and meeting the needs of children who were very damaged, are just some examples. Most, if not all, agencies are now aware of the difficulties raised by large-scale cases, but caution should be exercised lest

they assume complete confidence in dealing with more moderately-sized cases.

Many of the cases identified through the searches were family/relative-based and small-scale, involving two or three perpetrators. Whilst these cases were usually dealt with fairly adequately within existing procedures, even these cases raised additional problems: 31 cases (40 per cent) identified through the searches were family/relative-based cases that would meet the criteria of more restricted definitions of organised abuse, in that at least one of the perpetrators did not live with the child (La Fontaine, 1993). Small-scale, family/relative-based cases are significant, both in terms of practice and the development of a complete understanding of organised abuse.

References

Bashir, M. (1990) 'Public Eye Survey', BBC press release, 19 October 1990.

Bird, T., Withers, S., Smith, J., Gallagher, S. and O'Laughlin, T. (1990) 'Child sexual abuse networks – a shared response', workshop given at the 'Protecting Children into the 1990s' Conference, Harrogate, February 1990.

Burgess, A.N. and Clark, M.L. (1984) *Child Pornography and Sex Rings*, Lexington: Lexington Books.

Clayton, N. (1992) 'In the firing line', *Community Care*, 2 July.

Cohen, P. (1993) 'Conviction not comfort', *Community Care*, 16 September.

Community Care (1993) 'Disturbed girls assaulted', 30 September.

Creighton, S.J. (1993) 'Organised abuse: NSPCC experience', *Child Abuse Review*, 2, 232–42.

Department of Health (DoH) (1992) *Children and Young Persons on Child Protection Registers Year Ending 31st March 1991*, London: DOH.

Faller, K.C. (1987) 'Women who sexually abuse children', *Violence and Victims*, 2, 263–76.

Fawcett, J. (1991) 'Organised abuse: management implications', paper presented at conference on ritual abuse, Manchester, September.

Finkelhor, D., Williams, L. and Burns, N. (1988) *Nursery Crimes: Sexual Abuse in Day Care*, Newbury Park, Calif: Sage.

Gallagher, B., Hughes, B. and Parker, H. (1994) 'The Incidence of Known Cases of Organised and Ritual Child Sexual Abuse in England and Wales (1988–1991)', report to the Department of Health.

Hughes, B., Parker, H. and Gallagher, B. (1995) *Policing Child Sexual Abuse: Child Protection and Perpetrator Detection*, London: HMSO.

Hunt, P. and Baird, M. (1990) 'Children of sex rings', *Child Welfare*, 69 (3), 195–7.

Katz, I. (1991) 'Abuse victims tell of their childhood torment', *Guardian*, 27 September.

Kelly, L. and Scott, S. (1993) 'The current literature about the organised abuse of children', *Child Abuse Review*, 2, 281–7.

Kelly, L., Regan, L. and Burton, S. (1991) *Exploratory Study of the Prevalence of Sexual Abuse in a Sample of 16–21 Year Olds*, London: The Polytechnic of North London.

La Fontaine, J.S. (1993) 'Defining organised sexual abuse', *Child Abuse Review*, 2 (4), 223–31.

La Fontaine, J.S. (1994) *The Extent and Nature of Organised and Ritual Abuse: Research Findings*, London: HMSO.

Murray, N. (1993) 'A strategy of co-operation', *Community Care*, 13 May.

Myers, P. (1990) 'Return of eight children in abuse enquiry ordered', *Guardian*, 18 December.

Office of Population Census and Surveys (OPCS) (1992) *National and County Monitors*, London: OPCS.

Oliver, T. and Smith, R. (1993) *Lambs to the Slaughter*, London: Warner Books.

Parker, H., Gallagher, B. and Hughes, B. (1995) 'The policing of child sexual abuse in England and Wales', *Policing and Society*, forthcoming.

Redding, D. (1989) 'Smashing a sub-culture', *Community Care*, 1 June.

Warren, G. and Fowler, N. (1990) 'The scandal that shocked a county', *The Gazette*, 21 December.

Waterhouse, R., Kingman, S. and Cuffe, J. (1990) 'A satanic litany of suffering', *The Independent on Sunday*, 18 March.

Wild, N.J. (1989) 'Prevalence of child sex rings', *Paediatrics*, 83 (4), 553–8.

17 Child abuse which involves wider kin and family friends

Hedy Cleaver and Pam Freeman

Before the 1990s, research into child sexual abuse focused either on incest between father and daughter or paedophilia. But recent studies suggest a more complicated picture. The works of Margolin (1992) and Laviola (1992) show that in certain cases, fathers were not the only perpetrators. Children were also abused by other family members, and in some cases the abuse crossed generations. Furthermore, child abuse was not always contained within the family. For example, Faller (1991) found that it could involve both family members and outsiders.

Most recently, Gallagher (1993) and La Fontaine (1994) identified 149 cases of organised abuse, of which 'family-based' cases comprised the second-largest group. In these families, children were abused by both relatives and non-related adults, and women were frequently involved. The majority of children became victims, and neither gender nor age offered protection.

This wider perspective of child sexual abuse was the backdrop to our research into parents suspected of all forms of child abuse (Cleaver and Freeman, 1995). The close relationships developed with families allowed an exploration of related issues and led to the identification, in one family, of an abuse network. The expression 'abuse network' refers to a number of families and lone adults who are linked to one another for the purpose of child sexual abuse. The network differed from a group of abusers, because individual members did not necessarily know all those involved. As with Bott's (1971) analysis of social networks, there was a cell-like structure, where individuals used a particular person or family as a reference point. As a result, much of the network was hidden from most of those involved.

What we uncovered was not a new form of child sexual abuse but a unique context in which probably only a tiny minority occurs. This context was distinguished by two characteristics. First, the abuse extended to several adults and to more than one child. Children were abused within the family by par-

ents, grandparents, siblings and wider kin. Consequently, abuse could be said to have become normative. Second, it crossed generations. Sexual exploitation of children went on for years, and abused children became abusers. Thus the pattern of abuse displayed a cross-configuration: it extended vertically through the inter-generational family structure and laterally through the involvement of wider kin and family friends.

This chapter explores the network we studied. It assesses the extent of child sexual abuse and explores how individual members are related. It also looks at the way norms of abusive behaviour are established and seeks to explain how members make contact and communicate information. Furthermore, it analyses which members of the group are involved in the abuse and whether certain individuals avoid being drawn in. Finally, it considers the implications for social work practice.

Although subsequent work has allowed us to study a further eight networks which show similar features, it is important to recognise the limitations of this study. For example, we experienced difficulty in pursuing all allegations of sexual abuse: a few individuals had left home, we could not gain access to those in prison and some members were unforthcoming. This analysis therefore rests on a limited number of perspectives.

The network

It is clear from the family map in Figure 17.1 that the network is extensive, and a full description of every family and all the participants would be time-consuming and tedious for the reader. Our focus is the Latterley family, because the larger network was uncovered in the wake of a report of suspected sexual abuse involving 12-year-old Trisha Latterley. Trisha's teacher raised the alarm after he saw her kissing and cuddling a man old enough to be her grandfather.

An examination of social work records for the Latterley family showed a consistent focus on the women. Joyce, the great-grandmother of Trisha, was noted as promiscuous at the age of 12 – a circumstance which in today's climate would raise suspicions of sexual abuse. Joyce remained single but had a series of sexual partners and bore nine children. Her child-rearing was shrouded in suspicions of incest and neglect. The sons became delinquent, and the daughters' sexual behaviour mirrored that of their mother.

Alice, Trisha's grandmother, also bore many children and never married. She became a familiar face in the Children's Department, as social workers continued to register concern with respect to possible incest, violence and general neglect.

Veronica was the second daughter of ten children and was to become Trisha's mother. When Veronica was 12, a friend of her mother's, Nigel Zapp,

became the lodger. Alice was soon encouraging Veronica to visit Nigel's room – 'just for a cuddle because he's lonely' – with the result that, from Veronica's account, sexual intercourse became a regular after-school activity. Approximately a year later, Nigel announced his engagement to her 16-year-old sister, Lucy. The three sisters discovered that Nigel had abused them all, as well as seducing Veronica's friend, Mary Pritchard/Macdonald. The girls' friendship survived, but the ensuing row forced Nigel out of the house. A hundred miles away, he married another teenager and fathered two children. His abusive behaviour didn't change. An assault on his own daughter, although resulting in divorce, was kept secret from the police and Social Services.

Abuse within the Latterley family continued, with the sons physically and sexually abusing their sisters. Veronica sought escape in an early marriage to Bob Swann, the father of her first son, James. The relationship ended when, having for some time revealed himself a cross-dresser, Bob announced his intention to have a sex-change operation. A year later, Veronica married Roger Swallow, one of her brother's friends, and had two more children, Gary and Trisha. Trisha was found to have learning difficulties.

When the children were little, an old family friend, Harry Ollins, was a regular visitor, and Trisha became his 'special girl'. Veronica suspects that Harry was the first to sexually abuse Trisha, on the basis that, when Trisha was seven, an unconnected police investigation into a paedophile ring led to his arrest. Harry's sexual interest in children had been a secret from his family, and he was not suspected of abusing his own children.

Following the collapse of Veronica's second marriage, Nigel Zapp was reintroduced to her by another of her brothers, and they became lovers. He welcomed Trisha, now 9 years old, with open arms, but succeeded in ousting Veronica's two sons. Gary returned to his natural father, Roger Swallow, to live in poor conditions but safe from sexual abuse. James, the 13-year-old half-brother, whose natural father was now living as a woman, moved in to the sexually abusive household of Veronica's childhood friend, Mary Pritchard/Macdonald. This was a family where very young children were found to have been sexually assaulted (see Figure 17.1). Abused by Mary, he ran away to live rough, before hunger and cold drove him to seek shelter with his violent and sexually abusive uncles.

Nigel Zapp and Veronica Latterley had one child, Mary. At around this time, concern was expressed in social work records of Nigel's possible sexual involvement with four under-aged girls. It also transpired that he was involved in the abuse of the Macdonald children, as well as conducting a sexual liaison with Jenny Major, a single, lonely, middle-class parent, and abusing her 8-year-old daughter (see Figure 17.1). Veronica states that, in a desperate attempt to keep her lover's interest, she cajoled and coerced her daughter, Trisha, into a sexual relationship with him, thus repeating the pattern of her own childhood abuse.

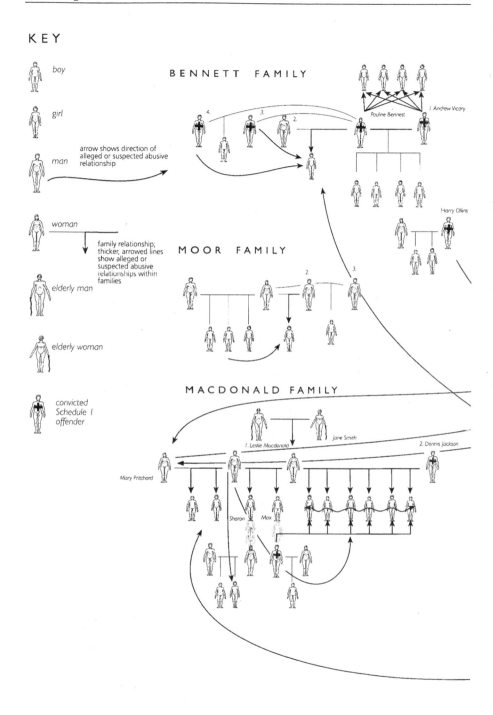

Figure 17.1   Family map – a network of abuse

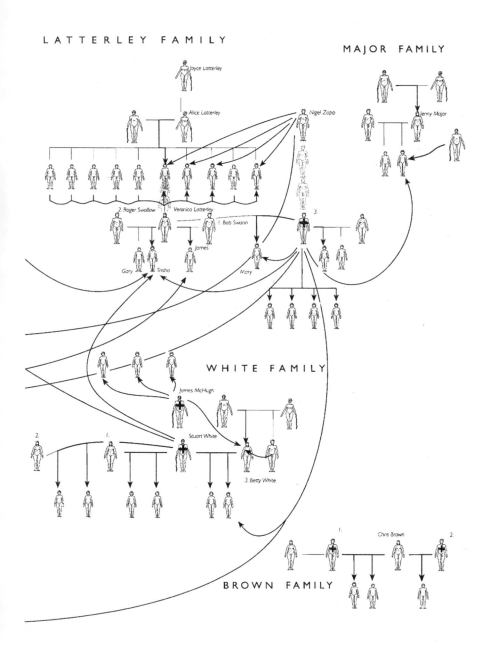

LATTERLEY FAMILY

MAJOR FAMILY

Joyce Latterley

Alice Latterley

Nigel Zapp

Jenny Major

2. Roger Swallow   Veronica Latterley

1. Bob Swann

3.

James

Gary   Trisha

Mary

WHITE FAMILY

James McHugh

2.   1.

Stuart White

3. Betty White

BROWN FAMILY

1.   Chris Brown   2.

Trisha's abuse was not confined to members of the family: by the time she was 11, Nigel's friends, including Stuart White (see Figure 17.1), were participating in her abuse. Stuart, a lay preacher and youth leader, had a history of sex offences stretching back 35 years. A borstal experience had originally brought Stuart and Nigel together, and re-housing in the same council flats reunited them, exposing children in both households to additional abuse.

Trisha's sexual encounters became routine; on her return each week from special school, a heavy drinking session heralded her sexual abuse. Her maltreatment continued until she was 12, when, as we have seen, her teacher's anxieties led to a child protection investigation. Nigel was convicted of abusing her and imprisoned for two months. Trisha and her half-sister, Mary, were taken into care. Veronica received family centre counselling, but her problems increased; she got into debt, lost her council flat and went to live at her brother's, where she moved into the bed of her son, James (then 16 years old). To evade the drunken physical and sexual attacks of her brother, Veronica and James frequently sleep rough. Mary was eventually adopted. Trisha remains a weekly boarder but spends weekends with foster-parents. There are suspicions that she has renewed contact with Nigel.

The nature and extent of the abuse

It emerged from our study that, in certain families, children were sexualised at an unusually early age. The sexual interaction might involve a child with adults, older children, their peers, or much younger children. As a result, the children in the network experienced many different forms of sexual molestation. For these reasons, we use the term 'sexual abuse' in its widest sense, to denote any form of sexual activity or encounter which involves a child. The type of abuse varied according to the age and gender of the child and the opportunity and the predilections of the perpetrator. Furthermore, the majority of children were 'groomed' and subsequently became victims of penetrative sexual activity, namely oral, anal or vaginal intercourse. In many respects, the picture is one of moral abandonment, in which stronger members of the group satisfy their needs at the cost of weaker participants.

Children were abused by family members and outsiders. Kinship defines who may sleep with whom (Harris, 1990), but unstable and complex patterns of kinship may contribute to a breakdown of sexual taboos. For example, in the network, relationships between adults were tenuous, and for any individual, serial partnerships were common. Since each relationship produced children, a degree of consanguinity existed between a high proportion of individuals. However, when relationships between adults are confused, the paternity of children may be uncertain. Moreover, the men's appetite for very young women blurred the divisions between generations, so that age

ceased to be a reliable indicator of relationships; the age of their later partners tended to be closer to their children's.

Our evidence suggests that, in families where the abuse was inter-generational, children were unlikely to escape; the majority of children, regardless
of their gender, were affected. Nevertheless, the few exceptions raise the
question of why some should escape and whether protective factors could be
identified. Whilst there is evidence to support Gill's (1971) and De Lissovoy's
(1979) premise that abuse is an interactive process between child and adult,
our data suggests something more complicated: situations influenced by the
idiosyncrasies of the individuals and prevailing circumstances. The very factors which protected some children made others vulnerable.

For example, the departure of brothers James and Gary was a consequence
of the same event – the infiltration of the family by Nigel. While James wan-
dered the streets, Gary was sheltered by his natural father, an inadequate but
non-abusive man. James's lack of a refuge and his vulnerability at a crucial
moment drove him back into the network and into the hands of an abuser.

A timely removal by Social Services of all the children sometimes protected the very young. Unfortunately, removal of the perpetrator cannot
guarantee safety of the victim. In the White family (see Figure 17.1), James
McHugh's imprisonment for abusing 13-year-old Betty White was not a
solution; clandestine visits to the prison allowed James to 'pass her on' to
another paedophile. In addition, recent problems involving children in residential care have shown that placement away from home cannot ensure a
child's safety.

Although in some cases abuse was routine, the children were not
assaulted continuously. As with all sexual activity, individual appetites differed, and activity was often determined by opportunity. For example,
Trisha's abuse followed a set pattern: each weekend on her return from residential school she was drawn into a drunken scenario of abuse involving her
mother, stepfather and family friends.

The abusers in the network

Men dominated the abusive activity but were not the only abusers. When
women were involved, usually mothers and grandmothers, the extent of
their participation ranged from recruitment or tacit acceptance to restraining
children or concealing its effects to being perpetrators themselves. There was
little evidence to suggest that women abused children alone; invariably, they
operated in the company of a male perpetrator. Nevertheless, some research
and adult recollections suggest that women do act independently (Margolin,
1986; Elliott, 1993).

Significant figures to emerge were a few 'satellite' men, who acted alone.

Their behaviour was opportunistic, establishing links between one abusive family and another, and in certain circumstances connecting it with other networks. For example, Harry's friendship with the Latterley family linked the network of families to a paedophile ring.

Given that the network is made up of a large number of participants allied to one another through their interest in an activity which is not only criminal but also socially tabooed, secrecy is vital. This raises the question of how members are safely recruited.

The recruitment of family members

In this context, members of the family can include blood relations who may have been the products of an incestuous relationship, as well as individuals linked through marriage. Although kinship has diminished in importance in British society, it still denotes membership of a group to which one owes and from which one can expect certain obligations (Nydegger, 1986). Thus recruiting blood-related kin presents few dangers to members of the existing abuse network, because they themselves have grown up in an abusive environment. In the context of the abuse network, the existence of kinship represented a secure underpinning, based on complicity and silence.

The introduction of new blood through marriage could place the network in jeopardy. The danger was minimised when liaisons were formed with people already *au fait* with child sexual abuse. Indeed, an element of self-determination was perceptible in the process of choosing marital partners. Just as common interests and similar backgrounds are components of relationships generally, so a similar process tended to govern the selection of partners by network members. By this means, Veronica Latterley was supplied with two sexual consorts by her abusive brothers.

The recruitment of outsiders

Those classed as 'outsiders' were either childhood friends or others with few, if any, prior connections. Childhood friendships are made in many different situations, but certain contexts, by congregating similarly vulnerable children, increase the probability of perpetuating the effects of childhood abuse. For example, there is a higher-than-average likelihood that the children of sexually-abusive parents will spend some time in care, or find themselves in care because of delinquent or disturbed behaviour (Finkelhor and Baron, 1986). In such contexts, children with similar experiences gravitate towards one another (Cleaver, 1991).

Associations formed in residential settings can endure. Indeed, because children in care are often isolated from their family, residential workers encourage leavers to stay in contact with each other. However, deviant

behaviour is just as likely to continue as more socially-acceptable traits – so it was with Nigel Latterley and Stuart White, whose shared experience of borstal cemented a friendship which was to last over a quarter of a century and become an important component in the abuse network. Nigel abused Stuart's children; Stuart abused Nigel's stepdaughter, Trisha.

Newcomers to the network were either lonely and depressed young women, many with a personal history of childhood abuse, or they were predatory men and women. Lonely women were befriended or preyed on by members of the network or exploited by male abusers, witness Jenny Major's experience. A proportion of all the women had a learning disability, which made them particularly vulnerable.

The predators, mainly men, lacked the channels of communication associated with organised paedophilia and had to rely on personal contacts in their pursuit of women and children. Certain pubs were notorious: although not used exclusively by child abusers, they served as meeting places where subsequent relationships might be negotiated. It emerged that many abusive relationships were based on a notion of exchange in which the male perpetrator's offer of love and financial assistance was traded for sexual access to the woman's children. A family centre worker told us: 'The women want the men and the men want the children.'

There were indications that, as outsiders were initiated into the network, their resistance to sexual activity with children was lowered by drink, drugs, pornographic videos and the prevailing sexual atmosphere. Once compromised, they were unlikely to retreat; with each step, the degree of complicity increased, and the likelihood of escape diminished.

Welfare and penal agencies inadvertently effect a link

In cases of suspected child abuse, one of the most helpful interventions is the referral of mothers and children to family centres (Cleaver and Freeman, 1995). Although for the vast majority this was a positive experience, for a few it brought unexpected dangers: childhood friendships were sometimes re-established between women who shared abusive backgrounds, and as a consequence, abusing families were drawn together.

On occasions, family centres were targeted by predatory men – the needy, lonely women with young children, who sheltered under a centre's caring wing, provided them with a ready hunting ground. Winkel and Koppelaar (1991) suggest that abused children may be seen as bullied. This would explain why, on occasions, lonely women exchanged sexual access to an abused child for acceptance into an apparently friendly group.

Local authorities' rehousing policy also put certain vulnerable mothers at risk. Limited public housing stock results in welfare agencies accommodating abusive families in close proximity – for example the rehousing of the

Latterleys and the Whites in the same council flats. In addition, the use of bed and breakfast accommodation by the Probation Service for certain newly-released men and by Social Services for destitute women and children aggravated the risks (NACRO, 1992). Neither agency is easily able to monitor occupancy, but communication between the services is essential if unintentionally dangerous liaisons are to be avoided.

The policy of segregating child sexual abusers (under Rule 43) in special prison wings may be necessary for their own protection, but there is evidence that it normalises deviance (NACRO, 1992). Friendships were established amongst like-minded prisoners, and information about children and families passed between them. In many instances, prisoners' friendships pre-dated their imprisonment. In the same way that the family centres linked certain women, so prison reworked the connections between certain families. On release, it was not uncommon to find men living near, if not with, the families of prison acquaintances. This combination of factors may help to account for the congregation within a small geographical area of Schedule 1 offenders and men with a history of suspected child sexual abuse.

Finally, in this catalogue of unintended consequences, the church emerged as another significant point of contact and exchange. In collaboration with the Prison Service, one church strove to establish links between parishioners and prisoners through a 'befriending' scheme. By this unexpected route, the names of certain vulnerable women with children passed between prisoners. Indeed, a number of released Schedule 1 offenders moved in with lonely and 'forgiving' new families and gained sexual access to children. We would emphasise that, in pointing out these effects, our aim is to alert practitioners of possible – although hopefully rare – outcomes, rather than to criticise the interventions.

The tenacity of the network

Many of the families were shunned by the larger community because of their reputation for violent feuding, drunkenness, chronic poverty and neglect of the children. Network membership appeared to supply a variety of instrumental and emotional needs. Adults baby-sat for each other, borrowed money or offered a bed in times of trouble. Even when violent quarrels erupted, the inter-dependence of individuals meant this seldom resulted in a permanent rift. In fact, individuals spoke of their deep commitment to friends and family.

Networks remained intact because children who grew up in a family where abuse was inter-generational internalised the notion that, although such activity was illegal and must be concealed, it was not necessarily morally wrong. A highly-charged sexual atmosphere and overt sexual activ-

ity between members of the family and visiting friends was accepted.

Similarly, deviant sexual norms of one family were reinforced through connections with like-minded others. The overlap of social and abuse networks strengthened the private code of behaviour and made it easier for families to legitimise their behaviour and discount its ill effects.

As in other contexts of sexual abuse, adults controlled children through a mixture of fear and rewards. Those considered unreliable were silenced, for example, by threatening to harm a pet, a younger sibling or a vulnerable parent. Some families were frequently very violent, and adults and children alike were intimidated. At a more subtle level, children were made aware of the danger to their parents of any disclosure. One child said: 'Although I hate him I didn't want me dad put in prison and he'd said that if I told they'd all be put away and I'd be taken into care.'

Women played a key role in the process of child-rearing and transmitting norms of behaviour. A substantial proportion of those who suffered childhood abuse chose abusive partners. The literature on marital violence offers some insight by suggesting that children nurtured on a mixture of love and abuse may equate one with the other and seek a similar combination in their adult relationships.

It would be wrong to assume that there is no escape for children who grow up in a network of abusive families. Some extricated themselves by marrying a non-abusing partner; but whenever such a relationship broke down, there was a tendency to retreat to the shelter and social support of the abuse network. Escape involved the loss of family and friends: a sacrifice many inadequate and isolated parents were incapable of sustaining. The combination of marrying a non-abuser and leaving the neighbourhood entirely was a better recipe for escape, since loss of contact forced individuals to establish a new social support system. Whether or not families were totally successful in extracting themselves, the combination of fear, shame and family loyalty deterred all but a few from revealing their abuse. In general, it emerged that since very few family members considered themselves entirely innocent, any action which might open the network to scrutiny was regarded as a threat to the safety of everyone involved.

Difficulties for social work practice posed by family network abuse

Networks pose problems of identification

It is difficult to establish identities because relationships between adults are unstable and complex, and households contain children who are related in a variety of ways, both to each other and to the adults. For each generation, the

pattern is repeated. The broader picture is still further complicated because adults are inclined to change their names with uncommon regularity – following marriages or in an attempt to avoid scrutiny.

Children are abused by many perpetrators, and to close an investigation after identifying a single perpetrator or a single thread of abusive connections may prove premature. However, everyone connected to an abusing family is not necessarily an abuser; there is a danger that once a network is uncovered, innocent individuals are labelled by association. Although they overlap, social and abuse networks do not necessarily coincide.

Working Together (DoH, 1991) offers some guidance when networks cross geographical boundaries, but even when they are contained within a single local authority, they present difficulties. For example, when all those involved do not live within the catchment area of one agency office, links between abusive families may be overlooked.

Mapping a network has implications in the area of professional ethics and civil liberties. Information obtained for one purpose, such as therapeutic family work, may end up being used for another: to help track someone's movement between families. The Department of Health (1988) Circular LAC(88)17 justifies the disclosure of confidential information without client consent in cases of child abuse. Nevertheless, in cases where so much detail is lurid and may be unreliable, problems of confidentiality are likely to arise.

Networks are difficult to destroy because of their cell-like structure (Bott, 1971). Irrespective of any willingness to co-operate, individual members will only have access to a limited amount of information. The connections between families may be obscure, and consequently very resilient. Added to which, families use strategies to safeguard the network: allowing an individual to be detected usually succeeds in diverting further scrutiny.

Network cases only make up a very small proportion of all child protection work. Nevertheless, because of their complexity, the unravelling process places considerable strain on the time and resources of child protection agencies.

Networks challenge common assumptions

The view of women as passive, dominated or psychotic does not always apply (Faller, 1987; Krug, 1989). Within a network, women can be responsible, not always unwittingly, for transmitting the abuse culture and recruiting new members. They may abet the abuse of children or actually engage in abuse.

The majority of treatment models for sex offenders are based on the notion that adult sexuality is specific in its focus. The evidence suggests sexual appetites so omnivorous that treatment which seeks to redirect sexual fantasy may be of little relevance.

Many of the network families were well known to social workers across several generations. This raises the question of whether long-term involvement, coupled with an understandable frustration when faced with chronic problem families, results in professionals accepting lower standards of childcare.

The 'satellite' men who establish connections between families, and the commerce of child pornography and prostitution, raise questions about current police and Social Services practices which deal with these trades as if they were discrete phenomena. The data suggest considerable overlap.

In an abuse network, the intensity and duration of maltreatment is extreme. No clear distinction exists between abuser and abused, and transfer between the two roles is common, even amongst the very young. Hunt and Baird (1990) show that the effect of multiple abuse can be devastating. Practitioners who have dealt with network cases find the children less capable of distinguishing between abusive and non-abusive relationships, and their sexualised behaviour may jeopardise both treatment and the stability of placements.

Abuse networks present problems for practitioners working within the spirit of the Children Act 1989. The degree of correspondence between abuse and social networks means that removal of a few adults or children is no solution. On the other hand, it is hardly feasible to lock up all the adults and place all the children in care. But keeping children at home and working with families to change ingrained attitudes and norms is an enormous task, requiring long-term commitments and extensive resources. There are, however, initiatives in a number of European countries where intra-familial sexual abuse is dealt with by voluntary, long-term therapy with the family rather than by prosecution (Sale and Davies, 1990; Philpot, 1991).

Conclusion

In this chapter, we have sought to extend practitioners' knowledge of one context in which child abuse can occur. Only a tiny minority of families investigated by child protection professionals will belong to such a network. None the less, the possibility that such a situation may exist has implications for case management in a particular geographical area and a bearing on the type of information that needs to be collated in order to provide a comprehensive service for children at risk. There is still much to be learned, not least about the exact nature and extent of the abuse, its precise impact on kinship networks and its wider functions for those involved.

References

Bott, E. (1971) *Family and Social Network*, London: Tavistock.

Cleaver, H. (1991) *Vulnerable Children in Schools*, Aldershot: Dartmouth.

Cleaver, H. and Freeman, P. (1995) *Parental Perspectives in Cases of Suspected Child Abuse*, London: HMSO.

De Lissovoy, V. (1979) 'Towards the definition of an "abuse provoking child" ', *Child Abuse and Neglect*, 3 (1), 341–50.

Department of Health (DoH) (1988) *Personal Social Services: Confidentiality of Personal Information*, Circular LAC(88)17, London: HMSO.

Department of Health (DoH) (1989) *An Introduction to the Children Act 1989*, London: HMSO.

Department of Health (DoH) (1991) *Working Together Under the Children Act: A Guide to Arrangements for Inter-Agency Co-operation for the Protection of Children from Abuse*, London: HMSO.

Elliott, M. (1993) *Female Sexual Abuse of Children: The Ultimate Taboo*, London: Longman.

Faller, K.C. (1987) 'Women who sexually abuse children', *Violence and Victims*, 2 (4), 263–76.

Faller, K.C. (1991) 'Poly-incestuous families', *Journal of Interpersonal Violence*, 6 (3), 311–21.

Finkelhor, D. and Baron, L. (1986) 'High-risk children', in D. Finklehor (ed.) *A Source Book on Child Sexual Abuse*, Beverly Hills: Sage.

Gallagher, B. (1993) 'Organised and ritual child abuse' (interim report to the Department of Health).

Gill, D.G. (1971) 'Violence against children', *Journal of Marriage and the Family*, 33, 637–48.

Harris, C. (1990) *Kinship*, Milton Keynes: Open University Press.

Hunt, P. and Baird, M. (1990) 'Children of sex rings', *Child Welfare*, 69 (3), 195–207.

Krug, R.S. (1989) 'Adult male report of childhood sexual abuse by mothers: Case descriptions, motivations and long-term consequences', *Child Abuse and Neglect*, 13 (1), 111–19.

La Fontaine, J.S. (1994) *The Extent and Nature of Organised and Ritual Abuse*, London: HMSO.

Laviola, M. (1992) 'Effects of older brother–younger sister incest: A study of the dynamics of 17 cases', *Child Abuse and Neglect*, 16 (3), 409–21.

Margolin, L. (1986) 'The effects of mother–son incest', *Lifestyles: A Journal of Changing Patterns*, 5, 104–14.

Margolin, L. (1992) 'Sexual abuse by grandparents', *Child Abuse and Neglect*, 16 (5), 735–41.

National Association for the Care and Resettlement of Offenders (NACRO) (1992) *Criminal Justice and the Prevention of Child Sexual Abuse*, London: NACRO.

Nydegger, C.M. (1986) 'Problematic son-in-law' in N. Datan, A.L. Greene and H.W. Reese (eds) *Life Span Developmental Psychology: Inter-generational Relations*, London: Lawrence Erlbaum Associates.

Philpot, T. (1991) 'Crime and Punishment', *Community Care*, 886 (24), 12–14.

Sale, A. and Davies, M. (1990) *Child Protection Policies and Practice in Europe*, London: NSPCC.

Winkel, F.W. and Koppelaar, L. (1991) 'Rape victims' style of self-presentation and secondary victimization by the environment: An experiment', *Journal of Interpersonal Violence*, 6 (1), 29–40.

18 A model for training and staff development

Anne Hollows and Jan Horwath

This chapter considers training and professional development of professionals who may need to work with cases of organised abuse. It contains a brief survey of key events in the development of training in child protection. It then considers the framework within which training and development must operate in order to play a successful part in preventing and responding to organised abuse. It suggests a strategic approach to both general and specific training, before reviewing the training and development contribution to the management of specific cases. Finally, it looks at the ways in which professional development can be maintained and enhanced.

Cases of organised abuse create major demands on individual agency and inter-agency resources in a number of ways. One of the first issues raised is that of the level of knowledge and skills available to meet the contingency. It has become almost a reflex action to think in terms of emergency training of key staff. A regular feature of the aftermath of such cases is the demand for training programmes to address organised abuse, so that any further occurrences of this kind will be more easily dealt with. A great deal is therefore expected of training about organised abuse: both ensuring that practice is right in the first place and ensuring that it is not wrong in the future. This chapter proposes a different way of considering the learning and staff development needs regarding organised abuse and draws on learning theories to suggest principles which should be applied to such learning.

A recent history of child protection training

Since the mid-1980s, there has been a steady development in the role of in-service training for work with child abuse. Initially, the focus for all child protection learning was one of awareness. This was an explicit aim of the

245

Department of Health's child abuse training initiative which led to the production and evaluation of training materials, particularly between 1987 and 1994. These included the Open University pack *Responding to Child Abuse and Neglect* (Open University, 1988) and the Nottingham University initiative *Multi-Disciplinary is Different* (Charles, 1991). The initiative also funded the Child Abuse Training Unit (CATU), based at the National Children's Bureau, which advised trainers about strategic and specific issues in the development of single-agency and multi-agency training. Both of the writers of this chapter worked for the CATU. They were often asked to advise on training for staff involved in investigating multiple or organised abuse, and this chapter draws on discussions and workshops with trainers during that period.

Training of social workers has been encouraged and enabled by the availability of government funding to local authority Social Services Departments under the Training Support Programme. Some of that funding has enabled the promotion of multi-disciplinary training programmes under the arrangements for ACPCs. These training initiatives have been supplemented by national training programmes around two key areas: the implementation of the Children Act 1989 and the implementation of the *Memorandum of Good Practice* (DoH/HO, 1992) in conjunction with the Criminal Justice Act 1991.

For some time, it appeared that, in many organisations, access to training had no particular rationale, and often interest or availability were the factors most likely to influence attendance on training courses. This led to a somewhat chaotic picture, where it was hard to predict who knew what or whether they had any opportunity to consolidate their learning with practice. Recently, there has been a tendency to adopt a more structured approach to identifying training needs in some local authorities. This has been based upon the twin notions that:

- The most experienced worker should tackle the most complex issues.
- Knowledge in the wrong hands could create problems – another version of 'A little knowledge is a dangerous thing.'

In general, these notions have much to commend them. Training undoubtedly needs to be constructed over time as a series of building blocks, and it is reasonable to assume that organised abuse *per se* does not form one of the foundation stones of such training. It is also true that training needs to relate to tasks which are currently being performed or imminently likely to be performed. At least in part, this is because the learning process requires implementation and reflection if it is to be effective. However, there have been less helpful consequences of this approach. First, it may have contributed towards the élitism of which child protection is sometimes accused in all the relevant professions. This may make it more difficult for staff who work in

the wider range of children's services to communicate their concerns to child protection professionals. This in turn has defined organised abuse as being within the domain of child protection, rather than focusing on the preventive work which should be undertaken in this area. Many of those who are most likely to encounter the first suspicions of complex, organised abuse are excluded from training, so that they are unable to recognise, let alone to act upon, what it is they are seeing. Meanwhile, the lack of any attempt to develop knowledge and awareness among managers has meant that, in the event of an organised abuse case coming to light, senior managers have struggled to provide effective leadership.

Beyond awareness

Awareness training has dominated child protection training for the past ten years, and it is sometimes difficult to move beyond that stage of training. Awareness can lead to identifying wider audiences who 'need to be made aware', as well as identifying further areas to learn about. There is always a risk that this will lead to a sense of being overwhelmed by awareness which has not been matched with the development of skills or by any sense of integration of knowledge and skills with values and attitudes. This creates a sense of powerlessness amongst professionals, which is unlikely to enable a positive response to child abuse – sometimes called 'conscious incompetence'. If this stage of learning persists, it can lead to burn-out. Whilst awareness training is critical in developing both knowledge and skills, it needs to be accompanied by relevant guidance on how to limit organised abuse through good prevention strategies, as well as how to respond, albeit at an initial level, if it does occur.

At the same time, other problems have arisen from training programmes which focus on the development of skills without any guarantee that those learning the skills will have any opportunity to put them into practice. For learning to be effective in the longer term, the learner has to be aware of the gap between the needs of the situation and the level of knowledge and skills with which she or he can respond to it. Learning, then, is the acquisition of knowledge and skills to meet that deficiency. It is important to relate the 'just in time' theory of training to organised abuse. Of course it is not possible to predict the occurrence of cases of this sort. However, it is possible to ensure that a widespread level of awareness is maintained and at the same time to guarantee that some staff will be highly trained and experienced in relevant knowledge and skills, for example investigating child sexual abuse. As we will see later in this chapter, these are the training cornerstones for building a response to organised abuse.

The components of an effective response

The creation of an effective staff development response to organised abuse requires much more than a training programme alone. There needs to be a backcloth of an appropriate learning climate within an organisation in which the development of staff can flourish. That development needs to incorporate awareness training at a wide level as part of a general preventive strategy in relation to child sexual abuse. There needs to be a comprehensive training programme for social workers who are involved in child protection activities. This should be supported and maintained through supervision policies and practices. There should be a commitment to ensuring that a strategic management consultancy group can be developed, with a commitment to maintaining expertise and offering consultancy in complex child protection cases, including organised abuse. Finally, there should be a clearly-developed strategic plan of how to respond to cases of organised abuse which come to light. Each of these points will be elaborated and discussed below.

The climate of learning

Effective learning

Learning takes place in a context, both organisational and individual. Those attending training will need to have opportunities to prepare for a course and to follow up their course work with practice and reflection. It will be of importance to ensure that the learning is facilitated by at least some people with local credibility and knowledge, who can relate to the local experience and respect the diversity of staff and service users. The relationship between teacher and learner is a critical feature of good learning. Trainers need to recognise this relationship as reciprocal (Smith, 1993) and to understand that they too will be learning from the training.

A further set of difficulties can be encountered when social workers or other child protection professionals find themselves professionally isolated because they alone in their team or organisation have specialist knowledge and skills in a particular area. This is particularly problematic in terms of enabling professionals to extend their learning through opportunities to reflect on their practice with peers or mentors. In this context, we suggest that the definition of training can be extended to include a wide range of *learning experiences* which are not necessarily linked to a formal training event.

In considering the issues around training and learning, it will be essential to remember that the response to organised abuse, whether preventive or investigative and beyond, will always be a multi-professional response. This increases the risk of conflicting agendas and diverse experiences. It remains

ironic that the agencies charged with statutory responsibility for investigating child abuse, the Social Services Department and the police, are staffed by those with the least professional training when compared, for example, with health visitors, psychologists and psychiatrists (Smith, 1993). In addition, there are differences in learning cultures and in arrangements for supervision and management.

There is a distinction which may be beginning to emerge between training and learning. It remains, in our view, impossible for a training course on its own to create effective learning, although it should start that process. No manager can ever abdicate responsibility for the development of professional practice to a trainer, however good or experienced.

This far from exclusive list of challenges to effective training and learning is noted here because it points to the need for us to be explicit about our own approach. As you read this chapter, you may find it helpful to consider the following ground rules for tackling training in this subject area:

- Effective learning combines work on knowledge, skills, attitudes and values.
- Skills learning can never be completed without supervised practice learning.
- Training is usually most effective when it takes place 'just in time', that is, when there is a realistic possibility of being able to use the learning in the immediate future.
- Training needs to be grounded in local knowledge and practice.
- Training must reflect and respect the diversity of participants and of the communities they serve.
- Where trainers come from outside the immediate vicinity, they should be supported by local knowledge.
- Management engagement with the commissioning of training should ensure that immediate line-managers of those being trained are prepared for their task in supporting the ongoing learning of the staff.
- The role of supervision in maintaining and extending learning is crucial.
- Whilst formal training events occupy an important place in the development of knowledge and skills, there are a wide variety of settings where teaching and learning may take place.

The problem of procedures

Another feature of training and professional development in recent years has been the position occupied by government guidance and local procedures in the teaching and learning process. Whilst national standards and clear procedures are obviously important strands in the delivery of an effective service, particularly at a complex multi-agency level, they can become

substitutes for critical thinking when unique constellations of problems occur. This is at its most acute where the response to cases of organised and multiple abuse is concerned. Much of the difficulty in responding to organised abuse has been in the attempt to find and then cling to an orthodoxy, without any evaluation of the origins or the implications of such an approach. It is important to recognise that clear procedural guidance needs to be partnered with carefully-developed knowledge and good supervision and support. Incorporating concepts of teaching and learning which can empower professionals to think critically will prepare them for both recognition and response in complex cases. Again, it will be important for staff to develop reflective practice in order to ensure that each new experience can be processed and incorporated into their practice base (Brookfield, 1987).

Portfolios of learning and experience

A relatively recent development in some Social Services and Health Departments has been that of the 'portfolio' of learning and experience. Originally designed as part of the NVQ system, these portfolios have proved to be a useful tool both for individual staff awareness and for the collation of training needs. Staff detail their training needs and log when they have received training. They are then able to document practice experience which has consolidated their learning. Over time, the system forms a running record of each staff member's professional development and may be of considerable assistance in judging their suitability to join a team constructed for a specific purpose, such as the investigation of organised abuse. At the same time, the portfolio provides a means of recording and storing their learning on the job, and for encouraging reflection and subsequent learning from their practical experience as a member of such a team.

Strategic planning in training

Accounts of cases of organised abuse offer detailed descriptions of the ways in which systems have been devised by abusers to avoid challenge. If we seek the objective of *preventing* as well as *responding to* organised abuse, then we must accept that learning will be required at some level throughout the statutory services and beyond. In designing training to meet the varying and widespread needs of staff at different levels and locations in organisations, we suggest a four-stage analysis:

1   What does this worker need to be aware of?
2   How do they need to be able to respond?
3   How will they be able to review their actions?
4   How will their work be maintained and supported?

It will be apparent from this analysis that, whilst a wide range of staff will need awareness training, a much smaller group will need to have the detailed knowledge and skills for response. At the same time, the need for careful supervision and consultation for those who may be called upon to provide a response is critical, both to the quality of the management of current work and for the ongoing development of learning.

Awareness training

If awareness training is to be more than a superficial process, then it must be constructed, both literally and metaphorically, as part of the process of prevention. The potential target audience for such training is wide. It may help in this context to draw an eco-map of awareness of the child's immediate needs (Figure 18.1). In the circle closest to the child will be those who provide their immediate care: family, or substitute carers. Social workers would only fall within this group if the child is already subject to some kind of intervention, for example being looked after by the local authority. Further out there will be those who deal with them on a regular or daily basis, including teachers, carers and friends. For children with special needs, there may be a wide range of specialist support. Then there will be those who come into contact with them on an occasional, or specialist, basis. This would include all those who may provide a particular input into the care of a child, such as a doctor, specialist teacher or a specialist therapist and the extended family. Finally, in the outer circle will be those who only come into contact with the child because a concern has been raised, such as social workers or police involved in child protection investigations. Where the people involved are professionals, they will have management structures intended to direct and support their work. The exact membership of each circle will need to be individualised for each child.

From this we can see that there is an important need for awareness training among a wide range of people, within both professional circles and the wider community, about the environments which may be vulnerable to organised abuse: for example schools where an individual staff member has disproportionate responsibility, or residential settings where sub-cultures are used to maintain discipline. They will also need to know the range of circumstances within the life of an establishment or organisation which would cause concern.

Much of this does not need to be learned within a framework of organised abuse. We have already noted that the enormity and scale of some aspects of child abuse (and this is a particular case in point) can be experienced as disempowering by many. Much of this material is more helpfully learned in a framework of good practice in relation to children's rights. Those who receive this kind of training need to know that, because infringements of

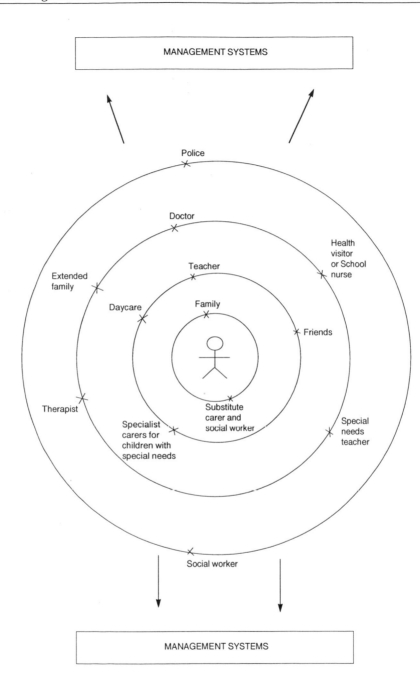

Figure 18.1   Eco-map of awareness needs

children's rights can have damaging consequences (including organised abuse), there are appropriate actions to take in circumstances which cause them concern. These responses need to be simple and clear, and staff need to be assured that their concerns will be heard without prejudice to their own position. Learning of this kind has an immediate value when it is structured around concepts of good practice, because it empowers the learner to use the learning immediately. It can take place on a 'whole-staff' basis, where establishments or projects can undertake audits of their strengths and weaknesses and develop action plans to implement. This achieves the dual purpose of making the organisation safer while at the same time providing the clues to recognising unsafe situations or behaviour.

The curriculum for awareness training can best be developed on a multi-professional basis. It may then be delivered as part of multi-agency foundation training for many of the staff involved, particularly those within the inner circles identified above. However, it is important to ensure that, if staff are not priority targets for multi-agency training, the training is provided on a single-agency basis. Using the four-stage model above, a curriculum can be determined as follows:

- need to be aware of

    - the existence of organised abuse;
    - how perpetrators operate;
    - signs and symptoms in children;
    - causes for concern in organisations;

- need to be able to

    - develop preventive strategies in the work environment;
    - understand their role in relation to local policies and procedures in the event of a case of organised abuse coming to light;
    - understand the impact on self and other staff;

- reviewing their actions

    - understand how to use supervision effectively;
    - be able to identify and use opportunities within the work group to discuss and reflect upon situations which cause concern;

- accessing support

    - be aware of sources of support, guidance and consultancy in cases which cause concern.

Coupled with this sort of basic awareness level for staff is the need to integrate a review of key points about organised abuse into other relevant train-

ing events: for example specific training for residential or daycare staff and community groups.

When staff responsibilities change, through promotion or re-location, it will be important to consider whether there will be a need to add a module of learning about organised abuse which ensures a role-specific awareness. In particular, this will apply to front-line and middle-managers. For this group, basic awareness training should be part of their induction to their new post (and a priority for all those in post who have not yet received it). An outline curriculum would include the following points:

- need to be aware of

  - the existence of organised abuse;
  - how perpetrators operate;
  - signs and symptoms in children;
  - causes for concern in organisations;
  - management implications of local policies and procedures;

- need to be able to

  - manage services for children in ways which encourage the prevention and the recognition of risks of organised abuse;
  - operate a first-line management response in cases of concern;
  - provide a supervisory environment where concerns can be discussed;
  - maintain accurate profiles of staff knowledge and skills;

- reviewing their actions

  - understand the need for reflection and review of their own practice, and appreciate how this can be used to support and teach their staff;

- accessing support

  - be able to access opportunities with their own line-managers or specialist professionals to reflect on and review their actions in this area of work;
  - be able to access local strategic management and consultancy teams.

It is important that awareness training is extended to staff working in quality and inspection teams in every agency. Inspection may be the catalyst to arousing suspicions of organised abuse in some establishments. Personnel staff are also important targets for this training, as they will be called upon to implement developments in recruitment and staff disciplinary action in

order to prevent and, where necessary, to respond to organised abusers within staff groups.

The need for awareness training to reach the senior management level of the relevant organisations will by now be apparent. In local authorities, this should also include the elected members, whose sole experience of organised abuse cases has often been one of delivering a response to media enquiries – sometimes with only very limited knowledge of the issues for the services involved. For this group, inter-agency learning will be an important part of the training process, providing a rare opportunity to share the implications of new knowledge for their relevant organisations. Their needs are particularly in the area of ensuring that policies in a wide range of areas enable them to prevent organised abuse, and where necessary, develop a strategic response to it. Senior managers will not, as a whole group, have time to address detail, neither will they have the opportunity to develop or maintain a specialist level of expertise. It will be essential for them to recognise the fast-changing nature of knowledge in this area and to be able to identify key individuals who can be relied upon to ensure that policies and procedures are in line with current research and practice. They will also need to ensure that arrangements are in place for a delegated group of senior managers to act as strategic advisers and consultants in complex cases. (This is discussed in detail below, under 'Organisational support'.) Given these constraints, their curriculum would include the following points:

- need to be aware of

    - the nature of organised abuse;
    - the ways in which perpetrators operate, and how this differs from intra-familial abuse;
    - staff as abusers and victims as abusers;
    - recent research and lessons from cases elsewhere;

- need to be able to

    - develop policies aimed at prevention of organised abuse through community and staff awareness, recruitment and supervision policies;
    - provide strategic leadership and support in cases of organised abuse;
    - deal with media enquiries;

- reviewing their actions

    - ensure multi-agency review procedures are effective;
    - ensure quality and inspection teams are integrated into all work in this area;

- accessing support
  - have knowledge and awareness about sources of support for work in organised abuse cases.

General training in childcare and child protection

The main plank of the response to organised abuse is that of a competent, confident staff team who have received an incremental programme of training, and whose learning has been maintained by opportunities to reflect on practice. It is in the continuing professional development of staff who are engaged in the investigation of and therapeutic response to child abuse cases generally that such competence will evolve. Knowledge and skills in work on organised abuse cases need to be incorporated into this picture of training and development. Staff who undertake investigative interviews will need to be aware of the possible indicators in an interview with one child which could suggest that this was part of a wider pattern of abuse. Cases of children who are both victims of abuse and have themselves abused should alert staff to the possibility of organised abuse. It is important to recognise the danger of overloading staff with knowledge, just as it is important to allow time for skills development to be completed to the point where staff have confidence in their ability to commence practice. Regular recall training has been found to be a more successful approach to ensuring continuing learning as well as to feeding in additional knowledge. Important, too, will be the regular opportunity to review practice in order to hone skills and identify gaps in knowledge. It is essential that the training course is not viewed as the sole opportunity for learning, but as a focal point around which a range of further learning opportunities are built. This puts at least some of the responsibility into the hands of practitioners themselves to maintain their own knowledge base and to take the initiative in becoming a reflective practitioner.

Critical in this approach is the emphasis on the parallel training for managers of front-line staff involved in child protection. They are perfectly placed to support practice, both through direct guidance and supervision and by providing opportunities and facilitating reflection on practice. As well as being a learning experience for practitioners, it provides line-managers with crucial knowledge and experience to shape their own practice.

Organisational support

One of the key features of the comprehensive approach to learning in this area will be the location of expertise within the organisations concerned with both preventing organised abuse and responding to it. There are significant differences between medicine and social work in this respect: in medicine,

the senior consultant is likely to be an expert in her or his field, whilst in social work, the director will be more likely to have current expertise in management than in an area of professional practice. In many Social Services Departments, the professional expertise is located well down the hierarchy, often at a point where there is little direct control over resources or access to them. Decision-making at a strategic level is therefore hampered by problems of knowledge and interpretation. Again, the concept of powerlessness applies: the expert child protection specialist may know what needs to be done but be powerless to achieve it because of their position within the organisation. There are further problems in terms of the nature of leadership. Senior staff members may be called upon to address public meetings, to deal with media enquiries and to speak to staff involved in providing a direct response. If their knowledge base is weak, this will be all too apparent to the staff who are actually doing the work, creating a potential for anger and hostility, particularly when things go wrong.

An approach which has proved effective in some areas has been the establishment of a small, high-level, inter-agency group which can operate as a consultancy resource in complex child abuse cases. The group is charged with maintaining a high level of current awareness regarding research and policy on child abuse issues. They would be expected to be available to act in a consultancy capacity in any difficult case, and to be a strategic planning and support service in cases of organised or multiple abuse. The group typically consists of people who are positioned within their respective hierarchies so that they can command resources and are able to deal with the media, as well as having the respect of staff. It is important to note that they do not take on line-management of staff, but hold responsibility for strategic planning and for consultancy and support to staff.

Operational outcomes

In the event of a case of organised abuse coming to light, how would the strategy described above operate?

First, there would be a strong baseline of awareness of organised abuse and of initial responses to be taken. An initial strategy meeting would be well informed by the presence of the consultancy team. Portfolios of learning and experience would provide information as to where key staff with appropriate skills and knowledge would be located. Once a course of action was agreed, the staff team would benefit from regular briefings, de-briefings and support sessions, so that their immediate experience could be processed in order to take the work further. Staff would have access to supervision from their own line-managers as well as to consultation with members of the consultancy team. This team would be well placed to identify additional or specialist resources to supplement or enhance the local effort. Staff could be

identified to co-ordinate and attend meetings of parents, if required, and there would be a consistent policy regarding responding to media enquiries. Throughout the inquiry, the therapeutic needs of the children involved could be considered and a plan made for responding to those needs.

At the end of the investigation, it would be possible to undertake a detailed review of the case. However effectively the case has been managed, there will always be lessons for front-line staff, for their managers and for the organisation as a whole. It is important that these lessons be identified and shared, both within the local organisations concerned and within the wider community of child welfare professionals.

It is through this continual reflection on experience that the learning organisation is formed. It is an approach which can replace anxiety with appropriate confidence, can replace uncertainty with tested knowledge, can pace the development of skills appropriately and can provide vital information for better prevention of organised abuse. From an organisational perspective, it builds mutual respect and a sense of safety and containment of practice and strategy in an area which remains full of complexities, risks and uncertainties.

References

Brookfield, S. (1987) *Developing Critical Thinkers*, Buckingham: Open University Press.

Charles, M. (1991) *Multi-Disciplinary is Different*, Nottingham: University of Nottingham Press.

Department of Health/Home Office (DoH/HO) (1992) *Memorandum of Good Practice on Video Recorded Interviews with Child Witnesses for Criminal Proceedings*, London: HMSO.

Open University (1988) *Responding to Child Abuse and Neglect*, London: Bedford Square Press.

Smith, G. (1993) *Systemic Approaches to Training in Child Protection*, London: Karnac Books.

19 An agenda for action

Peter Bibby

This chapter identifies a number of issues that I consider should be priorities for action over the next few years. By its nature, it is a personal list, and also excludes a number of important matters.

I have based my agenda for action on judgements made concerning the importance for children and the ease of achievement. Others may use different criteria to make their own judgements. What would not be acceptable would be to duck the need to make such judgements.

I have chosen the following six areas for priority action:

- stopping sexual tourism;
- improving public knowledge about organised abuse;
- making the judicial system more friendly towards children;
- changing methods of treatment in prison;
- developing a new form of life licence for convicted Schedule 1 offenders;
- transmission of HIV through organised abuse.

Once progress has been made on any or some of these fronts, then further areas will be added to my agenda.

Stopping sexual tourism

Paedophile behaviour is reinforced, and sometimes initiated, through sexual tourism. Just as many of us do things on holiday that we would not do at home, either because of different legislation or reduced restraint, many people are initiated into paedophilia on holiday, in particular in the poorer areas of the world. Indeed, it is a form of sexual colonialism. Such behaviour

is contrary to the United Nations' policy on the rights of children. A few countries have introduced childcare legislation that allows prosecution of actions that would be offences if committed at home, where they have been committed abroad. Attempts in early 1995 to introduce such legislation in the United Kingdom failed. Such legislation would not only make an important ethical statement, it would deter a number of abusers. In July 1995, the Home Secretary announced actions that would be taken against organisers of such holidays, but this action has been minimal to date, and shows no understanding of how paedophiles work. They travel privately and are unlikely to go to an ABTA-registered travel agent asking to go on a sexual tourism holiday!

Improving public knowledge

If we wait until the onset of a particular case before we consider informing the public of the existence and nature of organised abuse, we are already too late. If we leave public relations to the strategy group in any particular case, we have missed an opportunity. It is essential that Area Child Protection Committees' policy groups determine the local parameters around which relationships with the media will work.

It is vital that the approach taken locally be approved in general and sanctioned specifically by the senior managers. As it is possible that any complex case could become a high-profile case, it is vital that the strategy group (see Chapter 11) determines how it will be decided who will say what to whom and how. This is true even when the case has achieved its objectives. It is even more important when objectives have not been achieved.

For instance, it is possible that good local reporters may have obtained an indication that something is going on. It could affect the investigation if it is publicised. Decisions will then have to be made about whether anything is discussed, and on what basis: should the press be taken into confidence on the basis of an off-the-record briefing, or even on the basis that premature press publicity would adversely affect the children? The *quid pro quo* might be for the paper to have special access to information at a later date, when the case is over. Either answer to this dilemma is high-risk and will only work in the context of ongoing relationships with the media. These negotiations need to be undertaken on a joint basis and in conjunction with advice from the respective agency's press offices, under the leadership of the strategy group.

Another area that *must* be decided as a policy matter is the amount of information that needs to be given to politicians and how this will be decided in any particular case. Police operations are traditionally less affected by their committees than Social Services' are by their councillors. It is important that decisions to tell councillors are planned and implemented on the basis of

a joint agreement. It will be as necessary on occasions for the police to understand the importance of keeping politicians 'onside' as it is for local authorities to be aware of the concerns of the police over divulging sensitive information. This area is particularly sensitive when there are allegations about employees of the investigating council or even a councillor.

Nationally, it is also vitally important that organisations develop greater awareness in the community as a whole about the nature of this form of child abuse, the devices used to retain secrecy, and the many structural factors that inhibit the successful convictions of offenders and protection of children.

We are often naïve about the degree of contacts between abusers. We come across connections between abusers for which we have no explanation. Paedophiles work for each other 24 hours a day, seven days a week. Examples abound that include abusers clearing property as soon as friends have been arrested, or attending courts taking detailed notes that are then circulated around prisons as pornography. I am continually shocked at the single-mindedness and ruthlessness of these people.

I do not, in general, subscribe to the conspiracy theory of events in society, because it requires application and a degree of security that is not normally found. However, there is no doubt that paedophiles use a degree of organisation and security that we do not often come across, and we will never deal with them successfully unless we use a strategic approach.

Our knowledge on this topic is limited. Prior to 1991, there were no government guidelines about organised abuse. Dramatic examples existed of alleged 'satanic abuse'. The disclosures may or may not have been accurate, but on the whole, the evidence was discounted as figments of evangelical Christians' imaginations. It was not easy to get people to study 'boring, ordinary organised abuse'. The beginning of the 1990s, however, brought to light many examples of multiple abuse that had gone on for years without any preventative action being taken. There was, and still is, no central point to pull together what was known about the nature and extent of the phenomenon.

The research by Jean La Fontaine and Bernard Gallagher et al., combined with the training started by the Department of Health and a number of documentaries and dramatisations of high-profile cases (Dyfed, Peter Righton and a number of church scandals), has moved public opinion to the stage at which the general existence of organised abuse is felt to be credible. Society remains naïve about its extent and is resistant to believing it is occurring in any particular case where the person accused is well liked, respected or useful. Although childcare legislation is supposed to make the interests of the child paramount, a significant number of people and organisations are less clear-cut when the child's interest is in conflict with the employment rights of staff. (In this context, it is notable that the downfall of Albert Reynolds' government in Eire was triggered by the failure to take paedophilia seri-

ously, although there were no doubt other factors at play.) We are therefore some way down the road to establishing general credibility.

The increased awareness has ironically also been assisted by some of the more dramatic allegations which led to criticism of the investigators. In many cases, the residual feeling has been that the investigators may have done things wrong tactically, but somewhere in the case there *are* abusers.

It is sadly true that good work does not generally get publicity. Even where significant success is achieved, the media often focuses on the short-comings. In the 1994 Dyfed case, where a number of men were convicted of abuse, little reached the national media about the success. More space was given to a few case interviews, where it was suggested that interviewers may have led the child.

In order to counteract this, we need to have an understanding why this is so. Partly, it is because failures by people in authority are more newsworthy, and sell more papers; partly, it is because people who are on the receiving end of poor practice rightly want redress and understandably feel aggrieved; partly, it is because friends and relatives of convicted perpetrators and accused people do not, and indeed cannot, believe that this person they know has deceived them; for the paedophile, it is essential for future accep-tance to persuade others and oneself of one's innocence; and for some people, it is a valid strategy to undermine any attempts to convict pae-dophiles. We must not forget that paedophiles have a vested interest in sub-verting specific and general belief in the existence of abusing adults.

The next stage in our strategy must be to establish systems that give credi-bility to individual cases. This requires increases in training (see Chapter 18 in this volume) and in awareness, to at least first-line child protection man-agers and ACPC members. ACPC members must be familiar with the topic, as coping with the turbulence caused to normal work and the possible risks to organisational credibility cannot and should not rest with the tactical workers. This requires policies and procedures that legitimise the local approach. So many areas still do not have an understanding of the abusing process, have too rigid procedures (or none), and quite frankly, do not have the working culture that helps staff take the essential risk of going to the boundaries of social work knowledge.

The price for believing that a respected and trusted friend, colleague or rel-ative has abused may be the destruction of that relationship. People have a lot to lose in believing the worst. It takes a lot of courage to admit that one has been deceived. There are many examples of people being unable to believe that their partner/colleague has done something like this. As in fam-ily abuse and abuse in institutions, choices have to be made between their colleague or the children.

It is not uncommon for fellow teachers or residential staff and line-man-agers to disbelieve that a colleague has abused children, even after convic-

tion. This can sometimes be due to the cleverness of the abuser in deceiving colleagues. It also has much to do with the difficulty in coming to terms with their own responsibility for not noticing or acting. Such self-reproach is unfair because of the silencing techniques used by the abuser on colleagues. This will, I fear, be compounded by the approach being taken by the teachers' unions and the Council of Local Education Authorities (1994). These bodies seem to propound the view that it is much more likely that children are inventing allegations than being subjected to abuse. To them, children appear to be more powerful than teachers and spend all their time trying to subvert them. They do not appear to understand that abuse in schools is an abuse of the power and responsibility given to teachers by society.

Making the judicial process more child-friendly

When we get to court, we again discover the tension between the needs of the children and the needs of the defendant. Progress on behalf of victims has been made in the use of screens and closed-circuit television, but these are not in existence in all courts, nor can magistrates and judges be relied on to understand what children need. Defence barristers seem only too aware of what children need and do their best to make sure that they do not get it (all in the interest of the defendant, of course!).

The Pigot Committee (see Chapter 3 in this volume) looked into what was needed in courts and made recommendations that were welcomed by all child protection agencies. Among other things, it proposed, in an attempt to help children through the trauma of the delay in coming to court and the giving of evidence in court, that not only should video-taped evidence-in-chief be obtained as close to the time of disclosure as possible, but also that cross-examination should happen around the same time, out of court, in an informal setting. This would release children and their families for therapy as required, and in particular group therapy, where this was indicated as useful.

In the event, the changes which followed the Pigot Report bore little relationship to its recommendations.

The recent *Memorandum of Good Practice* on interviewing (DoH/HO, 1992) has produced a Kafkaesque situation where the children and their interviewers appear to be the people on trial, in a manner that does not apply even to subjects of rape. There is an increasing body of opinion which suggests that video-taped interviews do nothing to assist children, very expensively. Unless the Pigot Committee recommendations are fully implemented, an increasing number of people feel that personally-given evidence on closed-circuit television or behind a screen, together with any supporting evidence, is at present the best way of securing a conviction. At present, over 94 per cent of video-taped interviews do not get to court, and only one-third of

these result in conviction. Each unnecessary video-taped interview is a further abuse of the child. It could be easily argued that the resulting procedures in the *Memorandum of Good Practice* on interviewing (DoH/HO, 1992) have been turned into a success story for paedophiles; perhaps the conspiracy theory supporters were correct.

Sentencers need to understand how paedophiles work, and in particular, need to have a culture that believes that in any adult/child relationship, it is the adult who must have responsibility for any abuse of their power position. All too often, the defence claims that the child is more sexually active than the adult, or that previous abuse mitigates the blame of the adult. This may be a proper defence to run before conviction, although I doubt it. It is certainly not something that should mitigate the sentence.

There are a number of other features in the current child protection system that count against the successful protection of children. There is a tension between the need to protect children and the various legal processes set up to protect the accused. These include the right to silence, disclosure of evidence and the obsessive use of video interviews as the main form of prosecution evidence.

In most crime, the nature of relationship between the victim and the perpetrator is not as violatory as in child abuse, where the relationship is similar to that with rape victims and other people who have been violated. As we become more aware of the impact of crime on victims, we should be able to show people how very great is the impact on abused children and rape victims. Why is it that we treat the victims of these intrusive crimes in a different way from the victims of property crime?

If I am the subject of a theft, a police officer will assist me in preparing my statement. What has happened will be established in the privacy of my own home. The officer will direct the order in which items are written down, pulling out inconsistencies and allowing me to amend errors. It is quite unlike this for a child victim of abuse. First, the interview is held in a strange place (the interview suite), where every interaction is video-taped and every modification of the account is available to be taken apart later. If the video tape is used, then every detail of the interviewing technique used by the police and/or social workers is gone over in a way that never occurs when adults are the victims of property crime.

Changing methods of treatment in prison

We are all aware of cases of defendants who state, on a first conviction, that they did not know what came over them and that it had never happened before. It is quite clear from the work of Ray Wyre and others that paedophiles have high libidos and exhibit among the highest rates of recidivism.

Unlike many property offenders, the paedophile does not reduce offending on becoming an adult. Sentences and post-conviction treatment should take into account the high likelihood of future offending. Even 'first' offenders must be dealt with as people who put children at risk. It is likely that 'first offenders' have previously abused. Sentencing should therefore have the protection of children as a priority once someone has been convicted of a Schedule 1 offence.

This may result in longer sentences, but not necessarily so. There are other strategies that can be used. First, there is the manner in which the Prison Service deals with sexual offenders. There are rules banning the use of hard-core pornography in prisons; the use by sex offenders of child pin-ups, whether clothed, erotic or obscene, must be banned in prisons.

Having worked in a Rule 43 wing in a local prison, I am clear that sexual offenders do need to be protected against other prisoners, and even against some prison officers. However, the regime in such wings, or in specialist prisons, needs to be different from the present one. Ray Wyre has shown how paedophiles justify their behaviour by using fantasy to legitimise their actions (see Chapter 7 in this volume). This is a self-reinforcing cycle. It is therefore necessary to work with offenders to confront the fantasy with the reality of what they have done and to develop strategies to enable them to break out of the cycle. Such strategies are found to be effective mainly when offenders acknowledge the nature of their behaviour. They are also particularly effective when used with abusers at the time they start abusing, often when they are teenagers.

Whilst resources must be increased to confront these problems, like many preventative programmes, results will only show at a later stage, and the beneficiaries will not be at the cost centre that is required to justify the provision of therapeutic resources today.

Developing a new form of life licence

The approach in the section above will not make an impact on all, or even most, hardened paedophiles.

The public needs to be protected from the repetitious nature of paedophiles' offending: they are some of the most recidivist offenders that exist. This is more easily understood through the work of Ray Wyre. This shows the ways in which paedophiles reinforce the legitimacy of their actions through fantasy. This being so, it is unwise to think that any abuser will reform unless he takes responsibility for his actions, and has shown that he has worked through this to some degree of understanding and change in rationale. Resources are not made available for this to be achieved to any great degree.

This means that most paedophiles are released into the community completely free to go where they like and to disappear from the sight and jurisdiction of the authorities. There is a very persuasive civil liberty argument that once someone has served their sentence, they should be deemed to have repaid their debt to society. This might be appropriate to property offences, but it is not an approach that should be followed when children are at risk. It ignores what we now know about the nature of paedophile abuse. Paedophiles disappear from public surveillance for periods, only to reappear later. Short of perpetual electronic tagging, it is difficult to know how people can be released at the end of their sentence and watched constantly.

However, another area of concern arises where we are aware that convicted Schedule 1 offenders are known to be actively targeting and grooming children (there is a County Court ruling that grooming is abuse). Such behaviour or evidence is not enough for preventive action currently to be taken. Regular examples of behaviour that society chooses to allow include arranging for young children to be taken in to prison to see paedophile 'uncles'; convicted offenders being able to phone the children they have abused; teenagers taken as 'nieces' for approval as homecoming presents; photos of abusers' children being circulated to friends; paedophiles setting up young prisoners' support groups for teenage abusers or victims, or setting up children's charities or their own children's organisation.

As things stand at present, there is nothing to stop a convicted Schedule 1 offender from doing any of these things. Whilst respectable childcare societies will check their prospective employees, the public has no way of distinguishing these societies from paedophile-managed organisations. It is a reflection of our current priorities that the Charity Commissioners can stop an individual from setting up a charity if there is financial turpitude in the background. Society has no such control or lever on paedophiles.

This causes great concern and anxiety amongst professionals who are trying to protect children known to be in touch with these convicted men. At the moment, the protection agencies cannot be protective of children at risk, but can only react once offences have taken place. I do not believe that this should be allowed to continue. The best way of dealing with this is to develop the concept of a life licence for people who have been convicted of Schedule 1 offences.

There is a precedent in the life licence that is imposed on murderers. Even though they may be no risk to society, because of the importance that society attaches to this offence, this licence is imposed as part of the sentence. If someone commits a serious traffic offence, they can be disqualified from driving for life. If one is cruel to an animal, one can be disqualified from owning an animal for life. Paedophiles present a continuous danger to children, and unless we take serious action, we will continue to leave children at risk. I therefore believe that all those convicted of paedophile offences should be

disqualified from contact with children for an unlimited period after conviction. Rather like other disqualifications, there would be a process whereby this disqualification could be rescinded.

Such a child-contact disqualification order will give a useful resource to the child protection agencies. It would also allow preventive publicity to be propagated to carers and parents, without the current anxiety caused by the threat of civil legal action to stop the circulation of such information.

Failure to comply would make offenders liable to serve the balance of their original sentence again, or could even be made an offence in its own right. This would ensure that, where children were approached, protection agencies could take protective action as soon as they became aware of targeting activities by convicted paedophiles.

Transmission of HIV through organised abuse

As has been shown by Angela Thomas (Chapter 8 in this volume) and Anne Peake (Chapter 10 in this volume), there is much concern amongst children and their parents about the HIV status of the perpetrators. At present, perpetrators cannot be made to give this information, and neither can they be forced to have compulsory blood tests (and of course, a negative blood test can be a false negative). All the families can do is wait for six months after the latest abusive incident, before a test can be carried out on the victim of that abuse.

In fact, much more can be done. If we are clear about the specific nature of the abuse, we may find that it falls outside the high-risk activities – the abuse may involve penetration by hands, fingers or objects, rather than genitals. However, safer sex acts are unlikely in view of the power/domination issues that are integral to organised abuse.

Information about HIV status may have been given to people who are not bound by the same degree of confidentiality as the abusers' medical advisers. (The London Borough of Tower Hamlets has received some interesting advice on this topic (Redding, 1991).) A fair prediction of risk (but not absolute certainty) may be obtained by examining the lifestyle of the offender.

We therefore need to consider whether the needs of victims to have certainty – even the certainty of positive knowledge – should have priority over the traditional right of the perpetrator to confidentiality. If part of the solution to liberating children from the power of the abuser is to counteract the imbalance of power in the relationship, then the provision of this knowledge to the child will have a liberating effect. The other resource that victims and their families want and could find helpful is the offer of HIV advice and counselling in each case. They must also retain the right to decide whether

they themselves wish to have a blood test. This would be guided by the best current advice about having such tests as a matter of course.

At present, the balance in all these areas is tipped in favour of child abusers. We have begun to make inroads into one or two of these areas, but children will not be safe unless we deal with all of them. This requires dramatic changes in some of the major conservative institutions in our society, not least the judiciary, the Prison Service and parliament.

Failure in any one of these areas will result in a failure to protect children.

References

Council of Local Education Authorities (1994) *Guidelines on Practice and Procedure* (dealing with allegations of abuse made against staff).

Department of Health/Home Office (DoH/HO) (1992) *Memorandum of Good Practice on Video Recorded Interviews with Child Witnesses for Criminal Proceedings*, London: HMSO.

Pigot, T. (1989) *Report of the Advisory Group on Video Evidence* (The Pigot Report), London: HMSO.

Redding, D. (1991) 'Sexual abuse of nine children in Tower Hamlets by an HIV+ man', *Community Care*, January/February.

Index

Coping with Children in Stress

edited by Ved Varma

Childhood is a time of rapid change which can cause stress for many children, but those with special needs may have to face additional stresses, either at home or at school. This book investigates how to handle children with stresses derived from various sources – health, educational and social – looking at the causes and effects of stress, ways of preventing or minimising it, as well as coping strategies. The chapters focus on children with sensory impairments, physical disabilities, learning difficulties, emotional or behavioural difficulties, as well as gifted children and those from ethnic minorities.

This book is essential reading not only for special needs teachers but also for mainstream teachers of all age-ranges.

Ved Varma was formerly an educational psychologist with the Institute of Education, University of London, the Tavistock Clinic, and for the London Boroughs of Richmond and Brent.

1996　179 pages　Hbk　1 85742 252 X　£16.95
Pbk　1 85742 253 8　£32.50

Price subject to change without notification

A Handbook of Childhood Anxiety Management

edited by Kedar Nath Dwivedi & Ved Varma

Despite a large number of books dealing with problems of anxiety in adults, there is real scarcity of quality practical material for helping children with problems of anxiety today. This book aims to fill this important gap as a practical and comprehensive text written by a multidisciplinary team of experts in their respective fields. The book is aimed at assisting professionals in offering skilful help to children with problems of anxiety. The contents include descriptions of the causes, the nature and the distribution of anxiety problems in children and various approaches to treatment. A large variety of helping professionals working with children such as child psychiatrists, child psychologists, educational psychologists, paediatricians, school doctors and nurses, health visitors, teachers and social workers will find the book immensely valuable.

Dr Kedar Nath Dwivedi is a consultant in child, adolescent, and family psychiatry at the Child and Family Consultation Service and The Ken Stewart Family Centre, Northampton and is also a clinical teacher of the Faculty of Medicine, University of Leicester.

Ved Varma was formerly an educational psychologist with the Institute of Education, University of London, the Tavistock Clinic, and for the London Boroughs of Richmond and Brent.

1996   c 177 pages   1 85742 304 6

WORKING TOGETHER IN

Child Protection

An exploration of the multi-disciplinary task and system

MICHAEL MURPHY

This book is a resource for all practitioners, students, managers and trainers who work in the child protection field. It explores the detailed working arrangements of one child protection system and examines the roles and perspectives of the agencies and practitioners who make up that system. It uses examples that are drawn from current practice to outline crucial arguments in the text. It suggests that multi-disciplinary child protection work is both complex and difficult, claiming that a series of structural blockages exist to effective joint working, in particular that we all harbour an ignorance of the perspective and reality of the other agencies and practitioners within the system.

The work goes on to propose a number of measures to be taken by practitioner, agency and government departments that will promote multi-disciplinary working at all levels, suggesting that good multi-disciplinary communication, co-operation and action is synonymous with good child protection work.

The child protection system in England and Wales is used as a case study, but comparisons are drawn with child protection systems in other parts of the world. It is argued that the key concepts and conventions of effective multi-disciplinary child protection work are constant and go beyond the boundaries of single systems.

Michael Murphy is co-ordinator on a Multi-disciplinary Child Protection Resource project.

1995 224 pages Hbk 1 85742 197 3 £35.00
Pbk 1 85742 198 1 £14.95

Price subject to change without notification

arena

the **ABC** of
Child Protection

JEAN MOORE

"...an excellent source of information on the subject. If you buy this for your own reference shelf, you will take it down again and again to help you make sense of the child protection cases which all too often come your way." **The Magistrate**

The ABC of Child Protection examines four faces of abuse in detail: physical abuse, children caught up in marital violence, the much neglected subject of neglect, and sexual abuse.

The painful stresses experienced by the worker are not forgotten and emphasis is put upon the specific skills required in child protection work. There is a lively chapter on face-to-face work with abused children and the complexities of child protection conferences are helpfully analysed with particular reference to the attendance of parents and children.

The black perspective is given prominence with contributions from Emmanuel Okine and David Divine. A chapter by Caroline Ball describes the contents and implications of the 1989 Children Act. Issues relating to racism, sexism, classism, ageism and disabilityism are honestly tackled.

Jean Moore is a child abuse consultant and freelance trainer.

1992   224 pages   1 85742 027 6   £8.95

Price subject to change without notification

arena

The Children Act *1989* :
Putting it into Practice
Mary Ryan

This book provides a practical guide to those parts of the Children Act 1989 that relate to the provision of services by local authorities to children and families; the powers and duties of local authorities in such circumstances; care and supervision proceedings; and child protection issues.

The book is a unique combination of information on the legal framework contained in the Act, regulations and guidance and information on good social work and legal practice, relevant research and recent case law. It is grounded on the author's practical experience of providing an advice and advocacy service for families; providing training for social workers, lawyers and other child care professionals; being involved with the development of the legislation from the consultation period in the early 1980s, through the parliamentary process, and the subsequent consultation on regulations, guidance and court rules.

Mary Ryan, the Co-Director of the Family Rights Group, is a solicitor who after working in private practice as a family lawyer, was the Family Rights Group's legal advisor for 10 years.

1994   256 pages

Hbk   1 85742 192 2   **£30.00**   Pbk   1 85742 193 0   **£14.95**

Price subject to change without notification

arena

The Police and Social Workers

Second Edition

Terry Thomas

Social workers and police officers are in daily contact with one another in various areas of their work. This book offers a clear guide to that inter-agency work and critically examines how it is carried out in practice.

This second edition of the book has been substantially revised to take account of changes in the law, policy and procedures affecting both police and social workers. In particular the Children Act 1989, The Criminal Justice Act 1991 and the findings of the Royal Commission on Criminal Justice 1993. The opportunity has also been taken to revise parts of the original text to ensure as clear a light as possible is thrown on police-social work collaboration – illustrating both the positive and the negative.

Terry Thomas is Senior Lecturer in Social Work at Leeds Metropolitan University.

1994   346 pages   1 85742 157 4   £14.95

Price subject to change without notification

Personal Safety for Social Workers

Commissioned by
The Suzy Lamplugh Trust
Foreword by
Diana Lamplugh OBE

Pauline Bibby

This book is aimed at employers, managers and staff in social work agencies.

In part 1, *Personal Safety for Social Workers* deals with the respective roles and responsibilities of employers and employees are discussed, and offers guidance on developing a workplace personal safety policy. The design and management of the workplace are considered and guidelines provided for social workers working away from the normal work base. Part 2 contains detailed guidelines for use by individual social workers in a variety of work situations. Part 3 addresses training issues and provides a number of sample training programmes.

The message of this book is that proper attention to risk can reduce both the incidence of aggression and its development into violent acts.

1994   224 pages   1 85742 195 7   £16.95

Price subject to change without notification

arena